TO THE MOON INVESTING

Visually Mapping Your Winning Stock Market Portfolio

Kelly James Frank

WILEY

For general information on our other products and services or for technical support, please contact our Customer Care Department within the United States at (800) 762-2974, outside the United States at (317) 572-3993 or fax (317) 572-4002.

Wiley also publishes its books in a variety of electronic formats. Some content that appears in print may not be available in electronic formats. For more information about Wiley products, visit our web site at www.wiley.com.

Library of Congress Cataloging-in-Publication Data

Names: Frank, Kelly James, author.
Title: To the moon investing : visually mapping your winning stock market
    portfolio / Kelly James Frank.
Description: Hoboken, New Jersey : Wiley, [2023] | Includes index.
Identifiers: LCCN 2022043313 (print) | LCCN 2022043314 (ebook) | ISBN
    9781119911920 (cloth) | ISBN 9781119912019 (adobe pdf) | ISBN
    9781119912002 (epub)
Subjects: LCSH: Investments. | Portfolio management.
Classification: LCC HG4521 .F697 2023 (print) | LCC HG4521 (ebook) | DDC
    332.6–dc23/eng/20220923
LC record available at https://lccn.loc.gov/2022043313
LC ebook record available at https://lccn.loc.gov/2022043314

Cover Design: Wiley
Cover Image: © vovan/Shutterstock
Illustrator: Jocelyne L. Frank

SKY10036854_101922

This book is dedicated to all those who relentlessly create ideas to take their lives from what is to what could be.

CONTENTS

v

My *To the Moon* project was ignited by a simple question: "What should a person know about the market if they wish to achieve extraordinary investment results?" It became progressively clear on my journey to provide answers that I was blessed with incredible relationships that put me in a position to respond.

The book would not have soared without the visionary support of Samantha Enders at Wiley. Her talent for articulating the big picture and the best path to get there was remarkable. The editing process with Kim Wimpsett, Kamalini Christilda, Rahini Devi, Mike Isralewitz, and Donna J. Weinson was fun and integral to making the book the best it could be. Plus Purvi Patel, Samantha Wu, and Bill Falloon of Wiley were so supportive and reinforced to me why Wiley is such an outstanding publisher. I am indebted to all of you for your improvements to my manuscript!

I note the incredible treasure trove of information that I resourced from the Federal Reserve Bank of St. Louis, led by President and CEO James "Jim" Bullard. Their FRED database and its ease of use, along with the timely help from Adrienne Brennecke and Katrina Stierholz, is truly appreciated. The US Bureau of Labor Statistics, led by Commissioner William W. Beach, was also an information source, and I especially thank Jonathan Church and Malik Crawford of the BLS. The US Bureau of Economic Analysis, headed by Acting Director and Deputy Director Dr. Mary Bohman, had helpful data and Jeannine Aversa and Ann McDonel were kind to answer my questions.

Randy Nicholls (CPA, CA) was generous with his time on financial statement composition. The help of Talia Price and the Pew Research Center is greatly appreciated. Thank you to Joss Frank for the inspiration and artwork on the sketches and drawings, and Dylan Frank for views on option strategies.

There were many past colleagues, friends, and family that were instrumental to my personal development; they made me better. Chris Gardner, Ross Izzard, Philipp Gruner, Ken MacLean, Marie Ewasuik, Merrilee Ashworth, Bruce Hanson, Bob Murphy, Stephen Crocker, Alec Milne, Gene Schneidmiller, Ron Rattray, Al Balanko, Jim Cebuliak, Don Ikoma, Ryan Byrne, Stella Miranda, Pat Souliere, Dan Connelly, Tony Warren, Kathleen Cels, and Kevin Frank are all amazing and I'm grateful for our connection! My memories of my parents, Jim and Levine, and how they did everything possible to build my curiosity, is a gift that endures.

Despite all the oxygen provided by my phenomenal cadre, you may still find a ding or two in the rocket; I own them!

To my wife, Bonnie, and children, Danielle, Joss, and Dylan; the rocket sputtered at times, but your unconditional love made it go. Much love and gratitude back at ya!

After his corporate career, Kelly James Frank launched 13.8 Capital, an asset management firm focused on growth investments. He is active in finding solutions for the homeless challenge and gratefully wanders between the Rocky Mountains and Oahu.

The purpose of this book is to help you, whether you are a market rookie or a seasoned pro, become a better investor through an innovative set of exciting and intuitive investment maps.

Figure P.1 shows the trajectory of the book. Part I launches by explaining risk and how it affects you as an investor, the elements of preparation-thinking, and figuring out *Why* you want to invest. Then, in part II, we fuel up our financial literacy and dovetail into corporate growth versus value strategies. In part III, we burst into setting your radar for opportunity and look at vital financial metrics and business models, including our Five-Stack Discovery of Macro, Indices and Sectors, Value, Technical, and Brand elements for asset evaluations. In part IV, we complete our visual maps and enable you to boldly rocket to the Moon! Finally, in part V, we activate your flight with practical investment considerations.

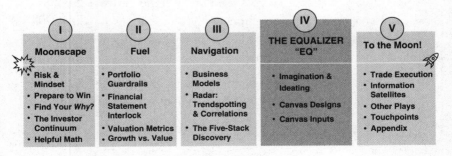

FIGURE P.1 Trajectory of *To the Moon Investing*

This book and its approach are vividly different from the usual wall-of-words investment books:

- Each chapter ends with a useful note capsule.

- I resource and integrate brilliant guidance from leading-edge business authors.

- There are charts and sketches to supplement your retention with places for you to record your market observations and understandings.

- The book describes extrinsic factors of macroeconomic policy on investment decisions.

- Business books usually provide a glossary of keywords. Instead, there is a contextual dialogue between two investors written in an easy-to-read screenplay format.

- There is an elegantly simple illustration of accounting statement connectivity, along with crucial comparative ratio targets.

- Asset choices are illustrated through uncomplicated and adaptable maps (a.k.a. canvases) that optimize your market understanding and financial acuity.

- The complexity of options is deconstructed through sequence-thinking of your investment objectives.

This book's goal is to find that magic space of being both fun and informative, and if you read with a beginner's mind, i.e. knowing that all things are possible, you will get to the Moon that much quicker!

The metaphor of "to the Moon" for investing comes from the exciting influx of young investors that stoked the market in early 2021. In addition to their energetic investment strategies, they dropped a fresh word stack that brought vibrancy to the market patois.

Periodically, you'll come across a point or comment that should stand alone due to its importance, beginning with the one following on footnotes. There is a tremendous amount of source information that I'm thankful for, and all are referenced for further review if you so wish.

The book's footnotes document from where certain Information is derived.
  Feel free to read the footnotes or keep your rocket at a constant speed and not read them, whichever works best for you!

Let's light the rocket!

Newspaper National Hockey League Reporter, post-game:
Derek, how can you check and fight those beasts out there?
I mean, you're not that big of a guy.
Derek, handing his hockey stick to the Reporter:
This is the great Equalizer.[1]

Derek Sanderson, Boston Bruins

This book provides the stock market version of the Equalizer (a.k.a. EQ); in effect, a strategy map for investors to reach a deeper understanding of markets, implement comparative financial tools, improve their trend forecasting, and create an optimal portfolio.[2]

The space trek to improved outcomes begins with a simple question: is it even possible to consistently achieve superior investment results? Well, the heavily debated efficient-market hypothesis proposes that it's impossible to

---

[1] Paraphrased from Derek Sanderson, "The Dead-End Kid Who Wants to Be a Superstar," *Maclean's* (November 1969), macleans.ca. Derek was a perennial All-Star during 22 years of professional hockey, winning two Stanley Cups, as well as the NHL Rookie of the Year, Calder Trophy, in the 1967–1968 season. Derek's O-Pee-Chee playing card lists his weight at 170 lbs. during his rookie season (https://www.ebay.ca/itm/393592125741?oid=165059036443). For a fantastic and fun read on hockey, and meeting life's challenges, I strongly recommend Derek's book *Crossing the Line*, with Kevin Shea (Harper Collins, 2012).

[2] Note that when I use the phrase "stock market," I'm referring to listed stocks on the NYSE, NASDAQ, OTC, and TSX, whereas "assets" refers to stocks as well as money-market instruments, derivatives, crypto, etc.

beat the market as stock prices reflect all known information. In other words, investors are not going to find undervalued stocks as current prices have already "built in" any and all impacting events specific to that stock. A parallel concept, known as the "efficient frontier," supposes that there is an optimal portfolio of diversified stocks that can yield the highest return for a given risk class.

> Both theories use the word "efficient" in the context of the market. But as an Investor, are you "efficient"? Do you have the curiosity, support network, intelligence, and tools to generate above-average returns?

To up our competitive game, many of us search through bookstores, pick at our cohort's experiences, or mine the internet for direction and answers. That's what I did, but there were always remaining questions:

- Are some financial indicators better than others?
- How can I leverage share volume into my analyses?
- Is there a way to de-risk my stock selection choices?
- What are the attributes that I require to be successful?
- How does sector rotation affect stock pricing and direction?
- How do accounting statements interlock (for stock selections)?
- Is there a way to, literally, map out my asset selection choices?
- What global economic (a.k.a. macro) metrics should I be aware of?
- Can the theories of business modeling act as an overlay for personal investing?

As I brainstormed my readings and analyses of asset selection best practices, it became clear that although the information gaps could be sealed, the leap toward choice actualization was across a chasm of risk, uncertainty, and confusion. Essentially, I needed a map that would guide my rocket through the fog of choices and toward superior outcomes.

Remember the world before Google? Say you were driving across the state to your college buddy's house. You might get a paper copy of a map, draw your route in red, and be on your way. Still though, for the "last mile" you were pretty much on your own. So you would call and get directions: "OK, so I turn left at the 7-11, drive four blocks till I see McDonald's, and then I turn right, and go for two more blocks and it's the one the left side with the orange b-ball hoop above the garage? Yeah, I think I got it." Today, anyone with a smartphone can arrive safely and on time: it's all laid out for you, both verbally and directionally on your screen. Similarly, imagine if you could create an X to Y illustrated asset-choice map that ranked your stock targets, crystallized your decision metrics, eliminated blind spots, and enlightened you to the best possible choices!

And that's where I come in: my quest to bridge that divide yielded a set of visual canvases that scale up your stock-selection acuity, collectively referred to as the Equalizer (**EQ**).

The **EQ** guides are prompted from three talented backdrops:

- The visual thinking logic of Dan Roam (*The Back of the Napkin*)[3]
- The creative idea generation from Michael Michalko (*Thinkertoys*)[4]
- The business modeling canvases from Alex Osterwalder and Team (*Strategyzer* book series)[5]

As a business executive, I frequently synthesized these three brilliant models to de-risk alternatives and drive superior outcomes. And now, the **EQ** will prepare you to blast through the efficient frontier to land on the Moon! Perhaps even more importantly, utilizing these canvases will level up your imagination toward what *could be* in your investment life.

Papa John's: Better Ingredients. Better Pizza.

EQ: Better Discovery. Better Outcomes.

Here's an **EQ** example: in early 2021, the market was excited about a bumper crop of Electric Vehicle stocks, comprised of companies that would build the vehicles and those that would provide the fuel source. Their CEOs

---

[3] Dan Roam, *The Back of the Napkin* (Penguin Group, 2008).
[4] Michael Michalko, *Thinkertoys* (Ten Speed Press, 2006).
[5] The Strategyzer series includes *Business Model Generation* by Alex Osterwalder, Yves Pigneur, and Alan Smith (Wiley, 2010); *Proposition Design* by Alex Osterwalder, Yves Pigneur, Greg Bernarda, Alan Smith, and Patricia Papadakos (Wiley, 2014); *Testing Business Ideas* by Alex Osterwalder and David Bland (Wiley, 2019); and *The Invincible Company* by Alex Osterwalder, Yves Pigneur, Fred Etiemble, and Alan Smith (Wiley, 2020).

all danced on the broadcast circuit trumpeting why they were best positioned to succeed in a market projected to exceed $800 billion in 2027.[6]

Everyone was keen on finding the next Tesla. Yet, when we retrace in figure I.1 how some of these organizations fared over an eight-month period, the yields were shockingly poor.

If you were an investor in any one of the nine companies and HODL'd for the eight months, what was your criteria for pressing Go in the first place on a particular stock? How did you layer in the competitive landscape? What did you forecast as a worst-case scenario? What was the X-Factor that separated your stock choice from the others? Or were you driven by fear of missing out (FOMO)?

My Electric Vehicle evaluation, using an **EQ** canvas that integrated possible macro effects, strategic financials, risk, and total addressable market considerations, concluded that the best choice was *not* to purchase any Electric Vehicle stock as the vertical was in its pre–Big Bang phase, primarily due to a lack of well-defined manufacturing schedules.[7]

As I continued to evaluate the entire group, I came to a Captain Obvious deduction: every vehicle, regardless of manufacturer, needed tires.[8] The Electric Vehicle **EQ** pushed me to a new canvas of tire companies, and I eventually moved forward with the Goodyear Tire & Rubber Company (GT). During that horrid 8-month Electric Vehicle stretch, I gained 71% with GT ($11.27 > $19.24) and then exited my position. My original **EQ**

		Feb. 2, 2021	Oct. 4, 2021	Change
Canoo Inc.	GOEV	$ 15.77	$ 6.81	−57%
Fisker Inc.	FSR	$ 14.85	$ 14.05	−5%
The Lion Electric Company	LEV	$ 27.58	$ 11.55	−58%
Lordstown Motor Corp.	RIDE	$ 24.76	$ 5.85	−76%
Lucid Group, Inc.	LCID	$ 32.14	$ 24.14	−25%
Nikola Corporation	NKLA	$ 23.00	$ 10.17	−56%
Nio Inc.	NIO	$ 55.77	$ 33.40	−40%
QuantumScape Corporation	QS	$ 42.58	$ 22.96	−46%
Workhorse Group Inc.	WKHS	$ 34.21	$ 6.93	−80%

FIGURE I.1 **EV Share Prices**
Source: Data from Yahoo! Finance 2021

---

[6] https://www.alliedmarketresearch.com/electric-vehicle-market.

[7] Of course, the clock is still running on these Electric Vehicle stocks, and some of them—perhaps even all of them—may eventually generate outsized returns. In fact, Lucid rose to ~$40 in early January 2022. Share prices were retrieved from Yahoo Finance! March 12–14, 2022.

[8] Captain Obvious is the amusing character, played by Brandon Moynihan, in the Hotels .com advertisements.

surpassed the efficient frontier. Of course, 71% gains are not the norm, but relatively small percentage changes can make an astonishing difference as explained by the "Rule of 72."

The Rule of 72 is a simple formula of 72 divided by a rate of return that approximates the number of years for an investment to double. For example, let's say you have your hard-earned money in a deposit certificate or bond, and assume the rate of return is 4% per year. The Rule of 72 suggests it would take about 18 years for your money to double. Or maybe you're already in the stock market and are accruing 9% gains a year, meaning an investment doubling of 8 years. If you could sharpen your decision tools and yield just 3 percentage points more per year, a 12% return would double in 6 years.

Setting aside tax considerations and risk factors, it is undeniable that to grow wealth *you must participate* in the asset market. Staying on the sidelines is the wrong move. The timing for entering the market, or expanding your commitment to it, couldn't be better! Recent and impactful factors are amplifying stock market opportunity through their collective "froth." Picture a resort island such as Martha's Vineyard off the coast of Massachusetts in summer versus winter. Even if you've never been there, you know that in the summer it's packed with free-spending people, businesses are open for longer hours, pop-up stores appear, tours become available for fishing and whale watching, there are new and broader restaurant menus, ferries offer more arrivals and departures . . . and the result is a profound increase in the circulation and quantity of money on the island. That's all due to tourism "froth."

Think of froth as the octane in your rocket fuel. Froth is what agitates and powers the market, and there are six catalysts that have accelerated market froth, as shown in figure I.2. Without them, the market would not be nearly as exciting, broad-based, wealthy, and accessible as it is.

■ Five Positive Catalysts

The following five market catalysts are positive inflection points contributing to investment opportunity.

Expanded Liquidity

There is more liquidity in America than ever before, as captured by the growth in the money supply (a.k.a. M2), helped by mighty stimulus bills and

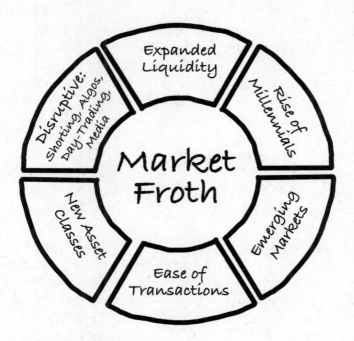

FIGURE I.2 Market Froth

Federal Reserve asset purchase programs. Figure I.3 shows M2's expansion from 1960 to December 2021.[9]

The astonishing visual is condensed to trillions for selected years in figure I.4. In just five years, from December 2016 to December 2021, the US money supply, M2, went from $13.2 trillion to $21.6 trillion, a 64% increase and a ballooning 41% in just the last two years! The Compounded Annual Growth Rate (CAGR, explained in chapter 3) highlights the accelerating pace of M2 expansion. Of course, there are many factors that contribute to M2's increase, including the US population rise from 179 million in 1960 to today's 332 million.[10] Still though, in stock parlance, since 1960, the population growth has been a 2-bagger, and M2, rising from $312 *billion* in December 1960 to $21.6 *trillion* in December 2021, is a whopping 70-bagger!

---

[9] M2 = M1 (currency in circulation + checking deposits) + savings/time deposits + money-market funds.

[10] https://www2.census.gov/library/publications/decennial/1960/population-pc-a2/15611114.pdf and https://www.census.gov/en.html as of January 5, 2022.

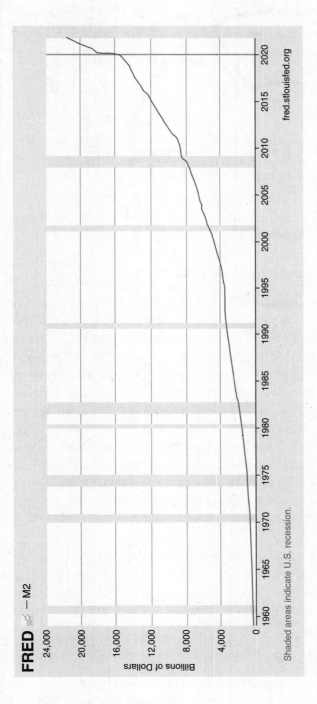

FIGURE I.3 M2, Seasonally Adjusted, 1960–2021[11]

Source: [11] / Federal Reserve Bank of St. Louis

---

[11] Board of Governors of the Federal Reserve System (US), M2 [M2SL], retrieved from FRED, Federal Reserve Bank of St. Louis; https://fred.stlouisfed.org/series/M2SL, May 19, 2022. The Federal Reserve of St. Louis is the eighth of the 12 Districts comprising the Federal Reserve System. FRED is the Federal Reserve Economic Data repository "created and maintained by the Research Department at the Federal Reserve Bank of St. Louis".

INTRODUCTION

USA Money Supply, M2							
in trillions	Dec. 1960	Dec. 2006	Dec. 2011	Dec. 2016	Dec. 2019	Dec. 2021	CAGR
M2	$ 0.3	$ 7.1	$ 9.7	$ 13.2	$ 15.3	$ 21.6	
1960 to 2021						6826%	7.2%
2006 to 2021						206%	7.7%
2011 to 2021						224%	8.4%
2016 to 2021						64%	10.4%
2019 to 2021						41%	18.8%

FIGURE I.4   M2 CAGR, Growth for Selected Years

Bottom Line: There is more money (a.k.a. liquidity) chasing stocks, and the sheer volume enhances and supports market dynamics.

Rise of Millennials

The last few years have witnessed an incredible and newfound participation of young people, generally referred to as Millennials or Generation Y, in the stock market. This digitally connected group of wealth seekers "piled into stocks like never before in 2020. Online broker Charles Schwab gained a record 4 million new clients last year. More than half of these new investors are under 40."[12] The Pew Research Center illustrates in figure I.5 how Millennials are now the largest US demographic per the most recent USA Census.[13]

Bottom Line: Younger adults are barging into markets with an aggressive (and, at times disruptive) intensity that accelerates market froth and opportunity. Although a survey by Investopedia concluded that "only 37% of Millennials do feel knowledgeable about the stock market"[14] (hence this

[12] Stephen McBride, "Millennials Will Propel Stocks Higher For Years," *Forbes* (February 8, 2021), https://www.forbes.com/sites/stephenmcbride1/2021/02/08/millennials-will-propel-stocks-higher-for-years.

[13] Pew Research Center, "Millennials Overtake Baby Boomers as America's Largest Generation" (April 28, 2020), https://www.pewresearch.org/fact-tank/2020/04/28/millennials-overtake-baby-boomers-as-americas-largest-generation/ft_20-04-27_generationsize_1/.
Note: Millennials refer to the population ages 23 to 38 as of 2019. Pew Research Center tabulations of U.S. Census Bureau population estimates released April 2020 and population projections released December 2017.

[14] Joetta Gobell, "The Affluent Millennial Investment Survey," Investopedia, November 20, 2019, https://www.investopedia.com/the-investopedia-affluent-millennials-study-4769751.

Projected population by generation
In millions

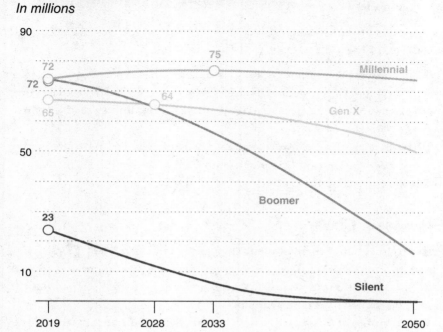

FIGURE I.5   **Millennial Population**
Source: [13] / Pew Research Center

book and the **EQ!**), their savvy technology skills empower them to easily participate and hunt for best-choice asset purchases in time frames that surpass older generations.

Emerging Markets

The Financial Times reports that "In a long-range forecast issued before the pandemic, the IMF said that between 2019 and 2024 China would account for 28 percent of global growth and India 15 percent—identifying them as the world's top two growth drivers, ahead of the US in third place."[15]

    Bottom Line: As emerging economies develop, their expanding middle classes will have capital to invest in their own countries, but also accretive

---

[15] James Kynge and Amy Kazmin, "Power Crunch in Asia and India Stokes Global Growth Anxiety," Financial Times (October 6, 2021), https://www.ft.com/content/b790d504-b77f-4370-81e5-5ba0d16008bc.

capital for US-listed stock purchases (subject to regulations issued by their own countries).

Ease of Transactions

Today, the buying and selling of stocks is accomplished with a few keystroke swipes. No more calling your broker or filling out multiple forms. Sure, the keystroke method has been around for a few years, but fintech platforms are increasingly easier to use.

Bottom Line: The elegant simplicity of asset selection motivates individuals to become traders/investors, with their resulting buy/sell volumes adding energy to the market.

New Asset Classes

The expanded buffet of investment choices—from Crypto to ETFs to fractionals to options—has never been larger, whereas in the not too recent past, the menu was a modest list of common and preferred shares, mutual funds, and money market instruments.

Bottom Line: Alternative ways to participate in the market adds momentum and traders in a "to the Moon" manifest destiny of wealth accumulation.

■ And One Disruptive Catalyst: Aggressive Approaches

Shorting, algorithmic-trading (a.k.a. high-frequency trading), breakneck day-trading, all often inflamed by social media messaging, are legitimate doppelganger subsets of market froth.

Bottom Line: When you're reviewing your stock prospects, remember there is a large and knowledgeable investor group on the other side of the trade-or-fade universe.

This book helps both entrants who are too fearful to participate in the market or don't know exactly how to invest, and are therefore wallowing in low-yield fixed investments, as well as seasoned investors who want to up their game and accrue a couple more return points. And given the increased breadth and depth of the market as driven by the catalysts, the window for a tailored approach to personal value creation couldn't be better.

■ Capsule

- Wealth creation through stock market participation is the right path, even when market confidence is getting slammed by potential recession cannonballs. It's both the rise and fall of markets that presents "to the Moon" opportunity.

- The dynamics of increased liquidity, new market players, and transactional ease of participation blend into a rich froth of opportunity, but you need an innovative, space-age tool to optimally participate in the market— which is what this book will give you in the form of the **Equalizer**.

PART I

MOONSCAPE

CHAPTER 1

Risk and Mindsets

He was an old man who fished alone in a skiff in the Gulf Stream and he had gone eighty-four days now without taking a fish. In the first forty days a boy had been with him. But after forty days without a fish the boy's parents had told him that the old man was now definitely and finally salao, *which is the worst form of unlucky, and the boy had gone at their orders in another boat which caught three good fish the first week.*[1]

Ernest Hemingway

Perhaps your stock selection experience is much like the fishing misfortune of Hemingway's old man. Maybe you view yourself being possessed by excessive *Salao*, real or imagined, and that prevents you from even attempting to play in the market; for sure, ineffective stock results wear on you and destroy your confidence.

The truth is that we all have *Salao* in our DNA. Unfortunately, some of us appear to have more *Salao* than others. Sure, you can shake the Magic 8 Ball harder or yell at the sky for celestial intervention, but the record may still show that your assets don't even get you to the next county, let alone the Moon. So you intentionally compromise by not playing in the game and you ghost your own rocket.

---

[1] Ernest Hemingway, *The Old Man and the Sea* (Scribner/Simon & Schuster, 2003; Copyright 1952 by Ernest Hemingway): 9

In addition to the *Salao* risk you bring, there is the investment risk the market brings per the assets you select. In simplified market portfolio theory, these two investment risks are referred to as *systemic* and *unsystematic*. Systemic risk is common across all investments, whereas unsystematic risk is specific to the investment choices you make.

How do you straitjacket systemic and unsystematic risk? Regarding the former, you really can't, other than closing your position and perhaps moving the cash to money market instruments. But unsystematic risk can be greatly reduced by having a diversified stock portfolio. Still though, there is your "unlucky" risk: *Salao,* and it must be confronted as it shall determine your rewards at the end of the day. Let's stretch our foreign language inputs to include another impactful word that is 180 degrees different from *Salao*, and that is the Finnish word of *Sisu*.[2]

> *Sisu* has a mystical, almost magical meaning. It is a Finnish term that can be roughly translated into English as strength of will, determination, perseverance, and acting rationally in the face of adversity.
>
> *Sisu* is not momentary courage, but the ability to sustain that courage. It is a word that cannot be fully translated. It stands for the philosophy that what must be done will be done, regardless of cost.

Your rocket to the Moon is very much dependent on your *Sisu*. Let's go backward to hear the story of a voyager and *Sisu,* and then we'll go forward to build yours.

> In 1914, going to the South Pole would be like going to the Moon today. Ernest Shackleton and his ship, the *Endurance*, sailed 12,000 miles from England to the Antarctica with his intention to be the first person to traverse the South Pole, end-to-end. However, the *Endurance* became stuck in pack ice, sank, and the 28 crew members had to live on an ice floe for six torturous months in frigid sub-zero weather, having only minimal food supplies and the mental strain of no-help-is-on-the-way. Knowing the ice floe would eventually melt in its drift North, Shackleton had to pivot.[3]

---

[2] https://www.finlandia.edu/about/our-finnish-heritage.

[3] For a great read on Ernest Shackleton, get *Endurance, Shackleton's Incredible Voyage* by Alfred Lansing (Basic Books, 2014), https://www.amazon.ca/Endurance-Shackletons-Incredible-Alfred-Lansingo. Other terrific reads that I sourced were: https://www.auroraexpeditions.com.au/blog/shackletons-endurance-expedition-timeline/amp/, https://www.coolantarctica.com/Antarctica, https://www.history.com/news/shackleton-endurance-survival.

There's more.

To save themselves, the entire crew squeezed into three open lifeboats, which they hauled over jagged pack ice and desperately rowed 350 miles for five days and nights through the howling Weddell arctic sea, vicious wind, and unrelenting cold to arrive at barren, snowy, Elephant Island.

Wow! Yup, there's still more.

Elephant Island had little food options and was far from shipping lanes—they had zero chance of being discovered. At latitude −61°, it would be the equivalent of where Anchorage, Alaska, is—except Down Under. After two weeks of living inside protective caves dug into a stunted hillside to avoid the often 75 mph winds, Shackleton decided their only chance was to take five men and row an astounding 825 miles north to South Georgia Island (a.k.a. the "Alps in mid-ocean") where he believed a whaling station existed. They arrived at South Georgia after two weeks of navigating the violent seas of the South Atlantic, considered the most dangerous and unpredictable on Earth.

825 miles! That's like rowing from Portland to Los Angeles! Not done though.

Since they landed on the uninhabited south shore, Shackleton and two of the crew had to hike 30 miles over an unexplored, glacier-studded mountain range to get to the northside whaling station. They completed the crossing in two days. Help was secured and all South Georgia and Elephant Island crew survived.

It takes *Sisu* to invest in the market. If you were in the market at the time, how did you react when it melted in March of 2020? "In barely four trading days, the Dow Jones Industrial Average (DJIA) plunged 6,400 points, a beatdown of roughly 26%."[4] Did you have the courage to see your investments through? Or did you panic and tap out? On March 18, 2020, the DJIA was 18,592. Yet, little more than a month later, on April 29, the DJIA finished the day at 24,634, a 32% increase from March 18. Too much *Salao* and not enough *Sisu* in your makeup? How can this be corrected? The formula for overriding *Salao* and leveraging up *Sisu* is quite simple: it was developed by the brilliant nineteenth-century chemist Dr. Louis Pasteur:[5]

Luck favors the prepared mind.

[4] https://www.ncbi.nlm.nih.gov/pmc/articles/PMC7343658.
[5] Paraphrased from https://www.nhlbi.nih.gov/directors-messages/serendipity-and-the-prepared-mind.

Preparation boosts *Sisu* and crushes *Salao*, leading to an increased confidence that enables a fresh prism of investment possibilities. Your investment rewards percolate between all the risk elements: systemic-unsystematic, plus your *Salao* versus *Sisu* mindset, as shown in figure 1.1.

Think back to any sport you played or any test you wrote. You likely prepared hard. And the day came for you to compete. You were ready to try out for a starting position on your high school soccer team. Or to take the SAT. The risk of failure was minimized, and your confidence maximized by putting yourself in a position to succeed. In the context of the stock market, the reduction of *Salao* and increase of *Sisu* through preparation moves you from being a gambler to being an investor. We've seen this model play out in other areas of life, for example, in the "peace through strength" diplomatic approach: you can achieve the objective of peace (lowered risk of war and increased benefit to humanity) through advanced military preparation.

The NASDAQ and NYSE together list about 6,000 companies and, on some days, a combined daily trade of over 8 billion shares.[6] How can the

FIGURE 1.1 **Risk and Reward**

[6] https://www.wsj.com/market-data/stocks/marketsdiary and https://www.statista.com/statistics/1277216/nyse-nasdaq-comparison-number-listed-companies.

FIGURE 1.2 *Salao* Versus *Sisu*

retail investor play in the same arena with the wolf pack of professional hedge funds, trading houses, banks, and mutual fund players and their obvious informational advantages? All your groundwork might still put you at a disadvantage to them. Again, that's where the **EQ**, which we create in part IV, gives you the support you require, because it's not just about the data, it's also how you plan, develop, and interpret your choices. In figure 1.2, your *Salao* and *Sisu* pivot on your preparation and completed **EQ**; as you paint the canvas with deep and wise market insight, your monetary gains will increase.

Of course, it's easy to say: Prepare More! If given the code to launch a rocket, it's useless unless you have the capacity to steer. Or in our case, the **EQ** canvases require that your training incorporates vital constructs, as gifted to you in the following chapters, so that you can maneuver to the Moon.

■ Capsule

- There is the risk the market brings: systemic and unsystematic.

- And just as important as market risk is the risk you bring: *Salao*.

- You must have a courageous mindset to win in the market: *Sisu*.

- Defeating your *Salao* and building your *Sisu* is a function of your preparation.

- Preparation + **EQ** = Rewards (optimal returns).

- Modern Portfolio Theory supposes that the maximum return for a specific risk class places one's portfolio on an efficient frontier curve; regardless, for us, we shall be guided by the following:

As a visual and motivational challenge, in our metaverse, we shall rocket to, and through, the efficient frontier to the Moon!

CHAPTER 2

Preparation

Unfortunately, there seems to be far more opportunity out there than ability....We should remember that good fortune often happens when opportunity meets with preparation.[1]

Thomas A. Edison

Our preparation is built through an awareness of *Why* we are on this journey, *How* we will complete our mission, and *What* we shall do. The linkage and order of first *Why*, then *How*, and finally *What*, was brilliantly developed and articulated by the *New York Times* best-selling author and thought leader Simon Sinek. Simon describes "The Golden Circle" that logically proceeds from the inside-out, that is, from *Why* to *How* to *What*. The premier importance of *Why* is described as:[2]

---

[1] https://www.thomasedison.org/edison-quotes.
[2] Simon Sinek, *Start With Why* (Penguin Group, 2011): 39; and Simon Sinek, David Mead, and Peter Docker, *Find Your Why* (Portfolio/Penguin, 2017): viii. I joined two statements and summarized them. I can't do his wonderful writings justice with my simple quotes here; please seek out Simon's books or google his inspiring TED talks.
Please note that my *Why-How-What* descriptions are my own interpretation and application of Simon's model.

> Some companies and people know *how* they do *what* they do. Very few can clearly articulate it. People and organizations who know their *why* enjoy greater long-term success . . . and are more forward-thinking and innovative.

Without the clarity of *Why* (i.e. a purpose, cause, belief), the firm or investor will float rudderless in a Red Ocean—a situational concept we discuss in chapter 8. In corporate speak, *Why* can also be thought of as the Vision, the *How* as the Strategy, and the *What* as the Mission (or solution-set). However, these terms tend to collide in interpretation, declaration, and usage across the corporate spectrum. No matter, they all serve as a rallying cry to their customer and employee base. Here are a few clips from some leading brands:

CATERPILLAR: At Caterpillar, we take pride in what we do and what we make possible—from the quality of our products and services to the people who stand behind them. But what matters to us most is how we help customers build a better world.[3]

COSTCO: Entrepreneurial spirit. Throughout the decades, the entrepreneurial drive for excellence has continued to define Costco staff at every level. From its management team to the people on the warehouse floor, everyone is united in a common goal to exceed member expectations.[4]

GOOGLE: Our mission is to organize the world's information and make it universally accessible and useful.[5]

EXXONMOBIL: Develops and applies next-generation technologies to help safely and responsibly meet the world's growing needs for energy and high-quality chemical products.[6]

LULULEMON: Our vision for our store was to create more than a place where people could get gear to sweat in, we wanted to create a community hub where people could learn and discuss the physical aspects of healthy living, mindfulness and living a life of possibility.[7]

---

[3] https://www.caterpillar.com/en/company/strategy-purpose/purpose.html.

[4] https://www.costco.ca/about-us.html?&reloaded=true&langId=-24.

[5] https://about.google/. Note that I will use "Google" and not "Alphabet Inc." in naming throughout the book.

[6] https://corporate.exxonmobil.com/About-us/Who-we-are.

[7] https://info.lululemon.com/about/our-story/history.

TESLA: Tesla's mission is to accelerate the world's transition to sustainable energy.[8]

WALMART: We aim to build a better world—helping people live better and renew the planet while building thriving, resilient communities. For us, this means working to create opportunity, build a more sustainable future, advance diversity, equity and inclusion and bring communities closer together.[9]

WILEY: Our community. Our responsibility. Unlocking human potential. We believe in sharing information to create a stronger, better informed, and more compassionate society.[10]

Each of us invests for different reasons. We typically cite *Why* in terms of financial objectives or gains, such as "I want to be up 10 grand by Christmas." But that is an outcome, not a Sinek *Why*. Your *Why* is the reason you turn on your computer to make trades even when you have the flu, the reason you PVR and faithfully watch your favorite business shows from CNBC while LeBron is playing, the reason you look at the changing product line at Costco for under-the-radar movers, and the reason you keenly listen to dull earnings report broadcasts. So rather than aiming for the 10 grand, an inspirational and authentic *Why* could be as simple as:

- To ensure my family has a joyous Christmas

- To invigorate my bucket-list fund for when I retire

- To kick-start my free library for underprivileged children

The inspirational *Why* takes you from the mundane to the adventure, from average to great, and from a one-time trophy to lasting fulfillment. You must create your own investment *Why*. Here's mine in terms of writing this book:

I believe the market exists for the benefit of all.
 And we need the market to grow personal wealth.
 I challenge the notion that retail investors can't surpass the efficient frontier.
 So I wrote this book.

---

[8] https://www.tesla.com/en_CA/about.

[9] https://corporate.walmart.com/purpose.

[10] https://www.WILEY.com/en-ca/corporatecitizenship.

Please think of your *Why* and write it in the space below. Do it in pencil as it may change over time:

MY *WHY*

Now the *How*.

Every company has proprietary inputs that contribute to *How* they build, provide, and differentiate their solution set, all executed to achieve a sustainable competitive advantage. Similarly, our *How* needs quality inputs, or in our case habits, to crush our *Salao*. There are three habits that should be a matter of practice on your journey to the Moon.

■ Curiosity

You have to like the business of business. Your mind should be in a perpetual search for why some companies grow and others fade. You must make this part of your personal radar system. In hockey and football, it's called "keeping your head on a swivel"—always looking for that opening (or that player coming to take your head off!). Let me give you an example of curiosity to explain what I mean. I was a latecomer to the *Yellowstone* TV drama and didn't start my binge-watching till early December, 2021. I was hooked immediately by the brilliant script of Taylor Sheridan, the exceptional acting, and the beauty of Montana. And I wasn't the only one:

> *Yellowstone* continues to defy gravity—and an industry-wide decline in linear ratings. The Season 4 finale of Paramount Network's hugely popular drama starring Oscar winner Kevin Costner hit a new series high with 9.3 million total viewers in Live+Same Day, up +81% vs. the Season 3 finale (5.2 million). The Jan. 2 closer eclipsed the previous L+SD viewership high mark set by the Season 4 premiere (8 million) to become the most

watched telecast on cable since *The Walking Dead* Season 8 premiere on AMC in October 2017 (11.4 million).[11]

On my TV screen, when the show starts, "Paramount" would briefly flash in the lower right-hand corner. What and who is Paramount? I did some quick googling and found they were owned by ViacomCBS (VIAC). It was clear that *Yellowstone* was a juggernaut. I completed my **EQ**, and came across some red flags, primarily a wide peak-to-trough share-price range of $28.29 – $101.97 over the past year. With the share price sitting flat at $28.40, I bought a few days before Christmas (2021) and pulled the 'chute in mid-February after its rip to $35. Agreed, not a multi-bagger, but a fine big wheeler in less than two months.

Imagine a tourist and a traveler going to an iceberg. A tourist would prance around the above-water peak and get their picture taken. The curious traveler scubas below to the bottom 7/8^{ths} and wants to see what the ice is like, how the nearby water changes color, and what fish swim close to it. The tourist is mindless, the traveler mindful.

Curiosity is a willful and fun exercise for your brain. Nurture it.

■ Support

Your orbit—that is, the people you live with, work with, and play with—are sources of ideas, testing of concepts, and helpful opinions. Seriously.

Now, you may say that your husband is a stock market idiot and thinks EBITDA is the newest COVID variant. Rather, view it this way: assume you were looking to buy Target (TGT). Perhaps he shops there, you could ask: Are the stores busy when you are there? Are the shelves stocked? Do you see newer and different product lines coming in? Are there enough clerks to handle the volume? How busy does it seem compared to the nearest Walmart (WMT)? Is the parking lot close to empty on Monday nights? Have you noticed prices rising or falling?

---

[11] Nellie Andreeva, "'Yellowstone' Sets New Ratings Records as Season 4 Finale Draws 9.3 Million Viewers," *Deadline* (January 5, 2022), https://deadline.com/2022/01/yellowstone-season-4-finale-ratings-highs-record-kevin-costner-paramount-network-1234904529. On February 15, 2022, ViacomCBS changed its name to Paramount Global; see https://www.nasdaq.com/articles/viacomcbs-changes-name-to-paramount-global.

Don't ignore the opportunity to ask questions of and test your thinking with anyone.

■ Intelligence

We all want to be smarter. But it's not about being IQ intelligent; rather, it's about putting in the effort to learn and understand the underpinnings of the market. If you don't know why the Fed is important, the difference between operating cash flow and free cash flow, how option volumes can portend share-price direction, how GDP is broadly calculated, the relationship between the 50 DMA and the 200 DMA, how many market sectors there are, what the Porter strategic model is, then maybe you should not invest directly and instead dial-in through an ETF. But the good news is that by purchasing this book and utilizing the **EQ**, you've taken important steps to add to your brain-power.

Your *How* of curiosity, support, and intelligence blend into a personal CSI of lifelong learning, an always-on radar mindset, and fun on your arc to superior market gains.

Finally, we come to *What* do we want to be?

The answer is simple: you need to be a driven professional and active Investor, which we join to Pro:Active. Both traits require little explanation; you've heard a thousand times someone who is good at their craft as being a "real pro." And by being "active," you're relentlessly involved in your stocks.

What does Papa John's do? They make pizzas.

What do you do? You professionally and actively invest. Think of yourself as a business, give it a name and use it as a moniker on community finance message boards. Even make up some business cards with your Pro:Active name to assist you in adopting the business mindset.[12]

To appreciate the mindset of the Pro:Active investor, let's jet through all investor types. We can broadly lump them into groups by their frequency of

---

[12] I'm not referring to establishing a sole proprietorship or incorporation: those entities have complicated operating and tax considerations that must be discussed with a professional accountant.

trading and stock selection approach per our Five-Stack Discovery (which emerges in chapter 9) that feeds the **EQ**:

- Macro (a.k.a. Economic Froth)

- Indices & Sector

- Valuation

- Technical (Momentum)

- Brand

By understanding the investor types in figure 2.1, we can fully grasp our journey:

	Algos	Day Traders & Swing Traders	Pro:Active	Buy 'n Hold	Buy 'n Forget
Trading Frequency	micro- seconds	daily to weekly	as required	upon major macro event	upon major personal event
Trade Trigger	Technical	Sector Technical	Five-Stack Discovery	Macro Valuation	Life

FIGURE 2.1 **The Investor Continuum**

Algorithmic trading was brought to America's general attention on a *60 Minutes* episode over 10 years ago and described by the *Wall Street Journal*:[13]

> High Frequency Trading: What You Missed on *60 Minutes*
> By Shira Ovide
> Oct. 11 2010 9:49 am ET
> *60 Minutes* last night ran a piece about high-frequency trading that piled onto doubts about such computer-driven rapid trades and whether they are an unfair gaming of the markets. These super computers, which actually decide which stocks to buy and sell, are operating on highly secret instructions programmed into them by math wizards who may or may not know anything about the value of the companies that are being traded, correspondent Steve Kroft said in the opener.

Some prognosticators suggest that machine-trading by Algos (a.k.a Quantitative analysts or Quants) account for ~70% of all American equity trading.[14] Their asset choices are made through instructions that sift through

---

[14] https://analyzingalpha.com/algorithmic-trading-statistics.

the momentum (technical) movements of stocks and screened against a complex set of buy-sell criteria. Cisco (CSCO) announced a dividend increase? Not that terribly important. CSCO Ask moved up one penny in the last 3 seconds? Very important. Freeport-McMoRan (FCX) announced a new mine in Wyoming? Not immediately important. FCX Bid and Ask narrowed from 6 cents to 4? Very important.

The NYSE and NASDAQ are usually open for 6.5 hours (9:30 AM – 4:00 PM EST) each trading day, or 390 minutes, or 23,400 seconds. If Ford (F) normally trades 60 million shares per session, equating to 2,564 shares per second, and suddenly blasts to 3,000 (or whatever parameter they've set), the Algos move to DEFCON alert.[15]

Day Traders and Swing Traders invest primarily on sector and technical flows, also known as momentum trading. They analyze share price, sector, and volume action through detailed, mathematical charting tools including RSI, MACD, Fibonacci, and Bollinger Bands; we will step into this realm in chapter 9.

Pro:Active investors navigate market opportunity by using a set of information-based tools that put them in a position to achieve superior market returns. These investors favor growth stocks and view market participation as part of their core-being. They don't marry their assets; instead, they use them to drive their *Why*.

Buy and Hold is a euphemism for, basically, letting your portfolio coast in a benign way. These types of investors are characterized by being overweight to dividend paying stocks. They set modest investment return goals with success being measured as a couple percentage points above a bank-issued term deposit.

Portfolio changes are triggered by major macro events: an oncoming recession foretold by a rising unemployment number or an increase in the Consumer Price Index might precipitate a Buy and Hold outflow to money-market instruments.

Buy and Forget is old or inherited money. These are Investors that socked away cash in shares years ago and left it there. It's on par with burying your money in coffee cans. You open the cans and sell some of your holdings when there is a major life change: a niece gets married and you want to give her a gift, your partner says it's time to tour Europe, etc.

---

[15]The Ford (F) exact average is 60,481,509 from Yahoo! Finance on July 8, 2022.

■ Capsule

■ Ignoring support opportunities and commanding your rocket in sub rosa mode will knock you off course.

■ In our investment approach, *Why* is the vision/cause/belief, the *How* is through our CSI inputs of curiosity, support, and intelligence, and the *What* is what we shall be: professional and active investors. And the fuel that makes it all go is the **EQ**, which we will engineer in part IV.

■ The push and pull tension in our market participation is portrayed in figure 2.2.

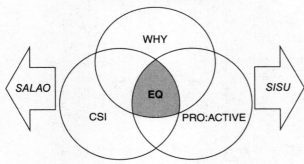

FIGURE 2.2   The Salao and Sisu Tension

CHAPTER 3

Some Helpful Math!

Waitress: "Mr. Berra, should I cut your pizza into 4 pieces or 8?"
Yogi: "You better make it four pieces; I don't think I can eat eight."[1]

Yogi Berra, New York Yankees

The stock market has its own passel of phrases and terms. Although "numbers" and their properties are not malleable like "words," they can still be thrown around with wild abandon and unintentionally cause confusion. Just to ensure we're all on the same math page, I corral a few subjects that sometimes stray.

■ Percentage Changes

The term *percent* is from the Latin per centum, meaning "hundred" or "by the hundred." When a number goes from "x to y," the percentage rate of change—or *delta*—is expressed as (y − x) divided by x, and multiplied by 100.[2]

---

[1] Numerous internet stories exist on this wonderful quote from the 10-time MLB World Series winner and 18-time All-Star.
[2] "Delta" also has a particular meaning in the world of options, and that will be discussed in chapter 14.

In November 2021, the US unemployment rate was 4.2% and the number of people unemployed was 6.7 million. For December 2021, the US unemployment rate was 3.9% with 6.3 million unemployed.[3] The unemployed people delta from November to December is:

$$[(6.3M - 6.7M) / (6.7M)] \times 100 = -6.0\%$$

The change from 4.2% to 3.9% is .3 "percentage points," *not* .3%. The change between the two percentages, in terms of percent:

$$[(3.9\% - 4.2\%) / (4.2\%)] \times 100 = -7.1\%$$

Keep it simple: use "percent" for the change in the raw data and "percentage points" for deltas in the actual percentages. It's important to understand this "% vs. points" detail as the application difference can swing your interpretation of data and charts.

Another concept is the increase in percentage compared to the decrease. For share prices, they can go up by several multiples of 100%, but they cannot decrease by less than their full value; i.e. they cannot decrease by more than 100% and go negative. If General Motors (GM) goes from $60/share to $120, the % increase is: $[(120 - 60) / 60)] \times 100 = 100\%$. If it goes to $240, then that is a 300% increase. But the most it can decrease to is $0/share, which is a 100% decrease.

■ Baggers

We often hear of "x baggers"; for example, assume you bought Tesla (TSLA) at $200 and sold when it hit $1000. To calculate share-price baggers, you divide your final share price by your original purchase price. For TSLA:

$$\$1000/\$200 = \text{a 5 bagger.}$$

Note that the percentage increase is not 500% though—it's 400% using the formula:

$$[(1000 - 200) / (200)] \times 100 = 400\%$$

Baggers and percentages are different.

[3] US Bureau of Labor Statistics, Economic News Release, Employment Situation Summary, https://www.bls.gov/news.release/empsit.nr0.htm.

◼ Multiples

Our **EQ** will have financial "categories": revenue, cost of goods sold, assets, and free cash flow, just to name a few. It will also have financial "metrics" to assess a category or company performance, and multiples (M) are just such a ratio metric:

$$M = \frac{\text{Numerator}}{\text{Denominator}}$$

As the numerator increases, M gets bigger. Conversely, as the denominator gets larger, M gets smaller. You can "freeze" M and forecast the numerator given a particular denominator input.

Likely the most popular valuation metric is the price earnings (PE) ratio, and it's basically what the market will pay "in times" for the earnings (a.k.a. net income) generated by the company:

M = Price per Share / Earnings per Share, or
M = Market Capitalization / Earnings

For example, the PE for Amazon (AMZN) on June 24, 2022, was 56 over the trailing twelve months (TTM).[4] This means the market is willing to pay a share price that is "56 times" Amazon's earnings per share. Multiples are especially handy as they are simple to calculate, widely adopted, and comparatively practical. But they can present a false positive, and making investment decisions on just one or two metrics can wreck your flight path.

◼ Compounded Annual Growth Rate (CAGR)

It's said that when Einstein was asked what his greatest discovery was, he allegedly replied to the effect of "the miracle of compound interest." This is the heart of the Rule of 72: earning interest on your interest and calculated through CAGR:

$$CAGR = (FV\ /\ PV)^{1/n} - 1$$

---

[4] Yahoo! Finance has it as 55.86, and I rounded to 56.

where:

FV   =   future value of an investment

PV   =   present value (a.k.a. starting value) of an investment

n   =   total number of compounding periods (months, years, etc.)

CAGR is easily determined in Excel or other workbooks. I mention CAGR only to familiarize you with the term and its background so that you can follow the "return" on your investments.

■ Present Value

CAGR tells us the speed of our investment and *present value* reveals what a future dollar is worth today. New companies are appealing to investors given their belief that they can get in on the ground floor at modest share prices that could leap in a few years when significant revenues and earnings are attained. In effect, the investor is saying: we have faith in your business model.

$$PV = FV / (1 + r)^n$$

where:

FV   =   future value of an investment

PV   =   the equivalent present value of the investment

n   =   total number of compounding periods (months, years, etc.)

r   =   the rate of return expected on your investment

Investments are on a clock in that a future dollar is not as valuable as a current dollar, given that today's buck can pump more money. The purpose of illustrating PV is not to time-measure your investment, but only to nail the damaging effects of inflation.

Occasionally, I will expand on a point using a fictitious company called ZettaByte Foods (ZBF). Here's an inflation example with ZBF and the Consumer Price Index year over year figures from the US Bureau of Labor Statistics:[5]

---

[5] CPI information sourced from the US Bureau of Labor Statistics is listed and attributed in appendix B.

- *Scenario A, February 2021*: You buy shares of ZBF and expect to reap $500 in four years. Inflation is 1.7% per year, compounded annually. What's that $500 worth today? Answer: $467.40

- *Scenario B, February 2022*: Fast-forward a year. Again, you buy ZBF and expect to net $500 in four years. Inflation is 7.9% per year, compounded annually. What is that $500 worth today? Answer: $368.88

Wow! Inflation rose 6.2 percentage points and the difference from Scenario A to B is a cash drop of over 20%. This elementary example should loudly resonate when we reach chapter 9 and align the inflation-fighting actions of the Federal Reserve to your investments.

■ The Numbers Tree

A look at how numbers are applied in this book ensures a more fluid read. Let's look at an example using ZBF.

> ZettaByte Foods (ZBF) released its Q1 Earnings Report this morning before the bell. Earnings rose to $15 million, up from $12 million the previous quarter. The market liked what it heard and pushed the share price up 10% giving a forward PE of 22.

Current or most recent period will be noted as "*n*" and a prior period, for example the previous Quarter would be *n* − *1*, two Quarters past would be *n* − *2*, etc. Figure 3.1 shows how ZBF shapes up.

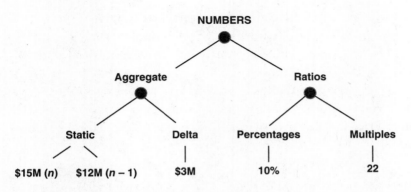

FIGURE 3.1   **Numerical Inputs**

■ Capsule

- ■ Dollar amounts, percentages, multiples (baggers), and deltas are contributors to the financial evaluation of companies on your radar.

- ■ Being confident in the math aids the shift from paper hands to diamond hands!

PART II

FUEL

CHAPTER 4

Portfolio Guardrails

Quantity to Own and Diversification

39

It is a beautiful and delightful sight to behold the body of the Moon.[1]

Galileo Galilei

An important question for every Pro:Active investor is how many stocks should you own at any one time? It's complicated because you're trying to calibrate two unrelated things: how much time you have and how much capital, and one can certainly eclipse the other. If you're working part-time, you have the off-hours to be involved in the market and manage a larger portfolio, but what are your capital constraints? If you're unemployed, you may have even more daylight hours than the part-timer, but what's your disposable income? Figure 4.1 is a consideration, and not a rule.

Regardless of your position in figure 4.1, there should be a degree of diversification in your portfolio. Even for an unemployed limited capital individual, holding three to four stocks is a solid de-risk (unsystematic)

---

[1] https://everydaypower.com.

	Unemployed (with limited capital)	Fully Employed (with capital)	Partially Employed (with capital)	Unemployed (with capital)
# of stocks held at any one time	3 to 4	4 to 8	5 to 10	10 to 15
Maximum capital % allocation to one Stock	50%	33%	25%	20%

FIGURE 4.1 Stocks Held and Capital Allocated

move. Note that figure 4.1's diversification is somewhat Goldilocks between the rival views of significant and reduced diversification:

Significant Diversification
Article by Mallika Mitra
June 16, 2021
   In 1970, academics Lawrence Fisher and James Lorie published their findings that a portfolio of around 30 stocks can provide enough diversification to limit risk while still raking in returns. And in the book *Investment Analysis and Portfolio Management*, Frank Reilly and Keith Brown wrote that owning about 12 to 18 stocks will give you more than 90% of the benefits of diversification. The sweet spot may be somewhere in the middle. Haran Segram, a clinical assistant professor of finance at the NYU's Stern School of Business, says between 20 and 25 stocks are needed for a diversified portfolio. Anything above 25 will only offer marginal benefits, he adds.[2]

Reduced Diversification
Thoughts of Warren Buffet
Given at the 1996 Berkshire Hathaway (BRK.A & .B) Annual Meeting
   Buffett declared that diversification is a "protection against ignorance." He went on to add that any investor who knows what they're doing should not feel the need to diversify at all, because they would only buy the companies they truly understand. If you know how to analyze businesses and value businesses, it's crazy to own 50 stocks or 40 stocks or 30 stocks, probably, because there aren't that many wonderful businesses that are understandable to a single human being, in all likelihood.
   And to have some super-wonderful business and then put money in number 30 or 35 on your list of attractiveness and forego putting more money into number one, just strikes Charlie and me as madness. And it's conventional practice, and it may—you know, if all you have to achieve is

[2] https://money.com/diversification-how-many-stocks/.

average, it may preserve your job. But it's a confession, in our view, that you don't really understand the businesses that you own."[3]

Our strategic preparation and tactical **EQ** execution allows us to operate closer to the reduced-diversification end of the spectrum.

A diversification addition to your portfolio could be an Exchange Traded Fund (ETF). These liquid investments track—even short—an index, a sector, other assets, or countries. Their intra-day liquidity and trading make them attractive investments; in fact, ETFs now account for over 10% of the entire NYSE and NASDAQ market capitalization.[4] And by the ETF being inherently diversified (some more than others) and not requiring much investment review-time, they could be the right choice for some part of your portfolio. But be wise and don't unknowingly glide into full-on passive investing; here are some recent comments from Cathie Wood and Elon Musk:[5]

Source: Twitter, Inc.

---

[3] https://finance.yahoo.com/news/warren-buffett-diversification-protection-against-164329437.html.

[4] Michael Wurston, "Global ETF Assets Hit $9 Trillion, Advises That US ETFs Are $6.6 Trillion," *Wall Street Journal* (August 12, 2021).

[5] Yun Li, "Elon Musk and Cathie Wood Knock Passive Index Investing, Saying It's Gone Too Far," CNBC (May 5, 2022), https://www.cnbc.com/2022/05/05/elon-musk-and-cathie-wood-knock-passive-index-investing-saying-its-gone-too-far.html.

It's table stakes for you as a Pro:Active investor to have portfolio diversification. If you own six stocks and four of them are banks, then you're not diversified as it's all about sectors, not companies. And inside the sector, if you have a couple stocks, there is an **EQ** way to detail your assignments even further—we'll get to that after we have some fun looking at financial reporting. Before you leave chapter 4, please scribble the names of any stocks or ETFs that you presently own.

CURRENT PORTFOLIO

_____

_____

_____

_____

■ Capsule

- Diversification is an inherent part of any portfolio, but over-diversification is an unnecessary governor on your engine. The **EQ** will help find the optimal setting.

- Your rocket requires continual maintenance. The quantity of held assets must align to both your capital and time limitations.

CHAPTER 5

Snapshot of Financial Statements

We were always focused on our profit and loss statement.
But cash flow was not a regularly discussed topic.
It was as if we were driving along, watching only the
speedometer, when in fact we were running out of gas.[1]

Michael S. Dell

A ll companies, whether listed on an exchange or not, keep a scorecard of their business performance through financial statements. The Securities and Exchange Commission (SEC), in its effort to ensure a fair, transparent, and robust market, requires dozens of time-sensitive forms in respect to a firm's financial condition, with the notable ones for your early-warning detection being:[2]

- 8K: major current developments in the company

- 10K/Annual Report: regarding the company's year-end financial condition

---

[1] Michael Dell is the Founder, CEO, and Chairman of Dell Technologies. https://en.wikipedia.org/wiki/Michael_Dell.

[2] https://www.sec.gov/forms.

- 10Q: regarding the company's financial condition at end of Quarters 1, 2, and 3

- 13D: filed when a person or group acquires more than 5% of a company's shares

- 13F: a quarterly report required from institutional owners having $100M+ in equity assets

- S-1: registration form for companies preparing to offer listed securities

Corporate financial submissions to the SEC include a trifecta of interrelated financial statements: the income statement, the balance sheet, and the cash flow statement. There's no need to tear apart the statements and prove our "accounting" knowledge; we shall aim for wisdom of evaluation over knowledge of Generally Accepted Accounting Principles (GAAP). Look, we're trying to make dough here, not deconstruct the chemical composition of flour.

Now is a great time to introduce a guiding principle known as Occam's Razor. There are myriad interpretations and translations of this fourteenth-century English philosopher's work; here's mine, which guides this book and the three financial statement summaries:[3]

The simplest way to explain something is usually the best way.

■ The Income Statement (Profit & Loss)

The income statement is like your household budget: list the money coming in the door and subtract your expenses, with the difference being your gain or loss at the end of the month. The income statement has four categories that are discussed by the corporate executive, as both point-in-time results and to previous quarters, at *every* Earnings Report (ER):

- Revenue: the "top line"

- Net Income: the "bottom line" (also referred to as earnings per share)

---

[3] https://www.merriam-webster.com/dictionary/Occam's razor. The "razor" refers to the act of shaving away excess information and unnecessary assumptions in the search for understanding, a.k.a. The Law of Parsimony.

- Growth: revenue increase to the previous period and guidance toward the future

- Margin % to Revenue: a ratio of any one (or all) of Gross Profit, EBITDA, Operating, EBIT, Net Income to Revenue[4]

Let's look at ZBF's *Occamized* income statement for the current year (n) and the previous year ($n-1$) in figure 5.1, but first a few notations:

- Cost of Goods Sold (COGS) are the variable costs associated with producing revenue.

- EBITDA is a common measure used by executives and analysts. If a company has asset impairments—such as a loss in the value of buildings—EBITDA may be mentioned as a pre-impairment amount (a.k.a. adjusted). Similar with Operating Earnings, there can be a pre and post adjustment number, and sometimes the difference is substantial.

- Depreciation, amortizations, and impairments are non–cash accounting terms to record the decline in value of an asset over a period of time.

- At the end of the fiscal year, the income statement is closed and the gain (after dividends, if any) or loss is transferred to the balance sheet as Retained Earnings. The income statement then starts the new fiscal period with a "clean sheet."

- Assume ZBF's current share price is $5.00 with 3,000 outstanding shares (i.e. market capitalization of $15,000 = $5.00 × 3,000).

ZBF had a good P&L per some selected valuation metrics in figure 5.2. Price to sales is reasonable at 3, YoY revenue growth was strong at 21%, and operating margin was a healthy 20% (especially given its consumer staples sector).

■ The Balance Sheet (Financial Position)

This sheet is a running total of what the company owns (assets), what it owes (liabilities), and the difference between the two (equity, a.k.a. net worth) at a point in time. The earnings report discussion would include:

- Capital Investment: expenditures adding to Fixed Assets (Property, Plant, & Equipment)

---

[4] Often, "margin" is expressed as an aggregate value as well as a percentage.

	n	n–1	FURTHER INFORMATION & AKA
Revenue	$ 5,100	$ 4,200	Topline ... aka: Sales
COGS	$ (3,000)	$ (2,600)	Cost of Goods Sold ... aka: Direct Costs
Gross Profit	$ 2,100	$ 1,600	aka: Gross Margin
SG&A	$ (1,000)	$ (900)	Salary, General, & Administrative Expenses ... aka: Indirect Cost
EBITDA	$ 1,100	$ 700	Earnings Before Interest, Taxes, Depreciation & Amortization
Depreciation	$ (100)	$ (70)	Non-cash charge for loss in value of fixed assets over time
Operating Income	$ 1,000	$ 630	Operating Margin %, expressed as Operating Income/Revenue
Non-Operating Revenue and/or Expenses	$ (5)	$ (10)	Items that are not core to the company's operations
EBIT	$ 995	$ 620	Earnings Before Interest & Taxes
Interest Expense	$ (75)	$ (65)	
Taxes	$ (166)	$ (100)	
Net Income	$ 754	$ 455	Bottomline ... aka: Earnings, Profit
Dividends Paid	$ (500)	$ (350)	
Remainder Transferred to Retained Earnings	$ 254	$ 105	
Tax Rate	18%	18%	
EBIAT (EBIT * (1 – Tax Rate))	$ 816	$ 508	Earnings Before Interest After Taxes
NOPAT (Net Income + Tax + Interest Expense + non-Operating Revenues/Expenses) × (1 – tax rate)	$ 820	$ 517	Net Operating Profit After Taxes

(note: EBIAT = NOPAT when Non-Operating Revenue and/or Expenses = Zero)

FIGURE 5.1 ZBF Income Statement

Price per Share (at time of Earnings Report)	$ 5.00
Earnings per Share	$ 0.25
Price Earnings Ratio, trailing 12 months	20
Outstanding Shares	3,000
Market Capitalization	$ 15,000
Price to Sales Ratio	3
Interest Coverage (EBIT/Interest Expense)	13
Year over Year (YoY) Revenue Growth	21%
EBITDA Margin	22%
YoY Revenue Growth + EBITDA Margin	43%
Operating Margin	20%
Profit Margin	15%
Dividend Yield	3%

FIGURE 5.2   ZBF Income Statement Valuations

- Debt: did the company add debt, especially long-term debt

- Liquidity: views on how the company managed its working capital

- Return Ratios: measuring selected income statement results to balance sheet categories

ZBF's balance sheet is shown in figure 5.3, but a few notations:

- Assets and liabilities are each separated into current and non-current groupings:

- Current assets includes cash, plus accounts receivable and inventory, as they can be turned into cash within a year (or are expected to).

- The same one-year horizon applies to current liabilities, such as accounts payable and short-term debt.

- Current assets minus current liabilities equals net working capital.

- Non-current assets and non-current liabilities are of a longer life cycle, i.e. their value or obligation extends beyond the current fiscal period.

- Assets are stated in "Mark to Market" values, that is, the value a company would receive if they sold the asset.

	n	$n-1$	$n-(n-1)$
Current Assets			
Cash	$ 300	$ 275	$ 25
Accounts Receivable	$ 400	$ 375	$ 25
Inventory	$ 900	$ 700	$ 200
Other, Prepaid Expenses	$ 100	$ 70	$ 30
Total Current Assets	$ 1,700	$ 1,420	$ 280
Non-Current Assets			
Property, Plant, & Equipment (PP&E)	$ 2,300	$ 2,000	$ 300
Accumulated Depreciation	$ 400	$ 300	$ 100
Net PP&E	$ 1,900	$ 1,700	$ 200
Intangibles (Goodwill, etc)	$ 525	$ 500	$ 25
Long-Term Investments	$ 60	$ 45	$ 15
Total non-Current Assets	$ 2,485	$ 2,245	$ 240
TOTAL ASSETS	$ 4,185	$ 3,665	$ 520
Current Liabilities			
Accounts Payable	$ 350	$ 325	$ 25
Short-Term Debt	$ 425	$ 400	$ 25
Other, Accrued Expenses	$ 150	$ 100	$ 50
Total Current Liabilities	$ 925	$ 825	$ 100
Non-Current Liabilities			
Other, non-Current Liabilities	$ 45	$ 40	$ 5
Long-Term Debt	$ 825	$ 675	$ 150
Total Non-Current Liabilities	$ 870	$ 715	$ 155
TOTAL LIABILITIES	$ 1,795	$ 1,540	$ 255
Equity			
Capital Stock	$ 936	$ 925	$ 11
Retained Earnings	$ 1,454	$ 1,200	$ 254
TOTAL EQUITY	$ 2,390	$ 2,125	$ 265

FIGURE 5.3 ZBF Balance Sheet

- Companies, per their charter, have a limit on the number of "authorized" common and/or preferred shares they can issue. A subset of authorized shares are outstanding shares, which comprises the restricted shares held by employees/insiders and the publicly traded "Float" shares.

- Market capitalization is normally based on outstanding shares, but some financial platforms use the float, so ensure you are assumption-consistent on cross-firm reviews.

The strength of ZBF's income statement is pretty-much matched by its balance sheet. Let's review some of ZBF's income statement and balance sheet metrics for period '*n*' in figure 5.4.

Although ZBF added debt during the year, it was easily carried by its EBITDA with a low 1.1 multiple and a good current assets to current liabilities ratio of 1.8. Returns are strong with its ROE well above its weighted average cost of capital (i.e. the debt and equity financing costs to operate the company). On the downside, the EV/EBITDA and price to book ratios are high—the market has lofty expectations.

Total Debt (ST + LT)	$ 1,250
Enterprise Value (Market Cap + Debt – Cash)	$ 15,950
Weighted Average Cost of Capital (assumed)	10%
Current Assets to Current Liabilities	1.8
Cash per Share	$ 0.10
Change in Short-Term & Long-Term Debt	$ 175
Debt/EBITDA, multiple	1.1
Debt/Equity	52%
Return (NI) on Assets	18%
Return (EBIAT) on Capitalization (as defined in figure 5.5)	22%
Return (NI) on Equity (must be > WACC)	32%
Enterprise Value to EBITDA, multiple	15
Book Value per Share	$ 0.80
Price/Share to Book Value/Share (aka, Price to Book)	6.3

FIGURE 5.4 Income Statement & Balance Sheet Metrics

The balance sheet is the origin for reckless definitions and usage of the word "capital" as shown in figure 5.5 with the numbers from ZBF. We'll swerve around this terminology black hole and ensure the **EQ** is *Occamized* wherever possible![5]

■ The Statement of Cash Flows

The cash flow statement is considered *the* record of a company's financial intelligence: are they generating cash or burning it? Although the math is a bit tricky, the concept is straightforward: how did the company source, manage, and invest cash throughout the year? The cash flow statement is chopped into operating, investment, and financing activities. Here's the ZBF view in figure 5.6:

- Build the Operating Cash Flow (OCF) with net income and add back those income statement elements that did not use cash (depreciation, amortizations, impairments).

- Next, capture the movement in working capital (excluding cash). If a current asset increased over the year, then deduct that amount from the tally. For example, in figure 5.3, ZBF's accounts receivable went from $375 to $400. By carrying more receivables, ZBF did not have "cash access," and it's an OCF deduction. If a current liability increased over the year, then that's a positive contribution to OCF. ZBF's accounts payable went from $325 to $350. By getting suppliers to carry those obligations, the $25 delta is added to the tally.

- Replicate the balance sheet deltas to Investment and Financing elements. The largest Investment entry is usually for PP&E.

- Subtract dividends paid from the income statement and include them in the Financing section.

---

[5] Note that Yahoo! Finance data is mostly sourced from Morningstar, and the following computations are typically used:

Net Debt = ST Debt + LT Debt (excluding ST & LT Capital Leases) − Cash

Total Debt = ST Debt + ST Capital Leases + LT Debt + LT Capital Leases

Invested Capital = ST Debt + LT Debt (excluding ST & LT Capital Leases) + Equity − Minority Interest

Total Capitalization = Invested Capital − ST Debt (excluding ST Capital Leases)

Enterprise Value = Market Capitalization (Share Price × Outstanding Shares) + ST Debt + ST Capital Leases + LT Debt + LT Capital Leases − Cash/Cash Equivalents

Debt to Equity = LT Debt + LT Capital Leases / Stockholders Equity (i.e. not total Equity)

	for period n	
Capital Structure	Debt to Equity (or Debt to Debt+Equity)	52%
Change In Capital Investment	PP&E change from Prior Year, ($n - (n-1)$)	$ 300
Working Capital	Current Assets – Current Liabilities	$ 775
Capital Stock	Issued Shares, aka Paid-In Capital	$ 936
Invested Capital (Finance Method)	Debt + Equity – Cash – Securities held in Other Companies – Retained Earnings	$ 1,826
Capital Assets	Property, Plant, & Equipment	$ 2,300
Invested Capital (Operations Method)	Fixed Assets + Current Assets – Current Liabilities – Cash	$ 2,775
Capital Employed	Assets – Current Liabilities or Equity + Non-Current Liabilities	$ 3,260
Net Operating Assets (aka, Net Capital)	Assets – Cash – Liabilities (excluding Debt)	$ 3,340
Capital Funding (the flipside of NOA)	Equity + Debt – Cash	$ 3,340
Capital (aka, Basic Invested Capital)	Debt + Equity	$ 3,640

Note: Debt = Short-Term & Long-Term Debt. Some Analysts only use Long-Term Debt in their metrics.
Note: Often, Capital Leases are excluded in Debt calculations.

FIGURE 5.5 Usage of the Word "Capital"

SNAPSHOT OF FINANCIAL STATEMENTS

OPERATING CASH FLOW (OCF)		
Net Income	$	**754**
Non-Cash Items: Add Back Depreciation	$	100
Changes in Working Capital (excl Cash)		
Change in Accounts Receivable	$	(25)
Change in Inventory	$	(200)
Change in Other, Prepaid Expenses	$	(30)
Change in Accounts Payable	$	25
Change in Accrued Expenses	$	50
TOTAL OPERATING CASH FLOW	$	674
INVESTMENT CASH FLOW		
Purchase of PP&E	$	(300)
Purchase of Intangibles	$	(25)
Purchase of Long-Term Investments	$	(15)
TOTAL INVESTMENT CASH FLOW	$	(340)
FINANCING CASH FLOW		
Increase in Short-Term Debt	$	25
Increase in Other non-Current Liabilities	$	5
Repayment of Long-Term Debt	$	(75)
Increase in (new) Long-Term Debt	$	225
Issuance of Capital Stock	$	11
Dividends Paid	$	(500)
TOTAL FINANCING CASH FLOW	$	(309)
OPERATING+INVESTMENT+FINANCING	$	**25**
Cash Balance, Previous Year ($n-1$)	$	275
TOTAL CASH FLOW + ($n-1$)	$	300
Cash Balance, Current Year (n)	$	300
FREE CASH FLOW (OCF – PPE Change)	$	374
Price/Share to OCF/Share (aka, Price to Cash Flow)		22
Enterprise Value to Free Cash Flow		43
Free Cash Flow to Enterprise Value		2.3%

FIGURE 5.6   ZBF Cash Flow Statement

- The previous year's $(n - 1)$ cash, plus the operating, investing, and Financing cash flows, equals the cash on the balance sheet in year n.

ZBF had strong operating cash flow, and the increase in PP&E was only minor, leading to healthy free cash flow. The EV/FCF multiple of 43 is hefty and suggests that the market may be paying a premium for ZBF.

The ZBF FCF calculation yielded what is sometimes called "owners earnings," and the formulation was developed by—you guessed it—Warren Buffett.[6] Often, FCF streams are part of a present value (a.k.a. discounted cash flow) analysis to determine an intrinsic share price or for buying a company.

Now, after all that, I'm putting some hair on this free cash flow thing. As you expected, there are other ways to calculate free cash flow, and we can group them as:

- **Levered:** known as free cash flow to Equity (FCFE): viewed as the cash left over after all bills are paid (ZBF FCF of $374 is essentially a Levered model).

- **Unlevered:** known as free cash flow to the Firm (FCFF): viewed as the cash a company has prior to making its debt (principal and interest) payments.

The free cash flow levered and unlevered computations can begin with OCF, EBITDA, EBIT, EBIAT, NOPAT, or net income. In the following levered example, assume ZBF's debt principal and interest repayments had an obligatory outflow of $150. You can see how different formulas drive different results in figure 5.7:

LEVERED FCF (Free Cash Flow to Equity)		UNLEVERED FCF (Free Cash Flow to the Firm)	
EBITDA	$ 1,100	Operating Cash Flow	$ 674
Taxes	$ (166)	Tax Rate	18%
Working Capital (excl Cash)	$ (180)	Interest Paid	$ 75
Capex	$ (300)	Tax Interest Shield	$ (62)
Mandatory Interest/Debt Payments	$ (150)	Capex	$ (300)
Levered Free Cash Flow	$ 304	Unlevered Free Cash Flow	$ 388

FIGURE 5.7 Cash Flow, Levered and Unlevered

---

[6] David Ahern, "Owner Earnings: Warren Buffett's Favorite Formula," GuruFocus.com (May 10, 2017), https://finance.yahoo.com/news/owner-earnings-warren-buffetts-favorite-173303913.html.

Just for fun, what are three financial valuation metrics that you really like? Drop them into the panel and let's see how the **EQ** measures up. We'll get to them shortly.

MY THREE FINANCIAL METRICS

_____

_____

_____

■ Capsule

- Knowing how financial statements "interlock" assists in developing and understanding comparative cross-firm financial valuations.

- Many ratios were presented in chapter 5; no worries, we're going to get to know them in subsequent chapters.

- _Occamize_ your FCF understanding to OCF + the annual change in PP&E (gross value).

- The **EQ** does not require any accounting mastery; rather, it only needs your higher-level CSI valuation efforts. Bookkeeping complexities just slow the rocket, ignore them!

- The **EQ** utilizes a set of superior valuation ratios with recommended "red flags." All you do is source the readily available metrics from one of many financial platforms.

CHAPTER 6

Financial Benchmarking

If you don't find a way to make money while you sleep, you will work until you die.[1]

Warren Buffett

All investments must be tethered to broader market performance, and there are numerous indices to illustrate the big picture. Although I list seven in figure 6.1 for their 2021 gains, the triple crown is the Dow Jones Industrial Average (DJIA), S&P 500, and the NASDAQ Composite.[2]

As a Pro:Active investor, you'll develop a CSI rhythm of stock-searching for radar prospects; that is, assets that have jump-started your curiosity. Is the market (index) rallying? Is my radar company in the mix, or am I on the outside looking in? How does my prospect compare to others? To which macro factors should I sensitize my radar stocks, and how does a particular factor benefit or slam a stock? Is there a way to easily summarize the value of each company? Damn, how does this company actually make money?

[1] https://www.goodreads.com/author/quotes/756.Warren_Buffett?page=2.
[2] Data amalgamated from: Gunjan Banerji, "In a Wild Year for Markets, Stocks Pull Off Big Gains," *Wall Street Journal* (December 31, 2021), https://www.wsj.com/articles/u-s-stocks-end-a-wild-year-with-big-gains-11640860206 and finance.yahoo.com/quote on January 24, 2022.

	Jan.4, 2021	Dec.31, 2021	% + in 2021	What Is It?
Dow Jones Industrial Average	30,224	36,338	20%	index of 30 NYSE stocks
S&P 500	3,701	4,766	29%	index of the top 500 NASDAQ & NYSE stocks
NASDAQ Composite	12,698	15,644	23%	index of the 3000+ NASDAQ companies
NASDAQ 100	12,686	16,320	29%	index of 100 non-financial NASDAQ companies
Dow Jones Transportation Average	12,230	16,479	35%	index of 20 transports ... is the oldest index
Russell 2000	1,946	2,245	15%	index of 2000 small cap NYSE, NASDAQ, & OTC stocks
Wilshire 5000	38,892	48,461	25%	index of 3500 HQ'd USA stocks

FIGURE 6.1 Indices

Source: Data from [2]

■ Company Groupings

Cross-mapping the capacities of your target companies to firms of like similarities and circumstances is where the **EQ** optimizes your diversification planning and financial rewards. Figure 6.2 heightens your "these outfits belong together" awareness so that comparisons are more effective.

Regions

Comparative companies should derive a similar percentage of their revenue from the same part of the world. If one gold company obtains 90% of its revenue from Canada/US, and the other is 90% from Mongolia, then your review is skewed from the outset. The Mongolian company brings

FIGURE 6.2 Corporate Groupings

Mega-Cap	$200 Billion +
Large-Cap	$10 Billion – $200 Billion
Mid-Cap	$2 Billion – $10 Billion
Small-Cap	$300 Million – $2 Billion
Micro-Cap	less than $300 Million

FIGURE 6.3   **Market Cap Groupings**

with it currency risk, logistic challenges, government unknowns, and possibly labor surety concerns: are these risks fully captured in the share price? Next, are you contrasting companies that have a similar market cap? Note that Wall Street classifies companies by their market cap size in figure 6.3.

Sectors

Are your two companies in the same sector? Per the Global Industry Classification Standard (GICS), there are 11 sectors sliced into 24 industry groups as shown in figure 6.4. Subterranean levels stratify the 24 to 69 industries and 158 sub-industries, and you'll see labels of "Durable" and "Non-Durable"; the former comprises goods that have a lifespan of three years or more, whereas the latter are consumed quickly. But there is no need for us to plumb the 69/158, and if you wish to see those groups, head to appendix H.

Figure 6.4 provides the approximate weighting of each sector in the S&P 500, along with a sample of the major ETFs that track that sector.[3] (You must be able to rattle-off all 11 sectors to be awarded the Pro:Active badge!)

Growth Versus Value

Wall Street hangs a moniker on companies: growth or value. *Growth* companies are expected to outperform the market, either due to their own excep-

[3] GICS information was sourced from: https://www.spglobal.com/spdji/en/indices/equity/sp-500/#data on March 11, 2022.
https://www.nasdaq.com/articles/the-11-sectors-of-the-stockmarket-their-biggest-etfs-2021-05-30.
https://www.msci.com/documents/1296102/11185224/GICS+Methodology+2020.pdf.
https://en.wikipedia.org/wiki/Global_Industry_Classification_Standard.

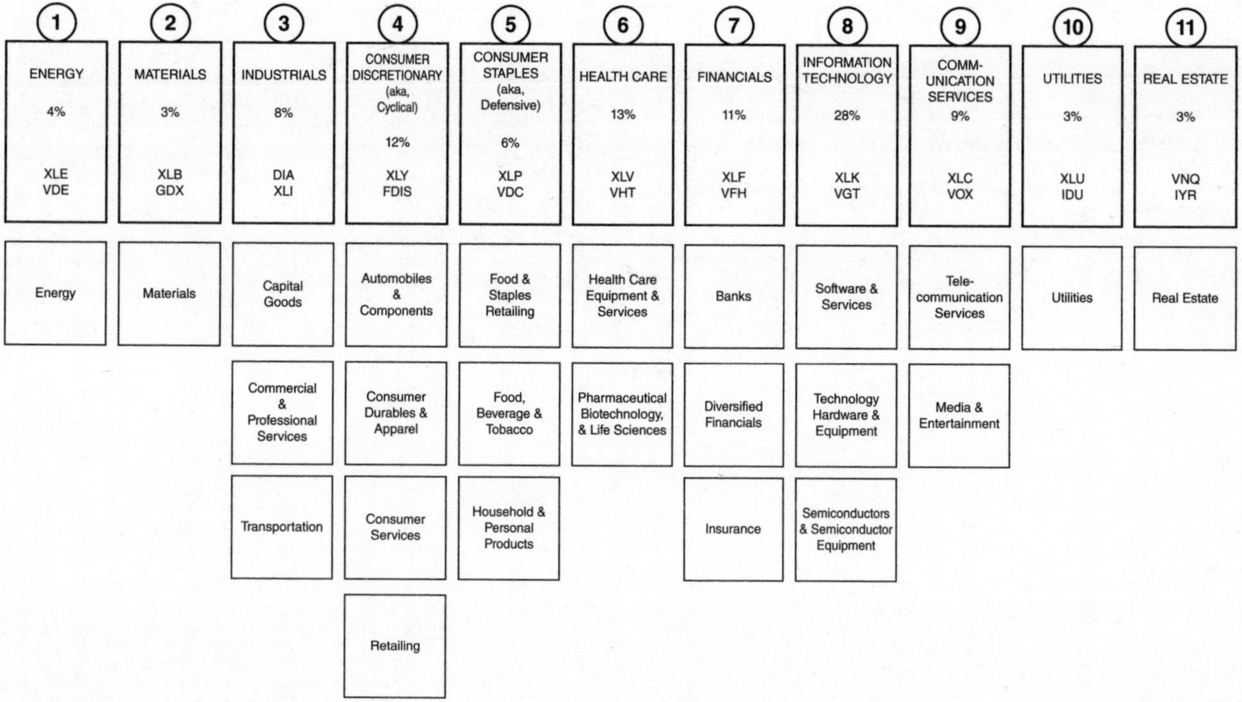

FIGURE 6.4 The 11 GICS Sectors

tionalism or because the ocean where they play is supposed to lift all boats. *Value* stocks tend to ripen at the sector average and have lower PEs. Often, they may be undervalued in that their share price neither reflects their "intrinsic" financials nor their future possibilities. Rightly or wrongly, the market perceives that growth companies will (eventually) provide higher returns and with these blue-sky expectations, the share price is pushed upward. Value stocks, for many reasons, have the shade of lower hope thrown at them, often to CEO and shareholder frustration.

Cyclical Versus Secular

Companies, whether growth or value, have revenue streams that are strongly affected by the general economy. So, two more labels arise, and we peel back the naming of *cyclical* versus *secular* to align with our **EQ** needs.

- *Cyclical* means the goods and services offered by that company track with the expansion and contraction of the economic cycle.

- *Secular* (a.k.a. defensive) is just the opposite: these steadier companies are less affected by the boom and bust of the economic cycle.

In chapter 4, you listed your current portfolio. Update the following box with those same stocks according to the cyclical and secular definitions.

Cyclical:	Secular:

The standard jargon is to varnish a company as cyclical or secular per its sector. For example, there are sectors of consumer discretionary and consumer staples, and by definition, the former is cyclical, and the latter is secular. But regardless of sector, some companies are more immune to the ups and downs of the economy as they're simply better run, or have more financial strength to withstand storms, or their solution set is bulletproof, or a host of other reasons. Take airlines in the *industrials* sector. When economic times are good, people enjoy more long-distance vacations, and airline revenues increase. It's very much a cyclical sector. However, within the established airline industry, it's true that some firms are more robust (e.g. Delta) than others (e.g. American Airlines), yet neither would be considered a growth company. Given this reality, the **EQ** slightly bends the branding application of cyclical and secular.

> The **EQ** rewards the more robust value companies (i.e. nongrowth), with a secular tag, regardless of the sector they operate in.

EQ Stock Groupings

The **EQ** integrates growth versus value and cyclical versus secular classifications to validate your diversification efforts. Understood, this is a bit of art mixed with science. But in our *Occam* model, we sometimes throw hand grenades and not darts. Figure 6.5 exhibits how we pop companies into four major groupings.

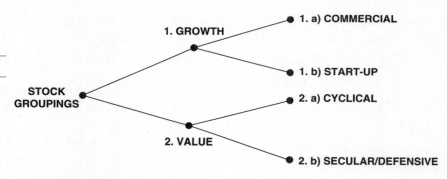

FIGURE 6.5 Stock Groupings

Here are details of the groupings:

■ **Growth Commercial:** These are newer listings with a top-line emphasis. Some evaluators use the "Rule of 40" to define a growth stock: the revenue growth plus the EBITDA (or Operating) margin should be 40% or higher. Growth commercial companies have positive EBITDA and could be bottom-line black. Geographic opportunities have yet to be fully realized. Their business model is solid, and their share price may exhibit parabolic moves. CEOs are often a brand in themselves.

   ■ Example: Tesla (TSLA)

- **Growth Start-up:** These are newer listings with an emphasis on telling their story by painting a no-worries, robust view of the future. They are at the early stages of their business life cycle and are focused on getting their solution set into production mode or a clinical trial approved. Often, they are a niche player. The difference between the float and shares outstanding is usually large, perhaps 15% or more. EBITDA may be negative. Shares often peak out of the gate and then flatten as operational or market-acceptance matters arise.

  - Example: Canoo (GOEV)

- **Value Cyclical:** These stocks surf with the economy's waves. If GDP and employment are rising, these stocks crest with them. Their dividend yields may have special payments in rising economies. Often, they are commodity or luxury-goods companies.

  - Example: Freeport-McMoRan (FCX)

- **Value Secular (a.k.a. Defensive):** These stocks are somewhat immune to the broader movements of the economy. They are often called "blue chips," a colloquialism from the early 1900s that associated a quality stock with the color of the highest poker chip (at that time). They pay a consistent dividend and enjoy strong brand recognition. Their massive balance sheets are a bulwark to economic downturns.

  - Example: Johnson & Johnson (JNJ)

In the following panel, I would like you to pencil in a few stocks that you have on your radar. We're going to blow out an **EQ** Canvas in chapter 11, but for now just assign your early-warning stocks to one of two groups: those that you believe are growth stocks and those that are value.

Growth:	**Value:**

■ Valuation

All companies on your stock radar will be sifted through the Five-Stack Discovery of macro (economic), indices and sector, valuation, technical, and brand reference points (a.k.a. evaluators or metrics). Although valuation will be fully reviewed in chapter 9, given our learnings from the financial statements, it would be shrewd to now examine a few metrics. By analyzing these now, along with some real company actuals, we can broaden our understanding of business models for subsequent chapters.

Valuation analysis is the financial deconstruction of a company's performance as pioneered by Benjamin Graham in his classic 1949 book *The Intelligent Investor*. Heads-up though, sometimes numbers—as Yogi Berra observed—can be deceiving and we accidentally fall into a "valuation trap." That's why our **EQ** sources from a Five-Stack model, and not only valuation. There are dozens and dozens of metric permutations and combinations, and the law of diminishing returns quickly arrives. To navigate the flotsam of data and get to a manageable set of evaluators, we *Occam* the cosmos to those that satisfy these conditions:

- Emphasize growth

- Can be computed simply

- Collectively source all three statements

- Are part of the terminology used in media

- Stand on their own merits and are not duplicative

Next, we categorize the evaluators to alpha, gamma, and omega in figure 6.6. I'm not saying that alpha is better than omega, it's that alpha data is the "go to," and I further strain alpha to a few acid tests. Of course, no metric exists in a vacuum; as noted, all data must be cross-referenced to a peer company that's in the same "stock grouping," and even better, of the same scale, geographic operating territory, sector, and sub-sector. Also, remember that every sector has its specialized indicators: netbacks in O&G, streaming subscriber growth, retail inventory turnover, cars shipped, price to book for banks especially, etc. You want to be aware of them as you explore companies.

The following are the alpha valuation acid tests, including the warning red flags. That's not to say that if your goal company is a metric outlier you should dismiss investing in it; more so, that you need other reasons to buy.

	MACRO (ECONOMIC)	INDICES & SECTOR	VALUATION	TECHNICAL	BRAND
ALPHA (Acid Test Metrics are Highlighted)	**Front Page News** **Fed: Inflation (CPI) &** **Unemployment** **GDP Q/Q** **Bond Yields, Oil** China PMI	**GDP Q/Q to** **Business Cycle** **S&P 500, with Hi-Lo** **ETF Weathervane** VIX	**PE (FWD), P/S** **EV/FCF, OM%** **Debt/EBITDA** 52 Range, Hi-Lo YoY Revenue ROE	**Float/Out-Shares** **50 DMA : 200 DMA** Beta RSI Short Ratio Puts to Calls	**Moat & Ocean** **Black Swans** **Guidance** **Upgrades & Downgrades**
GAMMA	Copper	DJIA & DJTA NASDAQ & NASDAQ 100 TRIN	PE (TTM), PEG P/CF, Div Yield EV/Sales, EV/EBITDA Market Cap/EBITDA Rule of 40 EBITDA Margin NI/Revenue	MACD Chart Visuals Maximum Pain	Share Buybacks/Splits Accounting Integrity ESG
OMEGA			ROA, R/Capital Price to Book Current Ratio, Cash/Share EBIT/Interest Expense Debt/Equity Turnover Ratios	Bollinger Fibonacci	Activists Meme

FIGURE 6.6 The Evaluator Matrix for the Five-Stack Discovery

Price-Earnings Ratio (PE)

This multiple is calculated as the share price to earnings per share and is often called a company's "valuation," which illustrates just how dominant PE is among all valuation metrics. PE is certainly the most quoted financial tool, and because of that, we dig deep on this one. Two of the first investment books I read—some 20 years ago—were *One Up on Wall Street* and *Beating the Street* by Peter Lynch; his books grew to be classics on interpreting market dynamics and the useful application of the price-earnings ratio:[4]

$$PE = \frac{\text{Price per Share}}{\text{Earnings per Share}} \quad or \quad PE = \frac{\text{Market Capitalization}}{\text{Earnings (aka, Net Income)}}$$

Market capitalization (market cap) is the price per share × the outstanding shares.

Peter supplemented the PE ratio with two observations: the price-earnings line and the PEG ratio.

The Price-Earnings Line "A quick way to tell if a stock is overpriced is to compare the price line to the earnings line. If you bought familiar growth companies—such as Shoney's, The Limited, or Marriott—when the stock price fell well below the earnings line, and sold them when the stock price rose dramatically above it, the chances are you'd do pretty well."[5]

The "price line" is the company's share price and the "earnings line" is the share price using a theoretical PE of "15 times" the earnings per share. If the price line <u>is below</u> the earnings line (or the earnings line is above the price line), it's a buy. For example:[6]

- Company X has a share price of $30

- Company X has EPS of $3

---

[4] "The Peter Lynch Approach to Investing in 'Understandable' Stocks." by Maria Crawford, *AAII JOURNAL* (January 1997), gives a terrific summary of Peter's work, https://home.csulb.edu/~pammerma/fin382/screener/lynch.htm.

[5] Peter Lynch, *One Up on Wall Street: How to Use What You Already Know to Make Money in the Market* (Simon & Schuster, 2000):164. Emphasis added. Peter also stated in the same paragraph, "I'm not necessarily advocating this practice, but I can think of worse strategies."

[6] Please note that my descriptions are my own interpretation and application of Peter's model.

- The 15 times earnings calculation, for this quarter, is $15 \times \$3 = \$45$

- Plot the changing share and earnings lines over several quarters

- Assuming the earnings line is consistently above the price line (share price), or jumps above it **dramatically**, it's a buy

At the time, 15 was a proven, historical valuation of price to earnings. Often, you'll hear "Company A is undervalued to Company B" with the comment supported by toggling PE ratios between them:

- Assume Company A has a price/share of $80 and earnings/share (EPS) of $4. PE $= 20$

- And Company B has a price/share of $32 and earnings/share (EPS) of $2. PE $= 16$

Say you have a fervent belief that B is as valuable as A. If B "traded 20 times" like A, then you can estimate B's what-if share price as, mathematically, share price $=$ PE $\times$ EPS.

Our what-if share price for B $= 20 \times \$2$, or $40: B is undervalued by $8 ($40 $-$ $32).[7]

The PEG Ratio   Given that the PE Multiple is a point-in-time calculation, Peter developed the Price Earnings to Growth (PEG) ratio to account for the projected earnings increase, with the principle below:[8]

$$PEG = \frac{PE}{\text{Earnings Growth Rate}}$$

The PE ratio of any company that's fairly priced will equal its growth rate . . . If the PE of Coca-Cola is 15, you'd expect the company to be growing at about 15% a year.

---

[7]The undervaluation can also be calculated as Company A's PE minus Company B's PE times Company B's EPS.
[8]Lynch, *One Up on Wall Street*: 199; also really well described in "Peter Lynch's Formulas for Valuing a Stock's Growth," by Joshua Kennon, *The Balance* (October 31, 2021), https://www.thebalance.com/peter-lynch-s-secret-formula-for-valuing-a-stock-s-growth-3973486.

Therefore, a PEG of 1 means the share price is fair valued, effectually at price equilibrium. *Over* 1 is *over*valued, *under* 1 is *under*valued. Let's stay with our A and B comparison by comparing the fictitious growth rates (g, of either EPS or Earnings) between the two companies:

- A's PE = 20. Assume g is 12%/year. PEG = 20/12 = 1.7
- B's PE = 16. Assume g is 11%/year. PEG = 16/11 = 1.5

Although both stocks have a sub-optimal PEG of being greater than 1, the notion that B is undervalued to A proves true per the PEG calculation.

Over the last decade, we've witnessed incredible advances in the building of mathematical models that quickly forecast g and allow the application of a forward PE (PE FWD) rather than a PE derived from the trailing twelve months (PE TTM). PE FWD provides the same conceptual output as a PEG ratio, and I prefer it due to its wide acceptance and usage.

Cash and PE   One more thing on PE. As shown, you can calculate the numerator in the PE formula by using the share price or market capitalization, and then adjusting the denominator to be either EPS or aggregate earnings. Some companies have such a war chest of cash, that by carving it out, you get a clearer sense of where their PE really sits.

$$\text{Market Cap} = \text{Share Price} \times \text{Outstanding Shares}$$

$$\text{PE, Adjusted} = \frac{\text{Market Cap} - \text{Cash (from The Balance Sheet)}}{\text{Earnings (Net Income)}}$$

Pfizer's (PFE, mega-cap) PE TTM is 15.5: $303.5B/$19.6B.[9] Backing out $29.7B of cash reduces its PE to 13.9, about a 10% drop. And if you're paying attention, Bueller, you'll note that we are now below Peter's 15 earnings line, ☺.

Finally, if you flip the numerator and denominator to, for example Earnings/Market Capitalization, you produce the "Earnings Yield."

Red flag: PE FWD greater than 25

---

[9]Yahoo! Finance, January 21, 2022.

Price to Sales (P/S)

When you purchase a stock, you are now an owner of that company. What could be more informational then knowing how the brand is selling in the marketplace given what you paid for it? The P/S ratio is not burdened by debt, capital structure, or accounting allocations (e.g. depreciation). Its elegant simplicity enables it to be a comparative evaluator across the entire base of listed companies.

$$P/S = \frac{\text{Price per Share}}{\text{Sales per Share}} \quad or \quad \frac{\text{Market Capitalization}}{\text{Sales}}$$

On the flipside, because P/S is determined from the top of the income statement, business execution, its capital investment legacy (depreciation), and earnings metrics do not play into the ratio. Regardless, P/S is a powerful descriptor for illustrating when a stock is undervalued or when its getting ahead of itself; i.e. there may be "irrational exhuberance" in respect to the firm's share price given its revenue engine.[10] P/S is grounded in current financials, whereas the previous evaluator, PE (FWD), is based on future financials.

Red flag: P/S over 5

Enterprise Value to Free Cash Flow (EV/FCF)

Enterprise Value (Market Capitalization + Debt − Cash)/FCF unveils the company's worth given its cash generation. FCF growth is considered by many analysts to be the ultimate guage of a company's wherewithal. There are other similar ratios: EV/Revenue, EV/EBITDA, and Market Cap/EBITDA. Note that EV/FCF is also known as the "Free Cash Flow Yield" when flipped and expressed as FCF/EV.

Because the PE ratio already incorporates market capitalization, and we've captured revenue in the P/S multiple, the EV/FCF view adds an unique dimension to the acid tests. One concern about EV is heavily leveraged companies enjoy the optics of a high EV; however, by removing cash,

---

[10] *Irrational Exuberance* by Nobel Prize winning economist Robert J. Shiller is a great read on overvalued markets. The phrase itself originated with Federal Reserve Chairman Alan Greenspan.

the inflated debt effect is dampened as presumably a heavily leveraged company is not raining money.

Red flag: EV/FCF greater than 40

Operating Margin (OM)

Operationally, the OM ratio of operating income to sales reveals the company's ability to execute its strategic plan, its discipline in cost control, and its commitment to build an enduring enterprise. Behind the OM curtain is the brand's cache of intellectual property, its competitive advantage, and the strength of its leadership. I believe the operating margin captures what Warren Buffett, the G.O.A.T. investor, meant when he stated:[11]

> The most important thing [is] trying to find a business with a wide and long-lasting moat around it . . . protecting a terrific economic castle with an honest lord in charge of the castle.

Don't envision the moat as a barrier between the company and its customers, shareholders, and suppliers; rather, view it as the impenetrable defense of the brand.

Some industries (e.g. grocery, retail) operate at very narrow OMs and warp to being more of a price-taker than a price-maker because the purchasing power of "the buy side" shoves them to a scale and volume model. This means the OM is the most sector-specific tool of the acid-test evaluators. Although margin computations can also be derived from gross profit, EBITDA, EBIT, or net income, the OM testimony is what we want to hear.

Red flag: OM% under 15%

Debt to Earnings Before Interest, Taxes, Depreciation & Amortization (Debt/EBITDA)

The debt to EBITDA ratio indicates the ability of the firm to pay its short-term and long-term debt and it combines an income statement category (EBITDA) with a balance sheet (debt) category. EBITDA is the right denom-

[11]Tae Kim, "Warren Buffett Believes This Is 'The Most Important Thing' to Find in a Business," CNBC (May 7, 2018), https://www.cnbc.com/2018/05/07/warren-buffett-believes-this-is-the-most-important-thing-to-find-in-a-business.html.

inator as it takes into account the costs (direct and indirect) to run the business before interest expenses are applied and without the murkiness that comes with depreciation expense. Also, its a go-to metric used by credit and lending agencies.

A common business word is "leverage" as used in the context of a company's operations, but more commonly, regarding its incurred debt. Operating leverage is the firm's mix of fixed and variable costs. A firm with high fixed costs but lower variable costs has stronger operating leverage in that if it were to expand production, the marginal cost on the next unit is lower than it would be at a firm with higher variable costs. Financial leverage is the firm's blend of debt and equity (a.k.a. capital structure). Purchasing high financially leveraged firms can be dangerous in bear markets as such companies are chained to their bank obligations in times of falling revenue. You may hear the phrase "Company X is leveraged to the hilt," it just means they are carrying a slew of debt and there is a concern on their ability to repay. Sometimes the debt numerator nets out cash and marketable securities.

Red flag: DEBT/EBITDA above 2.5

■ Valuation Test Flight

The optimal way to appreciate our valuation data is to crunch through a comparative spreadsheet of a handful of firms, as is done in figure 6.7. Populating a valuation sheet is uncomplicated as there are numerous financial websites that provide the data without having to plod through statements or SEC submissions. Figure 6.7 contrasts seven companies with approximate indicators aligned to the matrix of evaluators' design.[12]

Our Magnificent Seven companies are: Apple, Tesla, Freeport-McMoRan, Walmart, Kellogg, Disney, and Netflix. Before you look at the table, guesstimate four names to four panel categories. Here's a hint, they're four different companies!

---

[12] All data was pulled from Yahoo! Finance Statistic Tables on April 5, 2022, except Debt/EBITDA, which was pulled on April 27, 2022. No cross-checking was conducted to the actual Financial Statements. Ratios marked with "*" were calculated from Yahoo! Finance data. Note that the Debt/Equity figure from Yahoo! Finance is expressed without a percent sign, for example, 63 for Apple. All index and stock data in Chapter 9 was also retrieved from Yahoo! Finance on April 5, 2022 unless otherwise noted.

		Data is approximate, Balance Sheet is MRQ, Income/CF are TTM	APPLE	TESLA	Freeport-McMoRan	WALMART	KELLOGG	DISNEY	NETFLIX
			AAPL	TSLA	FCX	WMT	K	DIS	NFLX
		Grouping	Growth: Commercial	Growth: Commercial	Value: Cyclical	Value: Secular	Value: Cyclical	Growth: Commercial	Growth: Commercial
		Sector	Information Technology	Consumer Cyclical	Materials	Consumer Staples	Consumer Staples	Communication Services	Communication Services
		Current Share Price (SP)	$ 175.06	$ 1,091.26	$ 49.09	$ 151.47	$ 65.79	$ 135.62	$ 380.15
		Earnings/Out. Share (EPS)	$ 6.01	$ 4.90	$ 2.90	$ 4.87	$ 4.33	$ 1.68	$ 11.24
Values from the Statements BILLIONS		Revenue (Sales)	$ 378.3	$ 53.8	$ 22.8	$ 572.8	$ 14.2	$ 73.0	$ 29.7
		EBITDA	$ 128.2	$ 9.3	$ 10.5	$ 36.6	$ 2.5	$ 10.6	$ 6.4
		Operating Income	$ 116.9	$ 6.5	$ 8.3	$ 25.9	$ 1.8	$ 5.6	$ 6.2
		Net Income (Earnings)	$ 100.6	$ 5.5	$ 4.3	$ 13.7	$ 1.5	$ 3.2	$ 5.1
		Assets	$ 351.0	$ 62.1	$ 48.0	$ 244.9	$ 18.2	$ 203.6	$ 44.6
		Cash	$ 63.9	$ 17.7	$ 8.1	$ 14.8	$ 0.3	$ 14.4	$ 6.0
		Debt	$ 122.8	$ 8.9	$ 9.8	$ 58.4	$ 7.8	$ 54.1	$ 18.1
		Cash Flow: OCF	$ 112.2	$ 11.5	$ 7.7	$ 24.2	$ 1.7	$ 5.3	$ 0.4
		FCF (OCF - Capex)	$ 101.9	$ 3.5	$ 5.6	$ 11.1	$ 1.1	$ 1.5	$ (0.1)
Derived Values BILLIONS		Market Capitalization	$ 2,910	$ 1,180	$ 74	$ 416	$ 22	$ 252	$ 174
		Enterprise Value	$ 2,970	$ 1,130	$ 76	$ 458	$ 30	$ 292	$ 183
		Float	16.0	0.8	1.5	1.4	0.3	1.8	0.4
		Outstanding Shares	16.3	1.0	1.5	2.8	0.3	1.8	0.4
Alpha Acid Test		PE/FWD	30	115	15	22	16	31	36
		P/S	8	24	3	1	2	3	6
		EV/FCF*	29	324	14	41	26	197	−1,389
		Operating Margin/Sales	31%	12%	36%	5%	14%	8%	21%
		Debt/EBITDA*	0.96	0.95	0.93	1.60	3.11	5.13	2.83
Alpha Bold Additions		52 Low	$ 122.25	$ 546.98	$ 30.02	$ 132.01	$ 59.54	$ 128.38	$ 329.82
		52 High	$ 182.94	$ 1,243.45	$ 51.99	$ 153.33	$ 68.60	$ 190.40	$ 700.99
		52 Mid-Point*	$ 152.60	$ 895.22	$ 41.01	$ 142.67	$ 64.07	$ 159.39	$ 515.41
		Q/Q Revenue (yoy)	11%	65%	37%	1%	−1%	34%	16%
		ROE: NI/Equity	146%	20%	26%	16%	38%	4%	38%
VALUATION	Gamma	PE TTM	30	234	18	31	15	81	35
		PEG	3.5	3.3	n/a	3.1	2.6	1.0	1.8
		P/OCF*	$ 26	$ 103	$ 10	$ 17	$ 13	$ 48	$ 443
		Dividend Yield: Div/P	0.5%	0.0%	0.6	1.5%	3.5%	0.0%	0.0%
		EV/Sales	8	22	3	1	2	4	6
		EV/EBITDA*	23	121	7	13	11	27	29
		Rule of 40*	45%	82%	83%	7%	16%	49%	38%
		EBITDA Margin*	34%	17%	46%	6%	18%	14%	22%
		Profit Margin	27%	10%	19%	2%	10%	4%	17%
	Omega	Return on Assets (ROA)	20%	7%	12%	7%	7%	2%	9%
		Price to Book	40.6	39.2	5.3	5.0	6.0	2.8	11.0
		Current Ratio	1.0	1.4	2.5	0.9	0.6	1.1	1.0
		Cash/Share	$ 3.92	$ 17.13	$ 5.55	$ 5.36	$ 0.88	$ 7.93	$ 13.58
		Debt to Equity	63	28	42	64	184	52	114
TECHNICAL	Alpha Acid-Test & Bold	50 DMA	$ 167.61	$ 910.38	$ 45.17	$ 140.71	$ 63.44	$ 141.75	$ 382.49
		200 DMA	$ 157.16	$ 877.60	$ 39.21	$ 142.83	$ 63.61	$ 161.75	$ 533.65
		Short Ratio (to Float)	0.7%	3.0%	2.3%	0.8%	6.2%	1.0%	2.2%
		RSI	58	74	53	70	65	43	50
		BETA	1.2	2.1	2.0	0.6	0.6	1.2	1.0

FIGURE 6.7 Valuation Comparisons

Although there are a lot of point-in-time numbers presented in figure 6.7, a good way to get a feel for the data is to zero-in on a valuation cateogory, read horizontally, and then go to the company header names. Five things will become immediately apparent:

- No one metric tells the entire company story.
  A set of metrics is required to obtain a proper valuation view.

- Interpreting the data is simple once you group the information.
  Your reasoning becomes naturally focused.

- The metric dispersion across companies from different sectors is broad.
  Like-to-like comparisons are the most illuminating.

- Spreadsheeting the metrics of a radar stock to a best-in-class performer will generate a galaxy of penetrating questions.
  You will mentally stretch from looking-at-numbers to gaining company *empathy*.

- Selecting information from different fintechs/sites can be problematic.
  Be aware of their ratio and category definitions.

The power of strong operating margins with YoY revenue growth can't be overstated. Just for fun in figure 6.8, I took Einstein's seminal $E = mc^2$ and substituted OM for mass and YoY revenue growth for the speed of light. Yes, I created a Frank 'n' Einstein (FE) per the figure 6.8 results. What's not

71

FINANCIAL BENCHMARKING

	APPLE	TESLA	Freeport-McMoRan	WALMART	KELLOGG	DISNEY	NETFLIX
m = Operating Margin/Sales * 100	31	12	36	5	14	8	21
c = Q/Q Revenue (yoy) * 100	11	65	37	1	- 1	34	16
(FE = mc^2)	3,876	51,050	49,964	1	24	8,835	5,340
Divide by 100	39	510	500	0	0	88	53

FIGURE 6.8 **Operating Margin and Revenue Acceleration**

surprising is Tesla. What is surprising is how FCX popped, and Apple did not. If anything, the exercise reinforced the notion of sticking to intra-sector comparisons.

■ Capsule

- Company comparisons should be of like situations; this does not mean you avoid contrasting say a bank with an information technology firm, only that the valuation may not "line up."

- Not one of the valuation or technical indicators is valuable by itself. Teasing out intelligent guidance from a data set means analyzing a troop of metrics.

- All metrics are best examined through period-to-period deltas. The step-change POV is better than a one-and-done.

- The plug-and-play **EQ** is streamlined to optimize your asset selection choices through two tactics: a quick view (a.k.a. alpha acid test) of metrics or a more comprehensive view (a.k.a. alpha bold).

PART III

NAVIGATION

CHAPTER 7

Radar

Trendspotting and Correlations

If I were given one hour to save the planet, I would spend 59 minutes defining the problem and one minute resolving it.[1]

Albert Einstein

Having an always-on radar for investment opportunity is fun, like moseying through a rural garage sale searching for a pristine Velvet Underground album (with the Andy Warhol banana sticker) or retro Air Jordan 1 shoes—in your size, no less! Stock selection hunting is a bit trickier, but there are thinking patterns that can make the chase a whole lot easier. Consider your radar as the precursor to ideating stocks. (I came across the cool word "ideate" several years ago, and it fits our path!)[2]

First, though, I want to share some surprising market capitalization facts. The set of company market caps barbells to a handful of heavyweights at one end and an abundance of mid-size and smaller companies at the other. Just six of the NASDAQ 100 companies supply almost 60% of its 100-firm

---

[1] https://hbr.org/2012/09/are-you-solving-the-right-problem.
[2] https://www.merriam-webster.com/dictionary/ideate: "Like *idea* and *ideal*, *ideate* comes from the Greek verb *idein*, which means "to see.""

on April 22, 2022		MARKET CAP *trillions*
COMPANY	**SYMBOL**	
APPLE	APPL	$2.8
AMAZON	AMZN	$1.5
META PLATFORMS	FB	$0.5
ALPHABET C CLASS	GOOG	$1.6
ALPHABET A CLASS	GOOGL	$1.6
MICROSOFT	MSFT	$2.1
TESLA	TSLA	$1.0
TOTAL		$11.0
NASDAQ 100		$18.6
TOTAL/NASDAQ 100		59%
NYSE + NASDAQ Market Cap, est.		$51.0
APPL, AMZV, FB, GOOG/L, MSFT, TSLA		22%

FIGURE 7.1   NASDAQ Market Capitalizations

capitalization, as we see in figure 7.1.[3] To shine an intense light on this, NASDAQ has approximately 3,600 companies with $22 trillion of market cap and the NYSE 2,400 companies with $29 trillion of market cap. So, in early 2022, six companies out of 6,000 had one-fifth of the combined NYSE-NASDAQ $51 trillion capitalization![4]

The mental exercise of trendspotting and correlation begins with accepting your innate ability to "pump your mind" as described by Michael Michalko in his book *Thinkertoys*:[5]

> When you perceive trends and patterns of interest, begin to pump your mind for ideas, opportunities, and business possibilities. Look for connections and relationships between your content analysis and your business challenges.

[3] https://www.nasdaq.com/market-activity/quotes/nasdaq-ndx-index.
[4] https://www.nyse.com/network as sourced 4/24/22 states that it has over 2300 companies and $28.8 trillion of market cap. Also, see www.investopedia.com/ask/answers/difference-between-dow-and-nasdaq and www.nasdaq.com/solutions/nasdaq-equity-indexes.
[5] Michael Michalko *Thinkertoys*, 2nd edition (Ten Speed Press, 2006): 17.

■ Revving-Up the Five-Stack Discovery

Our CSI goal is to trendspot and correlate those stocks that we want to possibly buy or sell, i.e. how can we get some "inside baseball" for our radar before the rest of the investor pack arrives? There are many narratives that can feed the Five-Stack Discovery per figure 7.2.

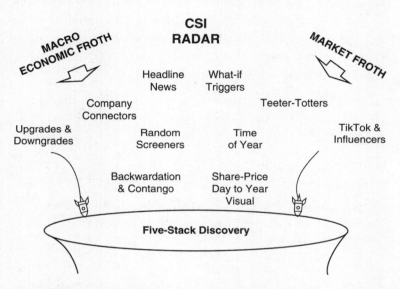

FIGURE 7.2   **Feeding the Five-Stack Discovery Model**

Upgrades and Downgrades

Immediately after quarter-end and annual earnings reports, the analysts that follow those companies issue tight summaries, along with a powerful Action or Trend descriptor. Each reviewing financial institution uses slightly different terminology, and it can be confusing as some of them are referring more to a Trend than a recommended Action. I link the Action and Trend words, and if you google a few equity reviews, you'll easily piece together a balanced outlook:

Action	Trend
Strong buy	Conviction, accumulate
Buy	Outperform, overweight, focus list
Hold	Maintain, equal weight, neutral, perform
Underperform	Underweight, moderate sell
Sell	Capitulation, rollover, tanking

The reviewing analyst may issue an update to the stock's price target (PT). The PTs don't come with any time frame, but a reasonable expectation for hitting-the-number is six to nine months out, i.e. in two to three quarters.

Company Connectors

Good news guidance is not only for the company that issued it! Assume Target (TGT), at its quarterly earnings report, issues strong guidance over the next few quarters due to its e-commerce website exceeding its expectations. With this better demand curve, who are the suppliers that TGT counts on? What "connected companies" could directly benefit?

- Is there a particular shipping supplier that has the TGT contract? Is it reasonable to assume they would have a revenue bump from TGT's e-commerce growth?

- Does TGT use any independent warehousing of its off-shore, imported goods at American seaports? Could they also see a revenue bump?

- What customer relationship management (CRM) platform does TGT ride on? Is the TGT development large enough to be causal to the share price of the CRM provider?

The idea is to unravel the guiding comments and find tailgating companies that might enjoy the same lift: if TGT had a terrific quarter, could that mean a strong ER from Walmart or Costco when they report a week or two later?

Headline News

The right news item can be radar candy:[6]

> (CNN)—President Joe Biden signed a $1.2 trillion infrastructure bill into law Monday, finalizing a key part of his economic agenda.
>
> It will deliver $550 billion of new federal investments in America's infrastructure over five years, touching everything from bridges and roads to the nation's broadband, water and energy systems. Experts say the

---

[6] Katie Lobosco and Tami Luhby, "Here's What's in the Bipartisan Infrastructure Package," CNN (November 15, 2021), https://www.cnn.com/2021/07/28/politics/infrastructure-bill-explained/index.html.

money is sorely needed to ensure safe travel, as well as the efficient transport of goods and produce across the country.

This announcement is in the wheelhouse of the materials and industrials sectors. Once you've made your list of several firms that could benefit, go to their websites and look for any press releases related to the headline news item. Pick up the phone and call their investor relations department for some event guidance. You'll likely get some type of canned response, but you might hear some swagger and that could be part of your Five-Stack Discovery. Even better, maybe you can connect at the VP or managing director level through LinkedIn with, "I see we both went to the University of Washington, yada . . . yada," and build a conversation!

Random Screeners

If the greatest retail investor access development of all time was the keystroke ease of purchasing or selling stocks through the many financial platforms, then the second might be the offering of consumer-friendly stock-screener programs. The power of being able to instantaneously conduct financial research across hundreds of companies through simple queries of a "PE between 10 and 15" or "dividend yields greater than 3%" is an awesome tool.

Imagine what it was like for your parents or grandparents to buy stocks in the 1980s. It was heavy lifting: going to the library and collecting and deciphering annual reports, paying $2.00 a minute to call long-distance for some insight from a company's investor relations team, stepping through the voluminous *Thomas Register* for supplier understandings, scratching for competitive corporate peers of targeted companies through the *Yellow Pages*, and slogging through the *Wall Street Journal* for any valuation numbers. Now, it's all there for you, and it's free! And if that wasn't hard enough for your parents and grandparents, stocks were fractionalized to $1/16^{th}$ of a dollar, not in pennies. Could it get more onerous?

The more you use a screener, the easier it gets. It can be fun to just make up something, say, today I want all companies that have less than $100 million of market-cap and with a Return on Equity of greater than 12%. You get a list, and some of the brand names will resonate. Geez, ZettaByte Foods is on here! I just read that they are opening 30 stores over the next year in the Midwest and Canada. Hmmm.

What-if Triggers

This is where you open the can of conjecture. Say you use an Apple phone and are continually wowed by their innovation. You hear on the news that Amazon is skunking self-driving vehicles. You believe the autonomous revolution is not about the engine; rather, it's about the freedom that technology brings. What events could pour out if Apple also went down this path? Figure 7.3 visualizes your brainstorming: Apple could develop the technology, buy a company that already has the technology, or not go forward at all on this front. These are Level 1 events that you note.

Level 2 refines Level 1. One stream is Apple "Purchases Technology." You know of Apple's stated commitment to the environment, so 2a could be "environmentally friendly" and at 3a and 3b, you tack on a couple of EV companies that Apple might buy. You can graft or lop limbs on the tree as you come up with ideas.

An appealing what-if workout is to map possible sector outcomes to US dollar strength, and then ratchet down to high import, export, and offshore revenue-sensitive companies. Interpreting the US dollar to other currencies goes like this:

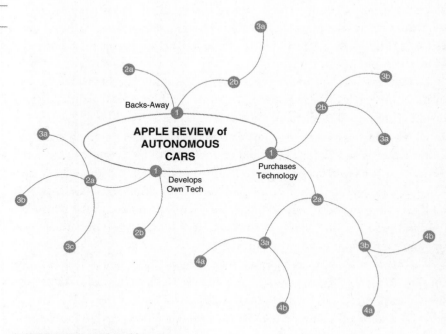

FIGURE 7.3 What-if Pattern

- There are seven "major" currency pairs, and the US dollar (USD) is in each one:

- (Euro) EUR/USD; USD/JPY (Japan); (Great Britain) GBP/USD; (Australia) AUD/USD; USD/CHF (Switzerland); USD/CAD (Canada); and (New Zealand) NZD/USD.

- The base currency is on the left, the quote currency on the right. For USD/Canada, USD is the base and the numerical relationship would indicate how many Canadian dollars (a.k.a. loonies) you could buy with one US dollar. Viewed from the other side, it shows how much Canadian currency is required to get one US dollar.

- Quoted currency pairs often go to four decimal places, with the 4th decimal swing called a pip (a.k.a. percentage in point). Assume the USD/CAD rate is 1.2513. If it went to 1/1.2514, that would be a change of one pip. Going to 1.2523 is 10 pips.

- Let's *Occam* it to 1/1.25. The currency posted change is in reference to the Base currency and the close of the previous day.

- So if the streaming ticker shows USD/CDN $1.25 −$.01, that means the USD weakened by one penny. At the previous close, one US dollar would have purchased $1.26 of Canadian currency, but today (at that moment), it's only getting $1.25.

What-if the USD strengthens to the Canadian dollar? What does that mean for US imports? Which sectors would benefit?

Another batch of what-ifs could be companies that you believe are ripe for a takeout or should be disaggregated due to the parts being greater than the whole.

I know you can quickly come up with a pile of what-if triggers. Throw down a few into the following box. Come back in three months or so and see if you called it!

| **FUTURE WHAT-IFS** |

_____

_____

_____

_____

_____

Time of Year

It's always a good time to buy stocks, assuming of course you did your **EQ** homework. There are a few well-worn Wall Street phrases regarding the clock: sell in May and go away; sell in spring and buy in the fall; here comes the Santa Claus rally; and get ready for the June swoon. Oops, the last one is not so much the market, but Cubs fans know what I'm sayin'.

But if the market believes that the optimal seasonal window is autumn, even if it's a self-fulfilling prophecy, why argue with it?

> Dec. 1, 2021 (Reuters)—A pileup of risks into year-end has some investors gauging whether December will continue its historical trend of a strong stock performance, even as markets face of worries over the Omicron coronavirus variant and a more hawkish Federal Reserve.
>
> November and December have been the S&P 500s second- and third-best months of the year since 1950, with the index rising an average of 1.7% and 1.5%, respectively, according to the Stock Trader's Almanac.[7]

Note that the best month is April, although here in 2022, that's not been the case. Another date-watch event is quadruple-witching day on the third Friday of March, June, September, and December. At this 4x a year spectacle, volatility increases as stock options, stock index futures, stock index options, and single stock futures expire on the same day. Some believe share prices rise before Witching Day as these derivative-based investments need to trade-around positions given the time-expiry of their securities. Finally, in addition to seasonal buying, there are also theories on what time to buy during the day or week or month.

Because we are Pro:Active investors over longer durations, those time cycles are not material. But there is one "time zone" that you should be very aware of, and that's the couple of weeks leading up to and after quarter end. Increased volumes with slipping share prices may foretell a broader exit or perhaps an opportunity to buy on the dip. Your **EQ** should have you positioned for a share-price move up or down.

Teeter-Totter

Some events have general A to B causal effects. If A happens, then B receives the pain or gain. There are many and most have empirical justification. Here are some of the more obvious ones.

---

[7] Lewis Krauskopf, "Analysis: History Says Expect Strong December for U.S. Stocks," Reuters (December 1, 2021), https://www.reuters.com/markets/europe/history-says-expect-strong-december-us-stocks-despite-omicron-fed-worries-2021-12-01/.

Helpful to Specific Sectors or Equities Overall

- Inflation increases: Gold prices and associated mining stocks go up

- Treasury demand and prices decrease/yields rise: Equities benefit

- Government fiscal spending increases: Equities (nervously) rise

- A few, major S&P 500 companies simultaneously give strong guidance: Equity risk-on

- Increased pace of Gross Domestic Product growth, quarter over quarter: Equity risk-on

- The economy enters a recovery: Transports start moving up, usually with the financial and consumer discretionary sectors

Neutral to Unhelpful to Equities

- Consumer credit availability shrinks: Durable Goods demand decreases and some sectors are broadsided

- Trade wars between major countries: uncertainty down-forces Equities

- Unemployment increases: Equities dip

- Inflation significantly increases: Equities sell off

- Bond demand and prices increase/Yields decline: Equity risk-off

- A few, major S&P 500 companies collectively give very weak guidance: Equities sell-off

- Global economy weakens: US Dollar increases and those US companies with most of their revenue from off-shore get hurt

Granted, these events are so high level to be of only minimum use. Just consider them as part of your looking-for-economic-clues mindset, that's all. If you have some that you'd like to add to the list, please do!

MORE TEETER-TOTTERS

TikTok and Influencers

TikTok now has one billion active users, and "It took Facebook roughly nine years to hit the billion-user mark, around eight for Instagram and seven for each of YouTube and WhatsApp. TikTok, launched in 2016, managed to reach the milestone in just five years."[8] More important is the connection of TikTok to "influencers":

> Rome Business School—Recent studies have disclosed that almost 80% of future marketing plans will focus upon at least one influencer marketing campaign in the upcoming year.
>
> Influencer marketing is a type of marketing that involves influential people that might hold sway over potential buyers. This may be because of the influencer's expertise, popularity, or reputation. In most of these cases, celebrities are often picked as points of reference because they have visibility and significant reach.[9]

The TikTok + Influencer bond is an entrepreneurial slipstream that can yank brand revenues up, very, very quickly. Being aware of what brands the influencers are flogging can be a good addition to your radar list.

Backwardation and Contango

The normal price-to-time commodities slope is for future deliveries to be priced higher than the current spot price, described as "contango." Future prices are higher due to speculation, product carrying costs, and cost input factors. Sometimes the price-to-time relationship enters "backwardation" as underlying conditions of significant near-term demand or supply challenges lead to higher spot than future prices. For example, the Russian invasion of Ukraine will cause backwardation on some crucial agricultural commodities:

> Food and Agricultural Organization of the United Nations—In 2021, either the Russian Federation or Ukraine (or both) ranked amongst the top three global exporters of wheat, maize, rapeseed, sunflower seeds and sunflower oil, while the Russian Federation also stood as the world's top exporter of nitrogen fertilizers, the second leading supplier of potassium

---

[8] https://www.economist.com/graphic-detail/2021/10/07/tiktoks-rapid-growth-shows-the-potency-of-video, October 7, 2021.

[9] https://romebusinessschool.com/blog/the-importance-of-influencer-marketing/, March 23, 2022.

fertilizers and the third largest exporter of phosphorous fertilizers. ... In Ukraine, the escalation of the conflict raises concerns on whether crops will be harvested and products exported. The war has already led to port closures, the suspension of oilseed crushing operations and the introduction of export licensing requirements for some products. All of these could take a toll on the country's exports of grains and vegetable oils in the months ahead. Much uncertainty also surrounds Russian export prospects, given sales difficulties that may arise as a result of economic sanctions imposed on the country.[10]

Backwardation is not the norm, and when it happens, there is a roiling effect to businesses that transform those commodities and to the consumers who ultimately use them. Interpreting these dynamics is part of your CSI.

Share-Price Visuals: Day to Annual

The beautiful simplicity of illustrating a day of share-price movements to its annual travels is a wicked way to get "deal flow" going in your head, and many platforms and fintechs provide that type of chart. Note that only the range numbers are indicated; you source the rest of the data from the ticker if you want exacts. Let's look at Apache in figure 7.4.[11]

The left side of the chart shows that Apache closed off its $44.28 high of the day. But wow, look at the right side. The high of the day was also the high of the year, and if you bought at $15.55, you're now running a 3-bagger! Here's Ford in figure 7.5.

Although Ford showed strength and wandered to $15.76, it fell below its $15.50 opening to close at $15.48. The right side tells you immediately that Ford is below its 365-day midpoint. Let's have a go at Apple per figure 7.6.

Apple fell more than $5 from its opening—still, though, it's on the upside of its annual range midpoint.

If you were reviewing a radar triple of APA vs. F vs. APPL, CSI questions begin:

- Might APA be getting toppy?

- Only APA closed above its open, was that true for the whole sector?

- If there was an announcement that day which gave F some strength, then why the fall-off?

[10] https://www.fao.org/3/cb9236en/cb9236en.pdf.
[11] Sourced from Yahoo! Finance, April 15, 2022.

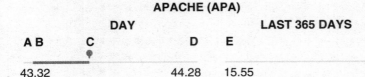

APACHE (APA)

DAY				LAST 365 DAYS		
A B	C		D	E		F G

43.32   44.28   15.55   44.28

A. Traded down to $43.32
B. Opened @ $43.37
C. Closed @ $43.68
D. Traded as high as $44.28

E. Range Lowest Trade: $15.55
F. Day's Close of $43.68
G. Range Highest Trade: $44.28
Traded narrowly within year's Range

FIGURE 7.4   Apache Share Price Record

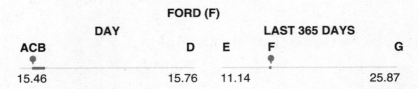

FORD (F)

DAY			LAST 365 DAYS		
ACB		D	E	F	G

15.46   15.76   11.14   25.87

A. Traded down to $15.46
B. Opened @ $15.50
C. Closed @ $15.48
D. Traded as high as $15.76

E. Range Lowest Trade: $11.14
F. Day's Close of $15.48
G. Range Highest Trade: $25.87
Traded narrowly within year's Range

FIGURE 7.5   Ford Share Price Record

APPLE (APPL)

DAY			LAST 365 DAYS		
AC		B D	E	F	G

165.05   171.27   122.25   182.94

A. Traded down to $165.05
B. Opened @ $170.62
C. Closed @ $165.29
D. Traded as high as $171.27

E. Range Lowest Trade: $122.25
F. Day's Close of $165.29
G. Range Highest Trade: $182.94
Traded a bit wider within year's Range

FIGURE 7.6   Apple Share Price Record

- What's stopping F from getting back to the upside of its annual midpoint?

- Why did APPL have a $5 open to close stumble?

- Which stock has the sweet momentum?

Of course, this triple trade would further benefit from an exospheric test to a peer. Regardless, there are many, many questions to sluice through and here's the toughest one: based on just the preceding three charts, which of the trey would you invest in? After you learn from the **EQ** in chapter 11, return and write your answer. Ponder why you did or did not change.

My Current Choice:	**After the EQ:**

■ Capsule

- The purpose of trendspotting and correlations is to ideate opportunity for your stock radar. Don't think of it as a "prediction" model, but more of a "prospect" model. If you were starting a business to sell a product or service, what is your initial target market—who are you *gonna call*? It's the same thing, but instead of being a sales leader, you are a Pro:Active investor!

- Scanning for radar stocks requires thinking. And thinking takes effort. The French philosopher René Descartes famously wrote in 1637, "I think, therefore I am." How about, "I think, therefore I am making money."

CHAPTER 8

Hitching Corporate Strategy to the EQ

Talent hits a target no one else can hit.
Genius hits a target no one else can see.

Arthur Schopenhauer[1]

To optimize our stock selection choices, we need insight into the most basic corporate question: *How* does the company make money? What does a company see that we might not see? The answer begins with feeling a company's strategy, and an ideal definition is given by A.G. Lafley and Roger L. Martin in their superb book, *Playing to Win:*[2]

A strategy is a coordinated and integrated set of five choices: a winning aspiration, where to play, how to win, core capabilities, and management systems.

---

[1] German philosopher, 1788–1860.
[2] A.G. Lafley and Roger L. Martin, *Playing to Win* (Harvard Business Review Press, 2013): 5. Note that in this strategy-context "Aspiration" is used, whereas Sinek emphasizes "Inspiration" in the *Why*.

If we recast the Lafley and Martin definition, we're trying to weigh one company's strategy versus another's for the right to have our investment dollars. Let me explain the picture in figure 8.1.

Our radar, through trendspotting and correlations, spawns target stocks for further review. With a target stock, you investigate its *Why*. If a company says that its *Why* includes supporting diversity, yet every member of their board and executive team is an older white male, then perhaps they're a phony outfit and not worthy of your investment dollars. You want to buy real companies that do real things in a real and honest way. Simon Sinek refers to this disconnect between what you say and what you do as failing the Celery Test, i.e. you say you like celery but never eat it![3]

Next, given the company's sector assignment, we tackle the four stock groupings. The market sets performance expectations pursuant to the company's placement in one of the four stock grouping swim lanes. For example, if your radar stock is a value-secular and it skips a quarterly dividend, there will likely be an investor backlash with a consequential downdraft to the share price. All your stock comparisons should ensure you're tumbling firms using the same stock grouping (and sector).

Companies are in a continual quest for competitive advantage. The *How* they do it, and the *What* they do, is the segue to the seminal work of Michael Porter and his description of three strategies for achieving competitive advantage:[4]

- **Cost Leadership:** be the lowest cost provider in that industry sector

- **Differentiation:** offer uniquely desirable products and services, usually at premium prices

- **Focus:** specialized services into a niche market, which are split to Focus/Cost and Focus/Differentiation

To further our corporate strategy empathy, I mash Porter's ideas with Chris Anderson's marketing theory from his book *The Long Tail: Why the Future of Business is Selling More for Less*.[5]

---

[3] Simon Sinek, *Start With Why* (Penguin 2009): 166–171. Simon advises (p. 168) that "Any decisions—hiring, partnerships, strategies, and tactics—should all pass the Celery Test."

[4] Michael E. Porter, *Competitive Advantage* (New York: The Free Press, 1985), Ch. 1: 11–15. Further sourced from an excellent summary at https://www.ifm.eng.cam.ac.uk/research/dstools/porters-generic-competitive-strategies/.

[5] Chris Anderson, *The Long Tail: Why the Future of Business Is Selling Less of More* (Hyperion 2006).

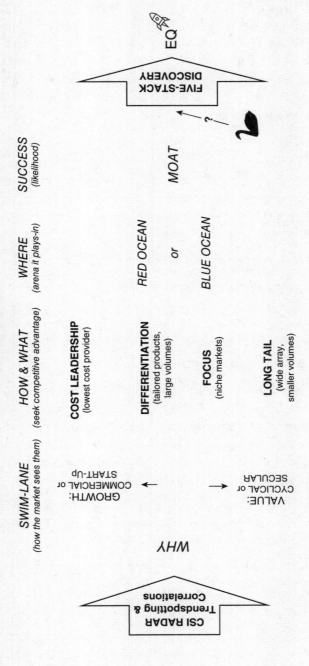

FIGURE 8.1 Business Models

- **Long Tail:** using technology to sell a wide array of niche products in relatively smaller volumes.

All companies can be inserted into one of these Porter/Anderson strategy buckets; knowing which one will assist with your empathy build for the **EQ**. Flip back to chapter 2 where the *Why* is provided for several companies. Assign Caterpillar, Walmart, and Wiley to one of the four following strategy groups, and then after you've read and reflected on the book for a week or so, revisit your thoughts.

Cost	Differentiation	Focus	Long Tail

Your Pro:Active preparation for the **EQ** dominoes like this:

- You scope out the target company's *Why*
- Picture the market's allocation of the company's to a stock grouping
- Build your awareness of the company's strategic *How* and *What*
- And move into *Where* does the company play?

And *Where* does not specifically mean the geographic or demographic markets that the company pursues; rather, is the company in an expanding vertical or more of a sunset industry? The meaningfulness of *Where* was a vital strategic component of a company's success according to Lafley and Martin, and this was further explored by W. Chan Kim and Renée Mauborgne in their brilliant book, *Blue Ocean Strategy*:

> In the red oceans . . . companies try to outperform their rivals to grab a greater share of existing demand. Products become commodities, and cut-throat competition turns the red ocean bloody.[6]

Blue Oceans, in contrast, are defined by untapped market space, fresh demand, and the opportunity for highly profitable growth.

---

[6]W. Chan Kim and Renée Mauborgne, *Blue Ocean Strategy* (Harvard Business School Publishing 2015): 4.

Kim and Mauborgne state:

> The creators of blue oceans, surprisingly, didn't use the competition as
> their benchmark. Instead, they followed a different strategic logic that we
> call *value innovation*. Value innovation is the cornerstone of blue ocean strat-
> egy. We call it value innovation because instead of focusing on beating the
> competition, you focus on making the competition irrelevant by creating a
> leap in value for buyers and your company, thereby opening up new and
> contested market space.[7]

The crux of their Blue Ocean versus Red Ocean model is that companies
can determine the color of ocean in which they operate through corporate
strategy; however, we shall flex their work toward our moon goal of optimal
stock selections. Essentially, we want to know: Is our radar stock sailing in a
Blue Ocean or a Red Ocean? Table 8.1 highlights some traits of the preferred Blue Ocean to the Red Ocean.[8]

TABLE 8.1   **Ocean Traits**

Blue Ocean	Red Ocean
Price-maker strength	Price-taker acceptance
Expanding vertical	Static vertical
Detailed differentiators among firms	Commonplace value propositions
Harbor growth stocks	Harbor value stocks
Dynamic growth choices	Organic developments
Mostly "out front" CEO's	Typically quiet CEOs
Wider share-price swings	Narrower share-price swings
Developing brands	Maturing brands
Disruptive products and services	Known proof-of-concept products and services

Stock investors gravitate to firms in the growing Blue Ocean vertical;
it's almost written in stone that the share prices of such companies will be
at a premium (i.e. high PEs). Organizations in the crowded Red Ocean
will often try to catapult into the Blue Ocean through M&As, attacking
underserved demographics and geographies, or extending their brand
through a halo effect. Review the *Why* in chapter 2 of ExxonMobil (XOM),
Google (GOOG), and Lululemon (LULU). Pencil in where you think
they cruise:

---

[7] Kim and Mauborgne, *Blue Ocean Strategy*: 13.

[8] Again, this is my interpretation of *Blue Ocean Strategy* and is not meant to be a total encap-
sulation of the work of W. Chan Kim and Renée Mauborgne.

Blue Ocean: _____

Red Ocean: _____

We can fuse the metaphors of oceans and moats for our **EQ**. The moat concept from Warren Buffett was introduced in chapter 6 and it's what separates the best-in-class company from its peers. The wider the moat (as a function of the attributes below), the greater the likelihood that a company is a cash-producing machine, both currently and ideally into the future.

- supply-chain surety
- patents held
- brilliant CEO
- engineering/technical specialized skill
- customer loyalty
- partnerships with other companies
- halo extender
- less mortar, more "net"
- consistent/dependable revenue stream
- youth-connected
- difficult to replicate products
- connected *Why*
- organic AND dynamic growth
- growing *What* pipeline of new products, new geographies, or new demographics
- risk-taking moonshot approach

- high ESG register
- disruptor/first mover
- employee and diversity engagement
- government support
- price maker not a price taker
- an honest "freemium" or razor-and-blade model
- transformative constructor and builder
- cross-branded to key demographics
- focused *How* strategy
- great call-center help
- large financial leverage and strongly capitalized
- limited competition
- broad geography served
- economies of scale and scope
- large total addressable market

There are many, many connected attributes that could give a company a wide moat, please add to the list!

_____

_____

_____

_____

_____

_____

Most of the previous moat attributes are self-explanatory, but a few require elaboration with an example noted:

- *Halo extender* is the company's ability to push its brand into new/unique products or services

  - Amazon and Alexa

- *Government support* could be a company that is operating a copper mine in a developing country under its protection and support

  - Freeport-McMoRan in Chile and Peru

- *High ESG register* (environment, social, and governance) is the company's commitment to societies changing norms

  - McDonald's and sustainable coffee sourcing

- *Vertical advantages* refer to securing upstream inputs and lowering costs

  - Costco and Kirkland Signature

- *Transformative constructor & builder* is a leap in the way a process, product, or service has traditionally been done

  - Canoo and the skateboard platform for vehicle production

- *Risk-taking moonshot approach* is an attribute of trying leading-edge products or strategies[9]

  - Pfizer, Moderna, and others on COVID vaccine production

_____

[9] Safi Bahcall, *Loonshots: Nurture the Crazy Ideas That Win Wars, Cure Diseases, and Transform Industries* (St. Martins Publishing Group, 2019). The book is a fun read on the importance of having people in an organization who are solely tasked with ideating new products, what-iffing, and coming up with better ways.

A company's moat can widen and narrow over time. New companies with fresh moats enter: Uber, DoorDash, Roblox. And if the moat narrows too much, the company (a.k.a. the brand) eventually disappears: Pan Am Airways, Blockbuster, Pontiac. The cascade of *Why* (vision), *How/What* (moat), *and Where* (ocean) raises a practical question:

What does success look like for your radar-stock company, now and in the future?

A company's success is confirmed through its reported financial metrics, corporate guidance, share price, and customer loyalty measures: collectively, these **lag** indicators are a function of the **lead** moat and ocean metaphors, as shown in figure 8.2.

Where would you put Tesla (TSLA) and Costco (COST) in figure 8.2? Arguably, A for TSLA and B for COST. Generally, we want to buy companies in quadrant A, but be mindful that their share prices could be highly overvalued. Companies in B can be awesome, and their moat width can more than make up for their Red Ocean; COST is a battleship in the Red Ocean of grocery and goods retail (sector: consumer staples). Companies in C may suffer from ineffective leadership or operational execution: the opportunity is there, but their Executive struggles to seize it, e.g. Intel (INTC), or they're fresh off the SPAC/IPO circuit and need to prove their moat, e.g. Luminar (LAZR). If your radar takes you into D, you're bottom-feeding—not that there's anything wrong with that! Companies in D are often subject to a high short ratio and unrelenting analyst downgrades, so be wary, e.g. Sears (SHLDQ).

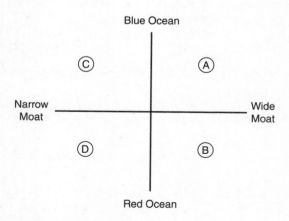

FIGURE 8.2 Moat & Ocean Location

Companies can drift from quadrant to quadrant on both positive and negative news. When you invest, you are making decisions based on "that moment" information. But things change, and at times, you pivot from your choice if the bad news is an overwhelming Black Swan, a phenomenon described by Nassim Nicholas Taleb:

> First, it is an *outlier*, as it lies outside the realm of regular expectations, because nothing in the past can convincingly point to possibility.
>
> Second, it carries an extreme impact.
>
> Third, in spite of its outlier status, human nature makes us concoct explanations for its occurrence after the fact, making it explainable and predictable.[10]

In effect, in Nassim's insightful and entertaining book, these unknown-unknowns are largely outside of our control, particularly as, "We concentrate on things we already know and time and time again fail to take into consideration what we don't know."[11] Much like the other writings I benefit from, I modify the tenets for our purposes: when targeting a stock, spend some noodling-time on Black Swan possibilities—from the elasticity of your radar company's customers to minor price changes to the company's ability to withstand a major supply-shock event, notwithstanding the randomness of occurrences and our own limitations of predicting them.

■ Capsule

- Being knowledgeable of a company's place in the Porter/Anderson business model channels to their *Why* and *How* for your **EQ** investment review.

- When you buy a stock, although you know the company's *What* (they produce), be mindful that you are approving their *Why* (vision) and *How* (strategy).

- A signal of a company's future success includes a view of its moat and ocean. These visuals telegraph whether you should pay a premium, or not, for the stock.

- Improbable, random Black Swan events *will* happen. Trendspotting and Correlations can assist your Black Swan conjectures.

---

[10] Nassim Nicholas Taleb, *The Black Swan: The Impact of the Highly Improbable* (Random House, 2007): xvii.

[11] Taleb, *The Black Swan:* book jacket copy.

CHAPTER 9

The Five-Stack Discovery

Well, that's just, like, your opinion, Man.[1]

The Dude, *The Big Lebowski*

Just the facts, Ma'am.[2]

Sergeant Joe Friday, *Dragnet*

Opinion is really the lowest form of human knowledge; it requires no accountability, no understanding. The highest form of knowledge, according to George Eliot, is empathy, for it requires us to suspend our egos and live in another's world. It requires profound, purpose-larger-than-the-self kind of understanding.[3]

Bill Bullard, Dean of Faculty,
San Francisco University High School

There are heaps of data all around us. By 2025, the amount of data generated each day is expected to reach 463 exabytes (EB) globally.[4] How much is that in practical terms?

---

[1] https://www.youtube.com/watch?v=Z-xI1384Ry4, Jeff Bridges as The Dude in *The Big Lebowski*, 1998. So funny!

[2] https://idioms.thefreedictionary.com/Just+the+facts from *Dragnet*, 1950s TV series.

[3] Ben Casnocha, quoting Bullard in "Three Things to Unlearn from School" (July 11, 2007), https://casnocha.com/2007/07/three-things-to.html. George Eliot is the pen name of English novelist Mary Ann Evans (1819 – 1880). A similar quote is attributed to Plato.

[4] One exabyte (a.k.a. EB) equals one quintillion (1018) bytes. https://seedscientific.com/how-much-data-is-created-every-day.

Per Indiana University:

> To hold 1 EB, you would need about 212,765,958 single-sided DVDs (a
> stack that's about 255.3 kilometers, or 158.65 miles, tall).[5]

And per Teradata.com:

> Some technologists have estimated that all the words ever spoken by man-
> kind would be equal to five Exabytes.[6]

For us, it's not the lack of available data; rather, it's the interpretation that
shapes our **EQ** quest. In our data mining, we separate opinion from fact and
trek into deep-space empathy through our Five-Stack Discovery model captured in figure 9.1. We use the five components to explore companies and
map the results to our **EQ**.

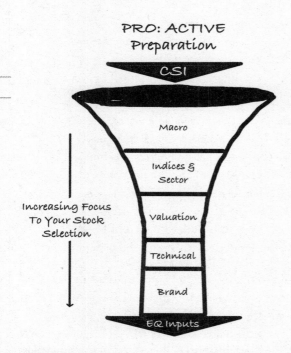

FIGURE 9.1 **Five-Stack Discovery Model**

[5] https://kb.iu.edu/d/apeq.
[6] https://www.teradata.com/Glossary/What-is-an-Exabyte.

The Five-Stack spills out two types of guiding data for the **EQ**:

- **Leads:** These data points are a predictive measure.
- **Lags:** These are the result of lead measures.

The distinction between leads and lags is drawn to assist our decoding of cause-and-effect relationships among events. Here's an example:[7]

Leads Versus Lags

March 4, 2022: Reuters publishes an article quoting the New York State pension chief on companies that should exit Russia, including McDonald's.

March 8, 2022: "McDonald's has decided to temporarily close all our restaurants in Russia and pause all operations in the market."

Lead: Restaurant closings.

Lag: Share price falls from $235.81 on March 4 to $223.58 on March 8.

The review of each slab in the Five-Stack Discovery is your "gimbal rig."[8] Sorry, there's no other way. If you wanna pilot the rocket, you gotta endure the training.

The Multiple-Axis Space Test Inertia Facility

Fondly called "the gimbal rig," these are simulated "tumble-type" maneuvers that might be encountered in space flight. Three tubular aluminum cages could revolve separately or in combination to give roll, pitch, and yaw motions at speeds up to 30 revolutions per minute, greater than those expected in actual space flight.

From February 15 through March 4, 1960, the gimbal rig provided valuable training for all seven project Mercury astronauts.

---

[7] Danielle Wiener-Bronner, "McDonald's, Starbucks and Coca-Cola Leave Russia," CNN Business (March 9, 2022), https://www.cnn.com/2022/03/08/business/mcdonalds-pepsi-coke-russia/index.html; Hilary Russ, "McDonald's, Pepsi, Others Should Consider Pausing Russia Operations—NY Pension Fund," Reuters (March 4, 2022), https://www.reuters.com/business/retail-consumer/mcdonalds-pepsi-others-should-consider-pausing-russia-operations-ny-pension-fund-2022-03-04/.

[8] https://www.nasa.gov/centers/glenn/about/history/mastif.html.

There's a comet of data coming at you in the gimbal rig, so rather than just one chapter-ending capsule, there is one after each Discovery block.

■ Macro (a.k.a. Economic Froth)

The Introduction described "market froth," but there is also "economic froth" in figure 9.2. Although the two interweave in several ways, economic froth directly affects where the economy is pinned in the business cycle. Macro events don't always impact Main Street and Wall Street in the same manner; for example, the US Bureau of Labor Statistics can announce a *decline* in the unemployment rate—great for Main Street—and on the same day, the market craters because OPEC announces a tightening of oil supply.

Macro events are part of your curiosity quest toward **EQ** creation. Once again, because of diminishing returns and the benefits arising from elegant simplicity, I handpick the best catalysts from the available macro data buffet. (The fact that the six market and economic froth wedges match the awesome Trivial Pursuit knowledge pie is a total accident, but I do love that game!)

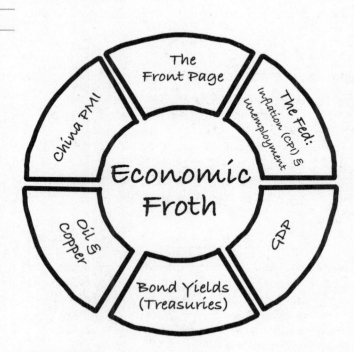

FIGURE 9.2 Economic Froth

Alpha/Acid Test & Bold (7 Metrics) and Gamma (1)

Assume you were taking the family to spend the day with your friends at their beach house 100 miles from your home. Before you leave, wouldn't you check your smartphone for the climate conditions? Even better, call your friends and ask, "How's the *weather* out there?"

Doing recon on the catalysts is like asking: "How are the *economic conditions* out there?" The following sections zip through those catalysts that visualize our economic froth.

The Front Page   News, whether it's print, broadcasts, podcasts, or video clips, affects markets. The COVID pandemic started in December 2019, and sadly, over 6 million lives have since been lost across the globe into Q1, 2022.[9] COVID impacted supply chains, office work, travel and vacations, visitations to care centers, social meetings, school and college attendance, and the entire way we live and interact. Some companies and sectors were severely impacted: brick-and-mortar stores, airlines, cruise lines, the hospitality industry, etc. Yet, many companies and sectors gained: e-commerce, delivery providers, remote meeting software makers, and others.

On March 12, 2020, the markets closed red as COVID economic pressures were more than investors could tolerate. The next morning, President Trump declared a COVID national emergency and the markets rebounded to a positive Friday close. But through the weekend, investor malaise returned and sent the market spiraling into a correction on March 16, per figure 9.3.[10]

	Thursday March 12, 2020	Friday March 13, 2020	Monday March 16, 2020	% Decline, 13th to 16th	Wednesday April 8, 2020
DJIA: DJI	21,201	23,186	20,189	−13%	23,434
S&P 500: GSPC	2,481	2,711	2,386	−12%	2,750
NASDAQ: IXIC	7,202	7,875	6,905	−12%	8,091

FIGURE 9.3   COVID National Emergency and the Market, 2020
Source: Data from [10]

---

[9] https://coronavirus.jhu.edu/map.html as of early March 2022.
[10] https://finance.yahoo.com/quote sourced on January 30, 2022.

Often, a Newtonian opposite force to the bad news arrives, and that's what occurred with a cavalry of COVID help, from more detailed vaccine plans to greater coordination from federal to state governments. On April 8, only 17 trading days after President Trump's declaration, all major indices surpassed their pre-declaration March 13, 2020, closings.[11] At other times, the market struggles to make sense of a cosmic event as investors nervously oscillate between fear and opportunity.

Here's a seesaw of investor responses to Russia's 2022 invasion of Ukraine, per figure 9.4:

	Friday February 18, 2022	Thursday February 24 (LOW), 2022	% Decline, 18th to 24th	Friday February 25, 2022
DJIA: DJI	34,079	32,273	–5%	34,059
S&P 500: GSPC	4,349	4,115	–5%	4,385
NASDAQ: IXIC	13,548	12,588	–7%	13,695

FIGURE 9.4 Russian Invasion of Ukraine and the Market

1. Markets closed on Friday, February 18, 2022, at healthy levels (wow, just look at those three index numbers in figure 9.4, as compared to April 8, 2020, in figure 9.3!).

2. Front-page news through the weekend and early into the week of February 21 began to reflect hostile actions in the separatist areas of eastern Ukraine, with Russia formally recognizing as sovereign nations the breakaway regions of Donetsk People's Republic and the Luhansk People's Republic.

3. In the early hours of Thursday, February 24, Russia invaded Ukraine and the indices reached their weekly lows that same morning.

4. President Biden spoke midday on Thursday in measured tones regarding the Ukraine invasion, and the market regained its footing, with all indices the next day retracing to the previous Friday.

5. Safe harbor from February 25 going forward? Not exactly. Two days later, February 27: "President Vladimir Putin put Russia's nuclear deterrent on high alert on Sunday in the face of a barrage of Western reprisals

[11] Actually, the NASDAQ Composite only needed until April 6, 2020, when it closed at 7,913.

for his war on Ukraine . . ."[12] The shock word "nuclear" jolted the markets on Monday and Tuesday, as shown in figure 9.5:

	Friday February 25, 2022	Monday February 28, 2022	Tuesday March 1, 2022	% Decline, 25th to 1st	Wednesday March 2, 2022	% Increase March 1st to 2nd	Thursday March 3, 2022	Friday March 4, 2022
DJIA: DJI	34,059	33,893	33,295	−2.2%	33,891	1.8%	33,795	33,615
S&P 500: GSPC	4,385	4,374	4,306	−1.8%	4,387	1.9%	4,363	4,329
NASDAQ: IXIC	13,695	13,751	13,532	−1.2%	13,752	1.6%	13,538	13,313

FIGURE 9.5   Russian Usage of the Word "Nuclear" and the Market

6. On the Tuesday evening of March 1, 2022, President Biden spoke to the nation in a confident State of the Union address. The next morning, Federal Reserve Chairman Jerome Powell supplied a "solid outlook" and markets snapped back at close on Wednesday, March 2.

> In remarks Wednesday before the House Financial Services Committee, the central bank leader said the war in Ukraine had "highly uncertain" potential impacts on the economy. But he said the Fed is still prepared to move forward with interest rate increases aimed at taming runaway inflation.
> Powell noted that **the lookout otherwise is solid**, with an "extremely tight" labor market and price pressures that he still expects to recede later in the year. He expects the Fed to raise its benchmark borrowing rate a quarter-percentage point at the March policy meeting, but added that he will consider potentially larger increases if inflation remains hot.[13]

7. However, on Thursday and Friday, the markets fell again as investors were increasingly alarmed by Russia's aggression and the spike in oil prices. Even a positive jobs report on Friday morning, March 4, did not help.

> Total nonfarm payroll employment rose by 678,000 in February, and the unemployment rate edged down to 3.8 percent, the U.S. Bureau of Labor Statistics reported today.[14]

[12] https://www.reuters.com/world/europe/russias-putin-puts-nuclear-forces-high-alert-2022-02-27.

[13] Jeff Cox, "Watch Federal Reserve Chair Powell Speak Live," CNBC (March 3, 2022), https://www.cnbc.com/2022/03/03/watch-federal-reserve-chair-powell-speak-live.html. Emphasis added.

[14] U.S. Bureau of Labor Statistics, Economic News Release, Employment Situation Summary, https://www.bls.gov/news.release/archives/empsit_03042022.htm.

The possibility of ongoing negative front-page news: COVID variants, Russia/Ukraine, China/Taiwan, and other headline news items can spin the market in unanticipated directions; our front-page curiosity quotient must be on steady alert. Front-page economic "breaking news" bulletins, streams, and reports frequently lever their story off a dominant headline word from the drawing in figure 9.6.

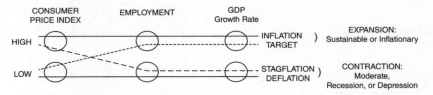

FIGURE 9.6 Headline Economic Words and the Preferred "Target" Outcomes

The headline words often career without context from one news outlet to another because the words themselves have different applications; some refer to the waves of the business cycle and others are in respect to broader economic conditions. Regardless, the **EQ** will bucket those headline words that are in the same blast radius for our bull and bear descriptors. Here are two summaries that provide helpful clarification of headline words:

National Bureau of Economic Research:
. . . **recession** is . . . a significant decline in economic activity that is spread across the economy and that lasts more than a few months. . .These include real personal income less transfers (PILT), nonfarm payroll employment, real personal consumption expenditures, wholesale-retail sales adjusted for price changes, employment as measured by the household survey, and industrial production.

The peak is the month in which a variety of economic indicators reach their highest level, followed by a significant decline in economic activity. Similarly, a month is designated as a trough when economic activity reaches a low point and begins to rise again for a sustained period. Expansion is the normal state of the economy; most recessions are brief. . .The NBER does not separately identify depressions in its Business Cycle chronology. The period between a peak and a trough is a contraction or a recession, and the period between the trough and the peak is an expansion.[15]

---

[15] https://www.nber.org/research/business-cycle-dating/business-cycle-dating-procedure-frequently-asked-questions. Per its website "The National Bureau of Economic Research (NBER) is a private, nonprofit, nonpartisan research organization dedicated to undertaking and disseminating unbiased economic research to public policymakers, business professionals, and the academic community." Emphasis added.

Ben Bernanke, Federal Reserve Chairman, on March 2, 2004:
During the major contraction phase of the **Depression**, between 1929 and 1933, real output in the United States fell nearly 30 percent. During the same period, according to retrospective studies, the unemployment rate rose from about 3 percent to nearly 25 percent and many of those lucky enough to have a job were able to work only part-time. For comparison, between 1973 and 1975, in what was perhaps the most severe U.S. recession of the World War II era, real output fell 3.4 percent and the unemployment rate rose from about 4 percent to about 9 percent. Other features of the 1929-33 decline included a sharp deflation—prices fell at a rate of nearly 10 percent per year during the early 1930s—as well as a plummeting stock market, widespread bank failures, and a rash of defaults and bankruptcies by businesses and households.[16]

How do you ascertain what front-page news will impact the market? There is no way to empirically explain the news, whether positive or negative. In chapter 1, unsystematic and systematic risk were presented. Visualize the front page in the same way. Remember, unsystematic risk can be diversified away. Systemic risk is a heavier burden. Your city announces an increase in property taxes; this affects you and is on the front page, but the citizens in the next burg could care less, and markets hum. Russia invading Ukraine affects everyone; it's systemic, and therefore grinds the market.

The register indicators and headline economic words will be explored, but first, is it possible to weigh the "front-page weather"? Maybe we can use one more tool, besides our gut, to measure the positive versus negative front-page pressure on stock selections. Does the approval rating of the president reflect the front-page weather? President Biden's approval rating determined by FiveThirtyEight on July 13, 2022, had it at a shallow 38.5%.[17]

Ratings swing during any administration and reflect a point-in-time feeling from the public on many personalized issues, including the overall economy, their own standard of living, and most importantly, the future.

Macro Register Target: Front Page

A Presidential approval rate of 51% or greater.

---

[16] https://www.federalreserve.gov/boarddocs/speeches/2004/200403022/default.htm. Emphasis added.

[17] "How popular/unpopular is Joe Biden?" FiveThirtyEight, "An updating calculation of the president's approval rating, accounting for each poll's quality, recency, sample size and partisan lean." https://projects.fivethirtyeight.com/biden-approval-rating/ at 12:01 PM.

The Fed: Inflation (CPI) and Employment The mandate and actions of the Federal Reserve System (a.k.a. the Fed), along with the clout of inflation and the hurt of unemployment, are a rocky belt that we fly through in figure 9.7.

The Fed is the central bank of the United States and has as its purpose through its 12 regional districts, "to promote the effective operation of the U.S. economy and, more generally, the public interest."[18] The Fed pursues a "dual mandate" of price stability and maximum sustainable employment with a targeted inflation rate of 2% and, until a couple of years ago, an unemployment rate of 4.4%.

On August 27, 2020, and reaffirmed on January 25, 2022, the Fed advised of a major policy shift on one of the two mandates, namely, its maximum sustainable employment rate:

> The maximum level of employment is a broad-based and inclusive goal that is not directly measurable and changes over time owing largely to nonmonetary factors that affect the structure and dynamics of the labor market. Consequently, it would not be appropriate to specify a fixed goal for employment.[19]

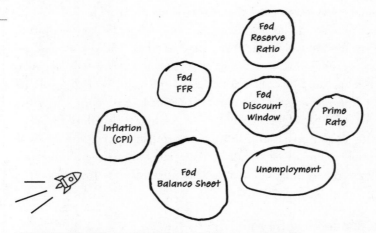

FIGURE 9.7 The Federal Reserve, Tools and Goals

---

[18] https://www.federalreserve.gov/aboutthefed/structure-federal-reserve-system.htm.

[19] https://www.federalreserve.gov/newsevents/pressreleases/monetary20200827a.htm and https://www.federalreserve.gov/monetarypolicy/files/FOMC_LongerRunGoals.pdf. Note that I frequently use "banks" as a catch-all term for all financial institutions that are regulated by the Federal Reserve.

The Fed has three monetary policy tools of open market operations, discount rate setting, and reserve ratios to accomplish its dual mandate.[20]

Open Market Operations: Balance Sheet and the Federal Funds Rate The Federal Open Market Committee (FOMC) affects the supply of money and credit rates by way of two mechanisms: sizing its balance sheet (see figure 9.8) through the purchase and sale of securities and calibrating the Federal Funds Rate (FFR).[21] Financial institutions (banks, S&Ls, etc.) must keep a "reserve" of funds to ensure they can meet their financial obligations, including depositor withdrawals. The FFR, with its lower and upper bounds, is the target range for these institutions to lend their excess reserve balances to each other.

To assist the expansion or contraction of the economy, the FOMC primes the level of institutional reserves to expand or contract the economy:

Expanding the Economy

- When the Fed *buys* securities, such as US government Treasuries from banks, the infusion increases bank reserves and expands liquidity (also known as quantitative easing in respect to longer-term securities).

Federal Reserve Balance Sheet

Assets	Liabilities and Net Worth
Treasury securities	Currency
Less-liquid assets	Bank reserves
Loans	Treasury deposits
	Capital

FIGURE 9.8 Federal Reserve Balance Sheet
Source: [21] / Federal Reserve Bank of St. Louis

---

[20] https://www.federalreserve.gov/monetarypolicy/fomc.htm.
[21] The Balance Sheet chart is from an excellent article, "Quantitative Easing: Entrance and Exit Strategies," by Alan S. Binder of the St. Louis Federal Reserve, https://files.stlouisfed.org/files/htdocs/publications/review/10/11/Blinder.pdf. Note that a "twist" is when the Fed adjusts its Balance Sheet through concurrently selling short-term bonds and buying long-term bonds to improve economic growth.

- With a reserve excess, banks may move funds among themselves at the suggested FFR range.

- The reserve **oversupply** makes more money available for business and consumer loan demand, which expands the economy.

Dampening the Economy Spools in Reverse

- The Fed *sells* securities (or does not re-invest maturing securities) and reduces its balance sheet (a.k.a. quantitative tightening).

- Bank purchasing of these assets lowers their reserves and increases the demand for interbank reserve funding.

- This **demand** reduces the money available for business and consumer loans, which contracts the economy.

The FFR range is the foundation for credit rates, and lowering the range is similar in market impact to the FOMC buying securities, and increasing the range has the same effect as the FOMC selling securities. The FFR is also expressed as an "effective rate," which is an average of all inter-bank reserve lending rates.

Figure 9.9 illustrates the effective FFR history.

Balance sheet adjustments are more impactful on longer-term Treasuries (a.k.a. the long end of the yield curve), whereas toggling the FFR is effectual on shorter-run Treasuries (a.k.a. the short end of the yield curve). A derivative of the FFR is the institutional prime rate (not to be confused with the primary credit rate), usually 3 percentage points higher than the FFR, as described by the Fed:

> **The prime rate is an interest rate determined by individual banks**. It is often used as a reference rate (also called the base rate) for many types of loans, including loans to small businesses and credit card loans. On its H.15 statistical release, "Selected Interest Rates," the Board reports the prime rate posted by the majority of the largest twenty-five banks. Although the **Federal Reserve has no direct role in setting the prime rate**, many banks choose to set their prime rates based partly on the target level of the **federal funds rate**—the rate that banks charge each other for short-term loans—established by the Federal Open Market Committee.[22]

---

[22] https://www.federalreserve.gov/faqs/credit_12846.htm. Emphasis added.

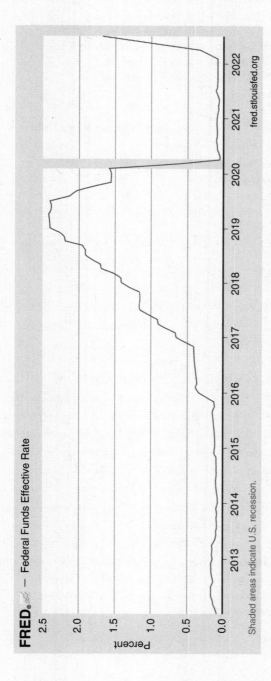

FIGURE 9.9 Federal Funds Effective Rate, Not Seasonally Adjusted, January 1, 2012–July 1, 2022[23]

Source: Board of Governors of the Federal Reserve System (US)

---

[23] Board of Governors of the Federal Reserve System (US), Federal Funds Effective Rate, retrieved from FRED, Federal Reserve Bank of St. Louis; https://fred.stlouisfed.org/series/fedfunds, August 21, 2022. The FFR is a FOMC recommended range and reserve lending rates are set among the banks themselves.

THE FIVE-STACK DISCOVERY

The Discount Rate Window Financial institutions can borrow from the Fed at its Board of Governors mandated discount rates:

> The discount rate is the interest rate charged to commercial banks and other depository institutions on loans they receive from their regional Federal Reserve Bank's lending facility—the discount window.[24]

The Fed has three discount window lending programs: Primary, Secondary, and Seasonal credit programs, each with a specific rate and set relative to the FFR, with the objective being:

> The Fed seeks to set interest rates to help set the backdrop for promoting the conditions that achieve the mandate set by the Congress—namely, maximum sustainable employment, low and stable inflation, and moderate long-term interest rates.[25]
>
> The **primary credit program** is the principal safety valve for ensuring adequate liquidity in the banking system and a backup source of short-term funds for generally sound depository institutions.[26]

A higher primary credit rate (PCR) rolls along with the FOMC selling securities and a higher FFR: the economy decelerates and hopefully inflation as well.

Reserve Requirements The Federal Reserve Board of Governors mandates the cash level that financial institutions are obligated to have in their vaults or with the Fed, calculated as a ratio to their customer deposits. Decreasing reserve requirements, as with a lowered FFR, makes more money available for commercial transactions and expands the economy. In an effort to spark the economy from its COVID malaise, "As announced on March 15, 2020, the Board reduced reserve requirement ratios to zero percent effective March 26, 2020. This action eliminated reserve requirements for all depository institutions."[27]

Given the immense weight of the Fed on stock market direction, it's useful to sift through its recent statements and actions, as there's market angst heading into 2022–2023 regarding the FOMC's plans for interest rates, both in terms of the quantum and the frequency (a.k.a. the "dot plot").

---

[24] https://www.federalreserve.gov/monetarypolicy/discountrate.htm.

[25] https://www.federalreserve.gov/faqs/why-do-interest-rates-matter.htm.

[26] https://www.frbdiscountwindow.org/pages/general-information.

[27] https://www.federalreserve.gov/monetarypolicy/reservereq.htm.

The FOMC announced on January 26, 2022:

> The Committee seeks to achieve maximum employment and inflation at
> the rate of 2 percent over the longer run. In support of these goals, the
> Committee decided to keep the target range for the federal funds rate at 0
> to ¼ percent.[28]

On March 16, 2022, at 2:00 PM, the Fed moved to torpedo inflation:

> The Board of Governors of the Federal Reserve System voted unanimously
> to raise the interest rate paid on reserve balances to 0.4 percent.
>   Undertake open market operations as necessary to maintain the federal
> funds rate in a target range of 1/4 to 1/2 percent.
>   In a related action, the Board of Governors of the Federal Reserve
> System voted unanimously to approve a 1/4 percentage point increase in
> the primary credit rate to 0.5 percent, effective March 17, 2022.[29]

The effective FFR would rise to .33%. At the post-meeting news confer-
ence, Chairman Powell advised:

> In addition, the Committee expects to begin reducing its holdings of
> Treasury securities and agency debt and agency mortgage-backed securi-
> ties at a coming meeting.
>   Fed Chairman Jerome Powell at his post-meeting news conference
> hinted that the balance sheet reduction could start in May, and said the
> process could be the equivalent of another rate hike this year.[30]

The market interpreted the Fed's March 16 actions as positive and consistent to previous statements, per the closing indices in the figure 9.10 snapshot.
   On April 6, 2022, the Fed released its March 15–16, 2022 Minutes noting a "balance sheet runoff":

> In their discussion, all participants agreed that elevated inflation and tight
> labor market conditions warranted commencement of balance sheet runoff
> at a coming meeting, with a faster pace of decline in securities holdings

---

[28] https://www.federalreserve.gov/newsevents/pressreleases/monetary20220126a.htm.
[29] https://www.federalreserve.gov/newsevents/pressreleases/monetary20220316a1.htm.
[30] Jeff Cox, "Federal Reserve Approves First Interest Rate Hike in More Than Three Years, Sees
Six More Ahead," CNBC (March 16, 2022), https://www.cnbc.com/2022/03/16/federal-
reserve-meeting.html.

	March 15, 2022	March 16, 2022	% Increase, 15th to 16th
DJIA: DJI	33,544	34,063	2%
S&P 500: GSPC	4,262	4,358	2%
NASDAQ: IXIC	12,949	13,437	4%

FIGURE 9.10 Indices Closing Prices on March 16 at 4 pm (EST) Following the Fed's 2:00 pm (EST) Rate Announcements

than over the 2017–19 period . . . Participants generally agreed that monthly caps of about $60 billion for Treasury securities and about $35 billion for agency MBS would likely be appropriate. Participants also generally agreed that the caps could be phased in over a period of three months or modestly longer if market conditions warrant.[31]

On May 4, 2022, at 2 pm EST, the Federal Reserve issued a FOMC statement that hoisted the FFR by 50 basis points from its .25% − .50% range to .75% − 1.0% (leading to an effective FFR of .83%):

The Committee seeks to achieve maximum employment and inflation at the rate of 2 percent over the longer run. With appropriate firming in the stance of monetary policy, the Committee expects inflation to return to its 2 percent objective and the labor market to remain strong. In support of these goals, the Committee decided to raise the target range for the federal funds rate to ¾ to 1 percent and anticipates that ongoing increases in the target range will be appropriate.[32]

The market's initial reaction was positive to the close on May 4, but then an investor earthquake rumbled through to the end of the week as captured in figure 9.11.

On June 15, 2022, the FOMC "decided to raise the target range for the federal funds rate to 1-1/2 to 1-3/4 percent," yielding an effective FFR of 1.58% and a PCR of 1.75%. On July 27, 2022, the FOMC moved the FFR range up another .75 percentage points "to 2-1/4 to 2-1/2", elevating the effective FFR to 2.33% and the PCR to 2.50%.[33]

---

[31] MBS is Mortgage Backed Securities. https://www.federalreserve.gov/monetarypolicy/files/fomcminutes20220316.pdf.

[32] https://www.federalreserve.gov/newsevents/pressreleases/monetary20220504a.htm.

[33] https://www.federalreserve.gov/newsevents/pressreleases/monetary20220615a.htm and /monetary20220727a.htm, and https://www.newyorkfed.org/markets/reference-rates/effr.

	May 3, 2022	May 4, 2022	% Increases 3rd to 4th	May 5, 2022	May 6, 2022	% Decline, 4th to 6th
DJIA: DJI	33,129	34,061	3%	32,998	32,899	–3%
S&P 500: GSPC	4,175	4,300	3%	4,147	4,123	–4%
NASDAQ: IXIC	12,564	12,965	3%	12,318	12,145	–6%

FIGURE 9.11 Indices Closing Prices May 3–May 6, 2022

Current Interest Rates	
Primary Credit **2.50%**	Secondary Credit **3.00%**
Seasonal Credit **2.55%**	Fed Funds Target **2.25-2.50%**

FIGURE 9.12 Federal Reserve Interest Rates, August 21, 2022[34]
Source: Adapted from [34]

The interest rate action of the Federal Reserve is captured in figure 9.12.

The remaining 2022 dot-plot actions by the Fed are the subject of great speculation, and you should be alert to sector responses.

The Federal Reserve's handiwork of balance sheet adjustments, FFR/Primary Credit Rate settings, and reserve requirements are a propellant, up or down, to equities. Hence, the mantra: Don't Fight the Fed!

MACRO REGISTER TARGET: THE FED

The macro register captures targets for inflation and unemployment, and by extension, it collars the Fed's monetary indicators.

Therefore, we will not specifically register the FFR, PCR, and the Reserve Ratio.

[34] https://www.frbdiscountwindow.org/

Inflation: The Consumer Price Index (CPI) Inflation, measured by the CPI, is defined and computed by the US Bureau of Labor Statistics (BLS), a unit of the Department of Labor, as:

> The Consumer Price Index (CPI) is a measure of the average change over time in the prices paid by urban consumers for a market basket of consumer goods and services. Indexes are available for the U.S. and various geographic areas. Average price data for select utility, automotive fuel, and food items are also available.[35]

Figure 9.13 presents the aggregated, approximate input weightings for the CPI.[36]

Housing & Household Energy	42%
Transportation, Vehicles, & Fuel	18%
Food & Beverage	14%
Medical Care	9%
Education & Communication	6%
Recreation	5%
Apparel	3%
Other Goods & Services	3%
Total	**100%**

FIGURE 9.13   CPI Components (Simplified)

As the FRED chart shows in figure 9.14, the Fed kept a lid on inflation from the mid-90s to Q1, 2021 as measured by the year over year (YoY) CPI movements. The chart goes all the way back to 1960 to show the recessionary periods in the US economy as indicated by the vertical grey bars.

---

[35] US Bureau of Labor Statistics, https://www.bls.gov/cpi/. Also see https://www.frbsf .org/education/publications/doctor-econ/2002/october/inflation-factors-rise/ from the Federal Reserve Bank of San Francisco for a nice read on the causes of inflation. And, from *Forbes*, George Calhoun (February 23, 2022) is a great backgrounder: https://www.forbes .com/sites/georgecalhoun/2022/02/23/the-31-flavors-of-inflation-do-we-really- understand-these-numbers/?sh=589683f31166.
[36] http://www.bls.gov/cpi/tables/relative-importance/2021.htm.

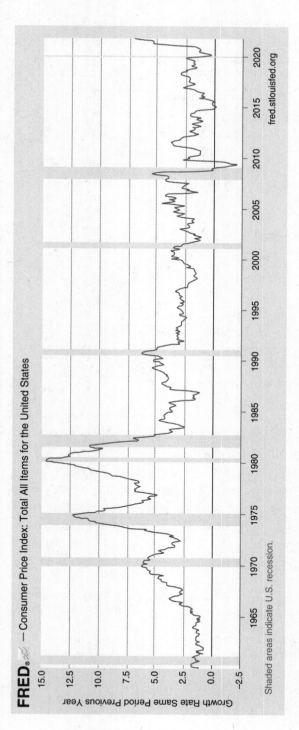

FIGURE 9.14 Consumer Price Index, Not Seasonally Adjusted, 1960–2021[37]

Source: Organization for Economic Co-operation and Development

THE FIVE-STACK DISCOVERY

---

[37] Board of Governors of the Federal Reserve System (US), Consumer Price Index: Total All Items for the United States, retrieved from FRED, Federal Reserve Bank of St. Louis; https://fred.stlouisfed.org/series/CPALTT01USM659N, May 19, 2022.

However, the CPI began to edge up in Q2, 2021 per figure 9.15.[38]

January	February	March
1.4%	1.7%	2.6%
April	**May**	**June**
4.2%	5.0%	5.4%
July	**August**	**September**
5.4%	5.3%	5.4%
October	**November**	**December**
6.2%	6.8%	7.0%

FIGURE 9.15   **CPI YoY Change by Month for 2021**
Source: Data from [39]

On February 10, 2022, at 8:30 AM (EST), the BLS advised of the January 2022 CPI YoY increase:

> The Consumer Price Index for All Urban Consumers (CPI-U) increased 0.6 percent in **January** on a seasonally adjusted basis, the U.S. Bureau of Labor Statistics reported today. Over the last 12 months, the all items index increased **7.5** percent before seasonal adjustment.[39]

With that 7.5% news, you would expect a corrective indices pullback from February 9 to the close on February 10, but the immediate fall was not as drastic as you might have predicted (see figure 9.16).

Why is that? Because, initially anyway, the market had largely priced-in forthcoming negative "economic" news. Just like Black Swan forecasting described in chapter 8, the forward-thinking people that run the hedge funds, ETFs, mutual funds, etc. (i.e. basically the non-retail investor group) had already digested much of the inflation reality. The market then further ruminated and took the indices to the woodshed the next day, February 11.

---

[38] US Bureau of Labor Statistics, Graphics for Economic News Release, https://www.bls.gov/charts/consumer-price-index/consumer-price-index-by-category-line-chart.htm.
[39] News Release, Bureau of Labor Statistics, US Department of Labor, https://www.bls.gov/news.release/pdf/cpi.pdf (February 10, 2022). Emphasis added.

	February 9, 2022	February 10, 2022	February 11, 2022	% Decline, 9th to 10th	% Decline, 9th to 11th
DJIA: DJI	35,768	35,242	34,738	−1%	−3%
S&P 500: GSPC	4,587	4,504	4,419	−2%	−4%
NASDAQ: IXIC	14,490	14,186	13,791	−2%	−5%

FIGURE 9.16   **Market Reaction to January 2022, CPI 7.5% YoY Increase**

Per the BLS March 10, 2022, Economic News Releases, the February 2022 CPI YoY was given as:

> The all items index rose **7.9** percent for the 12 months ending **February**. The 12-month increase has been steadily rising and is now the largest since the period ending January 1982.[40]

Inflation did not let up in March and April 2022 per the BLS Economic News Releases of April 12, 2022, and May 11, 2022:

> The all items index increased **8.3** percent for the 12 months ending **April**, a smaller increase than the **8.5**-percent figure for the period ending in **March**.[41]

Figure 9.17 provides the market reaction to the February, March, and April CPI announcements, both day of, and the following day.

Annualized CPI continued its torrid 2022 pace with May coming in at 8.6% and June at 9.1%.[42]

The cumulative effects of the high CPI rates monthly were a heavy burden for the market leading into mid-July, 2022. Inflation is particularly hard for growth stocks as these companies are anticipating future profits where a dollar is not as valuable as a current dollar. Inflation gorges at the economic

[40] US Bureau of Labor Statistics, Economic News Release, Consumer Price Index Summary, https://www.bls.gov/news.release/cpi.nr0.htm, retrieved March 10, 2022. Emphasis added.

[41] US Bureau of Labor Statistics, Economic News Release, Consumer Price Index Summary, https://www.bls.gov/news.release/cpi.nr0.htm, May 11, 2022. Emphasis added.

[42] https://www.bls.gov/news.release/cpi.nr0.htm.

	March 10, 2022	March 11, 2022	April 12, 2022	April 13, 2022	May 11, 2022	May 12, 2022
DJIA: DJI	33,174	32,944	34,220	34,565	31,834	31,730
S&P 500: GSPC	4,260	4,204	4,397	4,447	3,935	3,930
NASDAQ: IXIC	13,130	12,844	13,372	13,644	11,364	11,371

FIGURE 9.17 Market Reaction to February (7.9%), March (8.5%), and April (8.3%) 2022 CPI YoY Increase

pie and United Kingdom Prime Minister Margaret Thatcher said it best: "Inflation is the parent of unemployment and the unseen robber of those who have saved."[43] Economists generally agree, though, that some level of inflation is a good thing. If the specific target is 2%, is there an acceptable inflation range for our register? Let's have the cards speak:

- For some of our *Occamized* macro register targets, the backdrop of the last ten years is all we need. The massive changes in global trade and technology over the recent past makes earlier periods unimportant for the **EQ**.

- The 2012–2021 American economic growth was remarkable, and there is a thick line from the Fed's inflation and employment management to that growth. GDP was $16.6 trillion in Q1/12 and $24.0 trillion in Q4/21, an impressive 44% increase (with a CAGR of 3.7%, and illustrated in figure 9.20.).

- Logically, we want inflation data points that cluster around the inflation average as the economic engine ran beautifully at that rate, and our judgment call is to build an inflation desired range that contains two-thirds of the inflation data points.

A review of monthly CPI Y/Y data for 2012–2021 year generates a CPI average of 1.9% with two-thirds of the months in a range of .6% to 3.2% (for sure, 3.2% is well above the Fed's 2% target).

---

[43] https://quotefancy.com/quote/955977/Margaret-Thatcher-Inflation-is-the-parent-of-unemployment-and-the-unseen-robber-of-those-who-have-saved. Prime Minister of the United Kingdom Margaret Thatcher, 1925–2013.

A CPI range of .6% to 3.2%.

Unemployment/Employment   The Employment level can be summarized as a ratio of employed people to the non-institutional population over the age of 16.[44] The US Bureau of Labor Statistics issues its nicely concise Employment Situation Summary on the first Friday of each month (for the previous month), and on July 8, 2022, they advised:

> Nonfarm payroll employment rose by 372,000 in June, and the unemployment rate remained at 3.6 percent. Notable job gains occurred in professional and business services, leisure and hospitality, and health care.[45]

Unemployment rates have been low for several months: October 2021: 4.6%, November 4.2%, December 3.9%, January 4.0%, February 3.8%, and March to June, 3.6% per month. Figure 9.18 illustrates monthly unemployment rate for January 2012 to December 2021.

The unemployment rate is a window into the health of the economy and certainly a contributor to the expansion (or contraction) of the business cycle: the dark vertical bar on the chart is the COVID recession where unemployment spiked.

The 2012–2021 unemployment rates average 5.7% and it's 5.4% if we exclude nine COVID months, April to December. Two-thirds of the non-COVID months are in a band of 3.9% to 6.9%.

MACRO REGISTER TARGET: UNEMPLOYMENT

An unemployment range of 3.9% to 6.9%.

---

[44] https://www.bls.gov/cps/definitions.htm#lfconcepts. Noninstitutional means those in prisons, nursing homes, and the Armed Forces are excluded from the labor force calculation. Go to the link provided, US Bureau of Labor Statistics (a unit of the US Department of Labor) for a thorough description.

[45] US Bureau of Labor Statistics, Economic News Release, Consumer Price Index Summary, https://www.bls.gov/news.release/jec.nr0.htm, emphasis added.

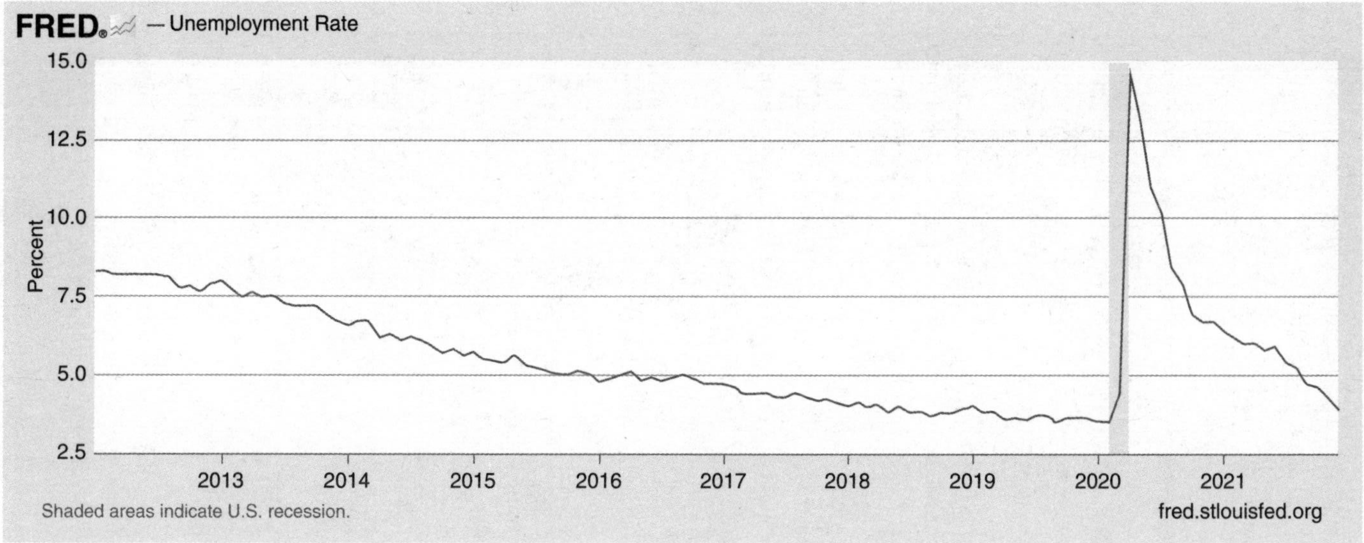

FRED® — Unemployment Rate

Shaded areas indicate U.S. recession.

FIGURE 9.18 Unemployment Rate, Seasonally Adjusted, January 2012 to December 2021[46]

Source: U.S. Bureau of Labor Statistics

[46] Board of Governors of the Federal Reserve System (US), Unemployment Rate, retrieved from FRED, Federal Reserve Bank of St. Louis; https://fred.stlouisfed.org/series/UNRATE#0, May 19, 2022.

Gross Domestic Product (GDP) GDP data is from the US Bureau of Economic Analysis (BEA), an agency of the Department of Commerce, and is described as:

> The value of the goods and services produced in the United States. The percentage that GDP grew (or shrank) from one period to another is an important way for Americans to gauge how their economy is doing.[47]

Arguably, the heavyweight of lag economic indicators is the annualized change in quarterly GDP, the value of all goods and services produced by the nation:

GDP = Government Purchases + Consumer Spending + Business Investments + Net Trade (Exports − Imports)

Figure 9.19 reveals the US Q4, 2021 GDP approximated to its major components.

in trillions	GDP COMPONENTS	
	Q4, 2021	Allocation
Government (G)	$4.1	17.2%
Consumer (C)	$16.3	68.1%
Business Investments (I)	$4.5	18.7%
Net Trade (N) (X+M)	−$.9	−4.0%
Total GDP	**$24.0**	**100.0%**
Exports (X)	$2.7	
Imports (M)	−$3.6	

FIGURE 9.19 GDP Components[48]
Source: [48] / Federal Reserve Bank of St. Louis

The FRED graph in figure 9.20 illustrates the significant GDP growth since 1960, reaching $24 trillion in Q4, 2021.

---

[47] Bureau of Economic Analysis, https://www.bea.gov/resources/learning-center/what-to-know-gdp.
[48] Board of Governors of the Federal Reserve System (US), Release Tables: Real GDP and Its Components, Quarterly, Seasonally Adjusted, retrieved from FRED, Federal Reserve Bank of St. Louis; https://fred.stlouisfed.org/release/tables?eid=155790&rid=269, May 19, 2022.

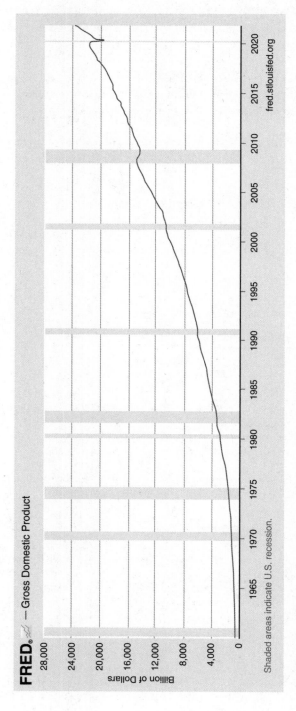

FIGURE 9.20 GDP, Seasonally Adjusted Annual Rate, 1960–2021[49]

Source: U.S. Bureau of Economic Analysis

---

[49] Board of Governors of the Federal Reserve System (US), Gross Domestic Product, retrieved from FRED, Federal Reserve Bank of St. Louis; https://fred.stlouisfed.org/series/GDP, May 19, 2022.

The GDP quarterly shifts help explain the waves in the business cycle and its series of peaks, contractions, troughs, then expansion, and peak again, per the Federal Reserve Bank of St. Louis:

> When compared with prior periods, GDP tells us whether the economy is **EXPANDING** by producing more goods and services, or **CONTRACTING** due to less output. It also tells us how the U.S. is performing relative to other economies around the world.[50]

Our macro register requires the change in GDP, not so much its total; in fact, the rate of GDP growth is conceptually similar to "g" in PE FWD and PEG.

The recent annualized GDP quarter-over-quarter shifts are shown in figure 9.21, with Q4, 2021 at 6.9% (Third Estimate), Q1, 2022 at −1.6% (Third Estimate), and Q2, 2022 at −.6% (Second Estimate):

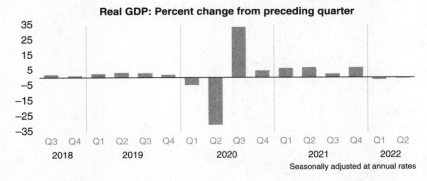

FIGURE 9.21   GDP Quarterly % Change to Preceding Quarter, Annualized, Q1 2018 to Q2 2022[51]
Source: U.S. Bureau of Economic Analysis

---

[50] https://www.stlouisfed.org/open-vault/2019/march/what-is-gdp-why-important.

[51] On April 28, 2022, the BEA provided a Q1, 2022 Advanced Estimate of a 1.4% annualized decline in real GDP. On May 26, they updated Q1, 2022 with their Second Estimate of a 1.5% decline, and on June 29 with their Third Estimate to a 1.6% drop. Q2, 2022 had a July 28, 2022 Advance Estimate of −.9% and adjusted to −.6% in their August 25 Second Estimate; https://www.bea.gov/data/gdp/gross-domestic-product, retrieved from the BEA, August 25, 2022.

A couple of interesting things about GDP: Warren Buffett developed the following metric as a general indicator of whether the market might be overbought or oversold.

$$\text{Buffett Indicator} = (\text{Total Market Capitalization} / \text{GDP}) \times 100$$

If the ratio is greater than 100%, then the market is encroaching into overbought territory. Total market capitalization of the NYSE and NASDAQ is about $51 trillion, and given GDP is $24 trillion, the Buffet Indicator yields 213%, i.e. very much over-bought.

To demonstrate the incredible size of Apple: Figure 9.22 illustrates the projected 2022 GDP for the largest economies in the world per the International Monetary Fund, to which I add Apple's Market Capitalization when it rang the bell at $3 trillion in early January 2022 (agreed, an Apple and oranges comparison).

PROJECTED GDP	
nominal, trillions, US$	**2022 (est.)**
USA	$25.3
CHINA	$19.9
JAPAN	$4.9
GERMANY	$4.3
UNITED KINGDOM	$3.4
INDIA	$3.3
APPLE	**$3.0**
FRANCE	$2.9
CANADA	$2.2
ITALY	$2.1
BRAZIL	$1.8
RUSSIA	$1.8
SOUTH KOREA	$1.8
AUSTRALIA	$1.7

FIGURE 9.22 **Apple's January 2022 Market Capitalization**[52]

[52] GDP figures are from https://en.wikipedia.org/wiki/List_of_countries_by_GDP_ (nominal) on 4/24/22 and Apple data is from https://www.barrons.com/articles/apple-3-trillion-market-cap-stock-price-51641225009. Apple's market cap dropped to $2.3 trillion in mid-May, 2022. Apple's annual revenues are about $378 billion.

Does the Federal Reserve or the Department of Commerce have a specific "all's well" GDP Quarter to Quarter (Q/Q) annualized target? No, they don't, so our GDP register is not grounded like inflation and unemployment, but we have guiding history:

- Per a C.I. Jones 2016 study (Stanford University): "For nearly 150 years, GDP per person in the US economy has grown at a remarkably steady average rate of around **2%** per year," and he further states "steady, sustained exponential growth for the last 150 years is a key characteristic of the frontier."[53]

- And from the Bureau of Economic Analysis: "between 2007 and 2019 . . . and real GDP growing at **1.7** percent per year."[54]

The 2012–2021 ten-year GDP annualized Q/Q average is 2.4%. Backing out the extreme 2020 COVID quarters of Q1 (−5.1%), Q2 (−31.2%), and Q3 (+33.8%) is material: the average then ladders up to 2.7% (chapter 3: an increase of .3 percentage points or 12.5%). As with the unemployment data set, nine months (three Quarters) are removed. Interestingly, the GDP 2020 outliers were from January to September, whereas for unemployment, it lagged April to December.

MACRO REGISTER TARGET: GDP

A GDP range of 1.0% to 4.4%.

Alternatively and similarly to our CPI output, we could have tightened up the GDP range to 2.0% − 2.49% per Appendix D, as 4.4% at the high end seems rich for an upper bound. But no need to be a perfect rocket scientist; being an excellent rocket astronaut works just fine!

Treasuries The Fed review underscored how interest rates can expand or contract the economy, and hence equities. Stepping behind the interest-rate curtain to look at directional Treasury movements is like getting our hands on the Fed's playbook. For the register, we are primarily interested in the 2- and 10-year Treasury Notes (a.k.a. T-Notes) from figure 9.23:

---

[53] https://web.stanford.edu/~chadj/facts.pdf, Stanford University. "The Facts of Economic Growth," pp. 5 and 6.
[54] https://apps.bea.gov/well-being/.

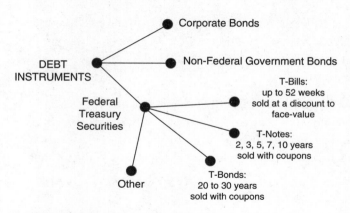

FIGURE 9.23 Debt Instrument Groups
Source: Adapted from [57]

The US Department of the Treasury, "as the steward of US economic and financial systems," has a broad mandate, including "the borrowing of funds necessary to run the federal government." Each day, they succinctly illustrate overall yield curves, averaged from different yields and maturities for that Treasury basket and displayed in figure 9.24:

Daily Treasury Par Yield Curve CMT Rates
02/25/2022

1 Month	2 Month	3 Month	6 Month
0.03	0.20	0.33	0.71

1 Year	2 Year	3 Year	5 Year
1.13	1.55	1.76	1.86

7 Year	10 Year	20 Year	30 Year
1.96	1.97	2.37	2.29

Daily Treasury Par Yield Curve CMT Rates
03/04/2022

1 Month	2 Month	3 Month	6 Month
0.15	0.21	0.34	0.69

1 Year	2 Year	3 Year	5 Year
1.05	1.50	1.62	1.65

7 Year	10 Year	20 Year	30 Year
1.70	1.74	2.23	2.16

FIGURE 9.24 Treasury Yields for February 25, 2022, and March 4, 2022[55]

---

[55]The averaging of yields and maturities results in the Constant Maturity Treasury (a.k.a. CMT) Rates. The quote and figures 9.24 and 9.27 were sourced from the U.S. Department of the Treasury; https://home.treasury.gov/about/general-information/role-of-the-treasury and https://home.treasury.gov/.

There are five things to know about Treasuries right at the launch pad:

- The US Treasury doesn't sell debt instruments, they *auction* them at pre-announced times as "the cornerstone of its debt management strategy."[56] These instruments can be traded after the auction, just like equities, in the secondary market.

- Treasury returns are counterintuitive in that the yield and pricing are inverse. (Hang on!)

- Generally, longer-dated Treasuries pay greater returns. This is the bargain arising from the investor tying up their capital (a.k.a. accepting an opportunity cost) and, rationally, the increased risk that comes with longer maturities. Note that in both CMT tables, as the maturity duration increases, so does the yield, except for the intriguing 20-year versus 30-year CMT.

- The Fed can easily spin the shorter maturity rate flywheel, forward or backward, through its careful manipulation of the FFR as those Treasury yields are quickly rolling over, whereas the 20- and 30-year bonds are anchored to earlier issued rates. Often, you'll hear "the Fed does not control the long end of the curve."

- As money moves **to** the safe haven of Treasuries, the luster **comes off** Equities. The 10-year T-Note yields are a Hubble telescope to inflation expectations and general economic direction.

Let's *Occam* through the yield and price relationship using T-Bills:

- T-Bills are sold at a discount to par value (a.k.a. face value), i.e. they do not have coupons.

- The yield (a.k.a. ROI) is the percentage difference between the par value and the purchase price per the following "Discount Yield" formula:[57]

$$\text{T-Bill Yield} = \frac{\text{Par Value} - \text{Purchase Price}}{\text{Par Value}} \times \frac{365}{\text{Days to Maturity}}$$

---

[56] Grant A. Driessen, Congressional Research Service (August 18, 2016), https://sgp.fas.org/crs/misc/R40767.pdf. For an excellent description of the process and the securities, go to https://www.treasurydirect.gov/instit/auctfund/work/auctime/auctime.htm.

[57] https://home.treasury.gov/policy-issues/financing-the-government/interest-rate-statistics/interest-rates-frequently-asked-questions: "Yields on all Treasury securities are based on actual day counts on a 365- or 366-day year basis." Analysts and other debt instruments often use 360 as the annual days rather than 365.

Assume you purchased a $1,000 T-Bill for $990 that matures in 3 months (applied as 13 weeks = 91 days), your return on investment is 4.01%:[58]

$$\text{T-Bill Yield} = \frac{\$1000 - \$990}{\$1000} \times \frac{365}{91} = .01 \times 4.01 = .0401 = 4.01\%$$

Bond pricing and yields can be thought of in terms of investor demand; here are some extreme examples to demonstrate the curious chain from demand to pricing to yields.

- In a **contracting** or **worried** economy, given T-Bills lower perceived risk, demand rises, prices rise, and yields decrease. Assume the $990 purchase price goes to $995:

$$\text{T-Bill Yield} = \frac{\$1000 - \$995}{\$1000} \times \frac{365}{91} = .005 \times 4.01 = .0200 = 2.00\%$$

- In an **expanding** or **confident** economy, investors have a bigger risk-appetite for Equities, so T-bill demand falls, prices fall, and yields track upwards. Assume the purchase price falls to $985.

$$\text{T-Bill Yield} = \frac{\$1000 - \$985}{\$1000} \times \frac{365}{91} = .015 \times 4.01 = .0602 = 6.02\%$$

The yield action is clean and clear, right? Well, there is a wrinkle. Read these three articles with emphasis added:

> (CNBC, September 30, 2021)—US Treasury **yields fell** on Thursday following **a sell-off** amid inflation fears. The yield on **the benchmark 10-year Treasury note slid 4 basis points 1.499%**. The yield on the 30-year Treasury bond dipped about 3 basis points to 2.058%. Yields move inversely to prices, and a basis point is equal to 0.01%.[59]

---

[58] If the Par Value denominator is replaced with the purchase price, the formula becomes the "Investment Yield Method: This yield is alternatively called the bond equivalent yield, the coupon equivalent rate, the effective yield and the interest yield," per the New York Federal Reserve description at https://www.newyorkfed.org/aboutthefed/fedpoint/fed28.html.
[59] Jesse Pound and Vicky McKeever, "U.S. Treasury Yields Dip Following Bond Sell-off," CNBC (September 30, 2021), https://www.cnbc.com/2021/09/30/us-bonds-treasury-yields-ease-back-slightly-following-sell-off.html.

(Barron's, January 18, 2022)—It isn't surprising that Treasury **yields are climbing** on the quickest pace of inflation in four decades. But the **selloff** in bonds isn't because of inflation fears. Instead, investors are betting the Federal Reserve will control prices with tighter policy. The market's moves are certainly notable, with yields of Treasuries from 2- to 30-year maturities at their highest point since at least the start of the pandemic. **The 10-year yield was trading Tuesday at its highest point since January 2020—at 1.84%.** At midday, it was up six basis points, or hundredths of a percentage point. It has soared 30 basis points so far this year.[60]

(Reuters, February 28, 2022)—US Treasury **yields fell** sharply on Monday as investors **sought safe-havens** after Western nations imposed tough new sanctions on Russia, including blocking some Russian banks from the SWIFT global payments system. US Treasury yields, which move inversely with prices, dropped sharply after the sanctions were imposed in response to Russia's invasion of Ukraine. The decline was led by the shorter-end of the yield curve, which is sensitive to interest rate expectations.[61]

The main point in the three articles:

- September 30, 2021: sell-off led to yields falling

- January 18, 2022: sell-off led to yields climbing

- February 28, 2022: demand (the reverse of a sell-off) rose, with yields falling

Again, our building-blocks:

- **Contracting or worried:** demand rises, prices rise, and yields fall

- **Expanding or confident:** demand falls (i.e. a sell-off), prices fall, and yields climb

- Longer-dated Treasuries pay greater returns

---

[60] Alexandra Scaggs, "Treasury Yields Are Rising. What's Causing the Selloff Isn't What You Think," *Barron's* (January 18, 2022), https://www.barrons.com/articles/treasury-bond-yields-rising-selloff-explained.

[61] https://www.reuters.com/article/usa-bonds/treasuries-u-s-yields-tumble-as-money-markets-%20scale-back-fed-rate-hike-bets-idUSL8N2V33EZ.

The yield directions between September 30 and January 18 sell-offs were different:

- The September 30 sell-off was fueled by inflation. Demand for Treasuries declined; but yields fell?

- The January 18 sell-off was driven by a market assumption of about-to-arrive higher paying securities. Demand for Treasuries declined; yields climbed.

February 28 was logical as the safe-haven (**contracting or worried**) pursuit meant more demand and subsequently falling yields.

Why did yields climb on January 18? The answer begins with a look back to the CMT's February 25 and March 4 yield change, as seen in the two CMT tables in figure 9.24:

- 1-, 2-, and 3-month yields rose.

- 6-month and 1-, 3-, 5-, 7-, 10-, 20-, 30-year yields fell.

We now add two points to our "Five Things to Know About Treasuries":

- Each Treasury basket has its own personality. They do not move in lock-step, neither in terms of direction nor in the pace of yield change.

132

- If significant inflation looms, rational investors often move in an interesting way when they expect the Fed to increase interest rates (to dampen inflation):

  - Shorter-maturity bond holders sell off as they believe higher return Treasuries are just around the corner. Similarly, sideline investors wait for the newer, higher return Treasuries. Lower Demand = Higher Yields.

  - Long-maturity bond holders and sideline investors accept current rates "at the long end of the curve" and lock in given the market uncertainty. Higher Demand = Lower Yields.

With the "normal" yield curve, the market believes GDP, employment, and inflation will develop at a conventional pace with yields on higher-risk, longer-term assets being greater. But when investors foresee an impending increased Fed interest rate move to counter inflation, the split between short- and long-run investor psyche can spur an "inverted" yield curve, like the backwardation effect in chapter 7. The yields at the long end drift lower, then "flatten," and eventually the long-run yield inverts to being below the shorter maturities, as drawn in figure 9.25.

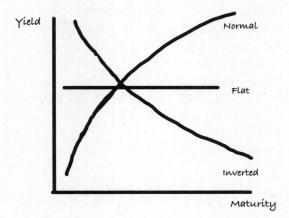

FIGURE 9.25 Yield and Maturity Relationship

And this is our "big learning" from the Federal Reserve Bank of San Francisco:

> Every U.S. recession in the past 60 years was preceded by a negative term spread, that is, an inverted yield curve. Furthermore, a negative term spread was always followed by an economic slowdown and, except for one time, by a recession.[62]

This narrowing phenomenon was echoed by bond expert Jeffrey Gundlach in a piece with Yahoo! Finance on January 4, 2022:

> As *Factset* recently pointed out, the spread between the 10-year and two-year Treasury yield narrowed to **79** basis points at the end of 2021. In March of last year—or well before the Fed signaled it would move into a period of tighter policy—that spread tallied 160 basis points. Looked at

---

[62] Michael D. Bauer and Thomas M. Mertens, "Economic Forecasts with the Yield Curve," Federal Reserve Bank of San Francisco (March 5, 2018). "A simple rule of thumb that predicts a recession within two years when the term spread is negative has correctly signaled all nine recessions since 1955 and had only one false positive, in the mid-1960s, when an inversion was followed by an economic slowdown but not an official recession." https://www.frbsf.org/economic-research/publications/economic-letter/2018/march/economic-forecasts-with-yield-curve/.

another way, the yield curve is flattening . . . starting the clock on a key recession indicator used by pros such as Gundlach.[63]

It's the narrowing spread between the 2- and 10-year Treasuries that acts as the recession canary in the coal mine, and the figure 9.26 FRED graph illustrates recent tightening between the 2-T and 10-T (a.k.a. 2s and 10s), with the basis point spread between them drifting and staying below 1% (a.k.a. 100 basis points) since November 26, 2021:

Let's pick at the Fed's March 16, 2022, announcement of increases for the:

- FFR: from 0 − .25% to .25% − .50%;

- PCR: from .25% to .50%; and,

- Reserve Ratio: from 0 to .4%.

How did Treasury yields react from March 16 to March 18? Lots of sloshing up and down in the Treasury pail, but a few observations from figure 9.27:

- For the one-, two,- and three-month Treasuries: lower yields, likely driven by contraction concerns

- The 5-T yield eventually flattened into the 10-T yield

- The 2-T and 10-T basis point difference over the three days went from 24 to 26 to 17

Generally, the yield movements were consistent with an investment community that had already baked-in the likely Fed actions. Still though, the 2-T and 10-T separation is slim and must be on your radar. The chart in figure 9.28 summarizes our Treasury understandings.

The 2-year and 10-year spread averages 113 (1.13%) basis points from 2012 to 2021.

MACRO REGISTER TARGET: 2-YEAR TO 10-YEAR BASIS POINT SPREAD

A normal yield curve.

NAVIGATION

---

[63] Brian Sozzi, "Bond King Jeffrey Gundlach: The Yield Curve May Be Sending a Recessionary Signal," Yahoo! News (January 4, 2022), https://ca.news.yahoo.com/bond-king-jeffrey-gundlach-the-yield-curve-may-be-sending-a-recessionary-signal-160935243.html and the Factset link goes to https://www.marketwatch.com/story/10-year-treasury-yield-pushes-back-above-1-5-to-kick-off-2022-11641213413. Emphasis added.

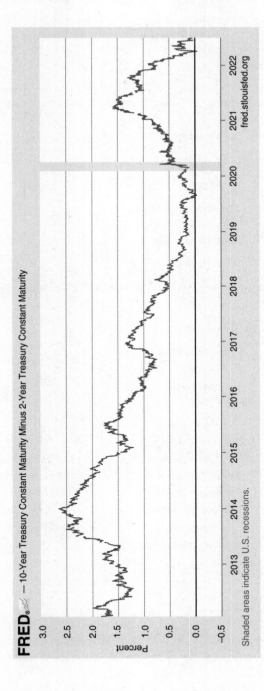

FIGURE 9.26 10-year and 2-year Treasury Yield Spreads, Not Seasonally Adjusted, January 1, 2012, to June 30, 2022[64]

Source: Federal Reserve Bank of St. Louis

---

[64] Board of Governors of the Federal Reserve System (US), 10-year Constant Maturity Minus 2-year Constant Maturity, retrieved from FRED, Federal Reserve Bank of St. Louis; https://fred.stlouisfed.org/series/T10Y2Y, July 14, 2022.

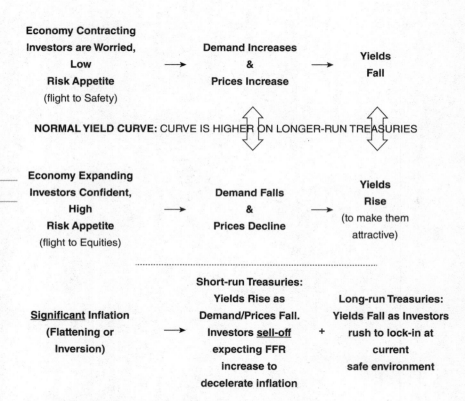

Daily Treasury Par Yield Curve CMT Rates 03/16/2022				Daily Treasury Par Yield Curve CMT Rates 03/17/2022				Daily Treasury Par Yield Curve CMT Rates 03/18/2022			
1 Month	2 Month	3 Month	6 Month	1 Month	2 Month	3 Month	6 Month	1 Month	2 Month	3 Month	6 Month
0.24	0.30	0.44	0.86	0.20	0.30	0.40	0.81	0.19	0.28	0.42	0.83
1 Year	2 Year	3 Year	5 Year	1 Year	2 Year	3 Year	5 Year	1 Year	2 Year	3 Year	5 Year
1.35	1.95	2.14	2.18	1.30	1.94	2.14	2.17	1.29	1.97	2.15	2.14
7 Year	10 Year	20 Year	30 Year	7 Year	10 Year	20 Year	30 Year	7 Year	10 Year	20 Year	30 Year
2.22	2.19	2.56	2.46	2.22	2.20	2.60	2.50	2.17	2.14	2.53	2.42

FIGURE 9.27   Treasury Yields for March 16, 17, 18, 2022

Economy Contracting
Investors are Worried,
Low
Risk Appetite
(flight to Safety)
→
Demand Increases
&
Prices Increase
→
Yields
Fall

NORMAL YIELD CURVE: CURVE IS HIGHER ON LONGER-RUN TREASURIES

Economy Expanding
Investors Confident,
High
Risk Appetite
(flight to Equities)
→
Demand Falls
&
Prices Decline
→
Yields
Rise
(to make them attractive)

Significant Inflation
(Flattening or Inversion)
→
Short-run Treasuries:
Yields Rise as
Demand/Prices Fall.
Investors sell-off
expecting FFR
increase to
decelerate inflation
+
Long-run Treasuries:
Yields Fall as Investors
rush to lock-in at
current
safe environment

FIGURE 9.28   Price and Yield Movements for Treasuries

Oil and Copper   Oil and copper are known as "hard" commodities in that they are drilled or mined, in contrast to "soft" commodities that are grown: wheat, barley, etc. All commodities are lead indicators of general economic direction.

Copper is called "Dr. Copper" as its pricing direction often reflects the ensuing strength of the economy. However, in contrast to Doc Copper, soaring oil prices may present the economy with a zero-sum game. Healthy production and high prices are good for the energy sector, but not always the consumer. And if oil goes too high, it can nudge demand destruction and users retreat. The bullseye is the right balance among cost, price, and national economic benefit in figure 9.29. If oil prices are overly squeezed, then accretive oil investment falls and jobs are lost with lower-cost producers from the Middle East filling the void.

The cost to produce an American barrel is about $45, per a Bloomberg report from December 2020.[65] Rystad Energy reported in November 2021 that "the average breakeven price for new oil projects has dropped to around $47 per barrel—down around 8% over the past year and 40% since 2014."[66] The figure 9.30 graph from the US Energy Information Administration (EIA) shows the widely varied cost inputs over several decades experienced by refiners.

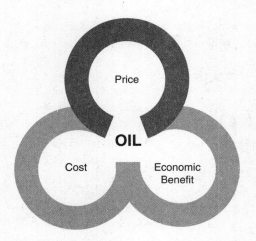

FIGURE 9.29   Price, Cost, and Economic Benefit Links

---

[65] https://oilprice.com/Latest-Energy-News/World-News/US-Shale-Patch-Reduced-Breakeven-Costs-By-20-This-Year.
[66] https://www.rystadenergy.com/newsevents/news/press-releases/as-falling-costs-make-new-oil-cheaper-to-produce-climate-policies-may-fail-unless-they-target-demand.

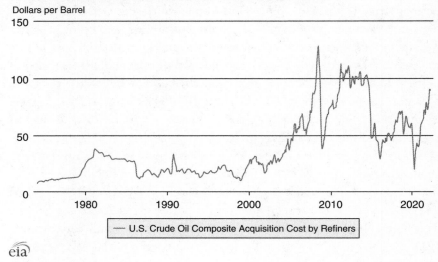

U.S. Crude Oil Composite Acquisition Cost by Refiners

Dollars per Barrel

— U.S. Crude Oil Composite Acquisition Cost by Refiners

eia

FIGURE 9.30   Refiner Costs from January 1974 to April 2022[67]

Source: U.S. Energy Information Administration / U.S. Department of Energy / Public domain

But what's the optimal per-barrel price for the economy? That's the essence for our macro register. A 2018 report, although dated, provides some context:

> Opinions on where the sweet spot currently lies differ widely, but analysts and strategists say it's probably somewhere between $60 and $70 per barrel. "If you are asking what price is high enough to sustain supply and low enough to sustain demand and perpetuate today's largely balanced global market, it is probably in the neighborhood of $65," said Sarah Emerson, a leading energy strategist at ESAI Energy. [68]

The average monthly spot price for West Texas Intermediate (WTI) from January 2012 to December 2021 per FRED was $65.72/barrel (appendix F). The Russian build-up on Ukraine's border in January and the invasion of late February led to the price per barrel smashing through $100 on March 1 and resulted in an H1 average price of $101.59. [69]

---

[67]"US Crude Oil Composite Acquisition Cost by Refiners (Dollars per Barrel)," https://www.eia.gov/dnav/pet/hist/LeafHandler.ashx?n=PET&s=R0000____3&f=M.

[68] https://money.cnn.com/2018/05/18/investing/oil-prices-best-price/index.html.

[69] Board of Governors of the Federal Reserve System (US), Crude Oil Prices: West Texas Intermediate (WTI)—Cushing, Oklahoma, retrieved from FRED, Federal Reserve Bank of St. Louis; https://fred.stlouisfed.org/series/DCOILWTICO (daily) and WTISPLC (monthly), May 19, 2022.

We'll likely slip 'n slide on high oil prices with the Ukraine crisis, although per Barron's, "it's worth noting oil hit a record $145 a barrel in 2008, a marker very much in play now. It is also worth noting where oil prices traded just five months after that record was reached: $31."[70]

Copper, a Gamma indicator, is not sufficiently impactful to our high-level macro register. For oil, the mix of production costs, worldwide supply, and general economic benefit collide into our register target.

▐ MACRO REGISTER TARGET: OIL

An oil per barrel price-range of $55 to $80.

China PMI   The influence of China as the world's second largest economy and its trade relationship with the United States is enormous: exports to China in 2021 were $151B and imports from China were $506B.[71]

Our macro register should recognize this US-China economic dynamic. Given the GDP catalyst already reflects the health of American international trade, a China-specific indicator would be their monthly Purchasing Managers Index (PMI), and per Moody's:

> The threshold of PMI is usually using 50 percent as the cut-off point for economic performance. If PMI above 50 percent, it reflects the manufacturing economy is expanding; if less than 50 percent, it reflects the manufacturing economy is in recession.[72]

Our register PMI is focused on American-China economics and not the political challenges inherent in the relationship (despite economics and politics being virtually inseparable).

▐ MACRO REGISTER TARGET: CHINA PMI

A China PMI of 51% or greater.

---

[70] Steve Goldstein, thebarronsdaily@barrons.com, March 7, 2022.

[71] https://www.census.gov/foreign-trade/balance/c5700.html.

[72] Moody's Analytics, https://www.economy.com/china/purchasing-managers-index.

Creating a Macro Register

Economic froth leads to a register of Leads and Lags per the sketch in figure 9.31 for our **EQ** mosaic. Note that the Fed wedge is separated to Inflation (CPI) and Unemployment.

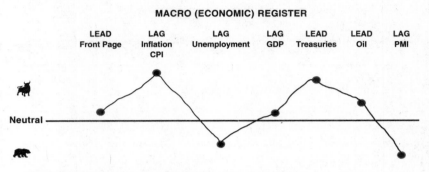

FIGURE 9.31   Macro (Economic) Register, Overview

Catalyst indicators that are above the neutral line angle to a bull market and indicators below the neutral line tilt toward a bear market. Let's play with the inflation catalyst. If inflation (CPI) is *low*, that would be a good thing for equities, so the inflation (CPI) datapoint would be above neutral and in bull territory.

For each of the seven catalysts, the **EQ** has targets above the neutral line.

The catalysts crystallize to an **EQ** acid test register per figure 9.32, with a few instructional comments.

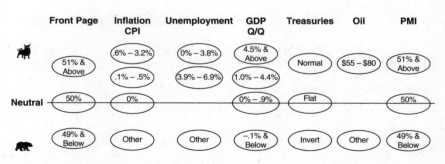

FIGURE 9.32   Acid Test Register

- There are many presidential approval surveys, and the rating difference among them is not material.

- Our target inflation range as measured by CPI is .6% to 3.2%. Most economists agree that some inflation is fine, that's why the .1% to .5% bubble sits above the neutral line.

- The unemployment and GDP target ranges have higher performance bubbles above them. For unemployment, the target range is 3.9% to 6.9%, but if it came in at say 2.5%, that's better and hence the upper location of 0% to 3.8%. The same logic applies to GDP; the 4.5% and above bubble is higher than the 1.0% to 4.4% bubble.

- Treasuries reflect the 2T to 10T yield curve.

- Oil and China PMI are straightforward.

- For both presidential approvals and the China PMI, the actual rates are often given to one decimal place, e.g. 52.2% rather than 52%. If you see them to one decimal place, just *Occamize* to the nearest whole number.

All these indicators are easily sourced online with a few keystrokes. Assume the presidential approval is 48%, CPI is 7.5%, unemployment is 3.8%, GDP growth 7%, the Treasury curve appears to be flattening, oil is $120/barrel, and the China PMI is 48%, here is how it looks in figure 9.33.

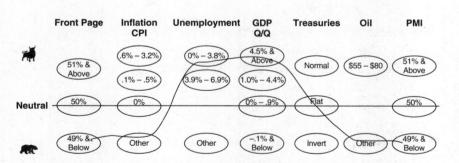

FIGURE 9.33   Acid Test Register, Populated

Our cockpit danger symbol would be flashing red, and that's pretty much what the Dow, S&P, and Nasdaq were telling us in early March, 2022. Some of you might want more detail, a bold view as shown in figure 9.34.

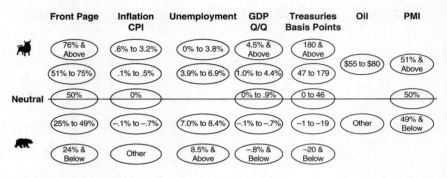

FIGURE 9.34 Bold Register

Minor note to figure 9.34: below the neutral line, there are two bubbles for CPI, unemployment, GDP, and Treasuries. The higher of the two CPI bubbles below the neutral line is two standard deviations from the average target. Let's use CPI as an example:

- The target is .6% to 3.2%, with an average of 1.9%.

- The standard deviation is 1.3.

- Two standard deviations below the average are −.7% (1.9 − 1.3 − 1.3 = −.7).

- −.7 becomes the extreme point for the first bubble below the neutral line.

- Given the other bubble points, the bookend to −.7% has to be −.1%

The same CPI range logic is applied to unemployment, GDP, and Treasuries. This is as statistical as we need to get! I just want you to appreciate there is honest rationale behind the bubbles. Please see the appendices for derivations.

Let's practice with one more, figure 9.35, using the bold canvas. Assume presidential approval is 48%, CPI is 8.5%, unemployment is 8.1%, GDP growth is negative 1.2%, the Treasury 2T − 10T differential is 21 basis points, oil is $108, and the China PMI is 41%.

Given the economic generalizations of inflation, deflation, and stagflation, what do you think the above example signals? (check figure 9.6 for an economic generalization reminder). In terms of the general business cycle, do you think it would be expanding or contracting? How might the Fed act to assist the economy? Sketch answers in below and read the following *Reuters* news bite and see if you got it. I have a feeling you did.

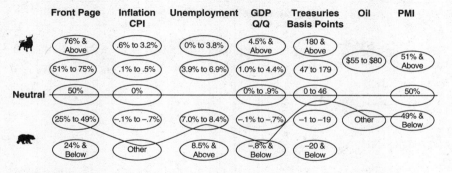

	Front Page	Inflation CPI	Unemployment	GDP Q/Q	Treasuries Basis Points	Oil	PMI
🐂	76% & Above	.6% to 3.2%	0% to 3.8%	4.5% & Above	180 & Above		51% & Above
	51% to 75%	.1% to .5%	3.9% to 6.9%	1.0% to 4.4%	47 to 179	$55 to $80	
Neutral	50%	0%		0% to .9%	0 to 46		50%
	25% to 49%	–.1% to –.7%	7.0% to 8.4%	–.1% to –.7%	–1 to –19	Other	49% & Below
🐻	24% & Below	Other	8.5% & Above	–.8% & Below	–20 & Below		

FIGURE 9.35   **Bold Register, Populated**

Inflation or Deflation or Stagflation?

Expanding or Contracting?

> BERLIN, March 22 (Reuters)—The German government will tailor its public spending plans to avoid stagflation in Europe's biggest economy and keep at bay the risk of sliding into a cycle of rising prices and anemic growth, Finance Minister Christian Lindner said on Tuesday. "The goal of the federal government is to support growth in Germany and mitigate the impact of inflationary risks," Lindner said in a speech at the Bundestag lower house.[73]

The macro register is your picture of the economy, and a picture is worth a thousand words, right? Worth more like a trip to the Moon!

This will all come together in the **EQ**. Let's recap and move to the indices and sector part of the Five-Stack.

---

[73] Joseph Nasr and Paul Carrel, "German Fiscal Policy to Stave Off Stagflation, Finance Minister Says," Reuters (March 22, 2022), https://www.reuters.com/business/finance/german-fiscal-policy-stave-off-stagflation-lindner-2022-03-22/.

The complete macro register erects seven totems to the **EQ**: Presidential Approval, CPI, Unemployment, GDP, Treasury 2–10T, Oil, and the China PMI.

Macro Register Capsule

- It's a good idea to create your own reminder calendar for CPI, unemployment, GDP Q/Q, and China PMI announcement dates.

- The macro register is a visual look at critical factors that churn the market. In May 2022, a swirling storm of lingering COVID effects, general supply-chain challenges, the Russia-Ukraine war, energy pricing shock, and inflation was a multiple compression on stock prices. The **EQ** goal is to ensure your stock selections are attuned to observed developments.

- The role of Federal Reserve monetary policy on equities cannot be overstated:

> April 22, 2022 (Reuters)—U.S. equity funds faced big outflows in the week to April 20 as concerns over economic growth, rising yields and prospects of aggressive monetary policy steps to stem inflation fanned risk-off sentiment. According to Refinitiv Lipper data, U.S. equity funds saw a net outflow of $16.57 billion, marking the biggest weekly outflow since Dec. 15.[74]

The Federal Reserve Bank of St. Louis provides a tight scoreboard that can feed the **EQ**, as shown in figure 9.36.[75] Personal Consumption Expenditures (a.k.a. PCE) are the Fed's preferred inflation measures. The Bureau of Economic Analysis produces the monthly PCE from GDP data

---

[74] Gaurav Dogra and Patturaja Murugaboopathy, "U.S. Equity Funds Post Biggest Weekly Outflow in More Than 4 Months," *Reuters* (April 22, 2022), https://www.reuters.com/business/finance/us-equity-funds-post-biggest-weekly-outflow-more-than-4-months-2022.

[75] The Fed also issues an "economic projections of Federal Reserve Board members and Federal Bank presidents, under their individual assumptions of projected appropriate monetary policy"; please see the June 15, 2022, projection at https://www.federalreserve.gov/monetarypolicy/files/fomcprojtabl20220615.pdf.

FIGURE 9.36 Economic Scoreboard[76]
Source: Federal Reserve Bank of St. Louis

whereas the Bureau of Labor calculates the Consumer Price Index from a narrower base of household surveys.

■ Indices and Sectors

Alpha/Acid Test & Bold (4 Metrics) and Gamma (5)

For this piece of the Discovery, our Alpha kit includes the S&P 500, GDP quarter to quarter growth progressions (as correlated to the business cycle), an ETF weathervane, and the VIX. Before we zigzag through them, let's look at the broader market.

The market has an ebb and flow, and colloquial terms have come to define the overall pricing action: dip, pullback, and correction. We also have bull and bear descriptors in regard to the broader market and these two lightning-bolt words refer to a sustained period of weakness or strength since the market's most recent bottom or top, with 20% up or down being the hurdle. Some outlets use more detailed definitions and tie-in the Dow Jones Transportation Average (i.e. it's a bull if DJIA and DJTA simultaneously and significantly move upward). Just note that in figure 9.37, the Descriptor and Delta names and percentages are not set in stone and different news outlets apply them in their own way.

Notionally, we want to know where the economy is in the business cycle: growing (*expanding*), shrinking (*contracting*), bottoming out (*trough*), or getting too toppy (*peak*)? The macro register is the precursor to the business cycle. If the macro register components, particularly GDP quarter over quarter (Q/Q) is rising, then you are on the expanding side, and the reverse for the contracting slope. Index levels and sector rotation are engineered from the business cycle and pictured in figure 9.38.

[76] Retreived from the front page of https://www.stlouisfed.org/, August 21, 2022.

MARKET ACTION	
Descriptor	**% Delta**
Dip	–2%
Pullback	–5% to –10%
Correction	–10% to –20%
Bear	–20% or worse
Bull	20% or more

FIGURE 9.37 **Market Descriptors**

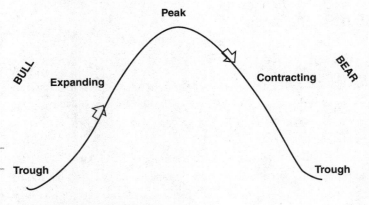

FIGURE 9.38 **The Business Cycle**

Let's shape our appreciation of the business cycle with some historical generalizations. A friendly reminder: these grouped terms, although more alike than different, are not fully interchangeable.[77]

Contraction, Bottom, and Bear

- Bear markets last about ten to 13 months.

- Bear market average decline is about 33%.

---

[77] I pulled information from three helpful sources: (1) Kat Tretina and Benjamin Curry, "Bear Market and Bull Market: What's The Difference?" *Forbes* (February 24, 2022), https://www.forbes.com/advisor/investing/bear-market-vs-bull-market/; (2) Mark Hulbert, "Bull Markets Usually Don't End with a Bang," *Wall Street Journal* (October 2, 2021), https://www.wsj.com/articles/bull-market-end-11633129950; (3) Thomas Franck, "A Look at Bear and Bull Markets Through History," CNBC (March 14, 2020), https://www.cnbc.com/2020/03/14/a-look-at-bear-and-bull-markets-through-history.

- There have been 14 bear markets since 1950.

- Bottoms tend to be a shorter duration than tops.

- We've had 12 recessions since 1950 and 4 since 1990.

- In the last 20 years, half of S&P 500 strongest days happened in bear markets.

- Many market seers suggest two consecutive GDP Q/Q of negative growth means the economy is contracting at a recession-type pace.[78]

Expansion, Peak, and Bull

- There have also been 14 bull markets since 1950.

- Bull markets average three to four years.

- Tops tend to be gradual with sectors taking turns in peaking, then falling.

A March 2019 study by S&P Global reviewed pricing dispersions among sectors and stocks, and advised of the importance of sector awareness when buying stocks:

> The fluctuating levels of sectoral dispersion, when combined with remarks in earlier sectors regarding the correlations, potential liquidity, and capacity of sector-based investment tools, reinforce the sense of a growing importance of sectoral perspectives in the construction of active portfolios.[79]

Sector rotation begins with a macro event, and it turns the associated ETFs, which can be a forerunner as to whether your radar stock price moves up or down, as symbolized in figure 9.39.

---

[78]This recession descriptor is from an August 28, 1974, *New York Times* article by Leonard Silk: "Julius Shiskin, the Commissioner of the Bureau of Labor Statistics, has sought to come up with quantitative criteria that would show whether a recession was actually in progress. On the basis of a study of past recessions, Mr. Shiskin concludes that a current decline in aggregate economic activity would qualify as a recession if: In terms of *duration* it lasts 9 months or longer as measured by a decline in nonfarm employment. In terms of *depth* it *includes a decline of at least 1.5 percent in real gross national product that extends over at least two quarters (six months),* and a rise in the unemployment rate of more than two points and to a level above 6 percent. In terms of *diffusion*; more than 75 percent of all industries sustain declines in employment lasting six months or longer." https://www.nytimes.com/1974/08/28/archives/recession-some-criteria-missing-so-far-there-will-be-no-recession.

[79]Tim Edwards and Craig J. Lazzara, "Sector Effects in the S&P 500®, The Role of Sectors in Risk, Pricing, and Active Returns," S&P Dow Jones Indices (March 2019), https://www.spglobal.com/spdji/en/documents/research/research-sector-effects-in-the-sp-500.pdf.

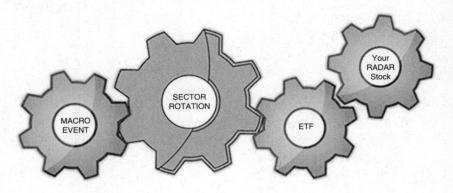

FIGURE 9.39   Key Relationships to Your Radar Stock

The S&P 500 is our foundational index for surveying the market's direction, and the **EQ** tops up our scrutiny with one of the most valuable observations of the market: sectors do not move in unison.

Being in front of sector rotation is a speedy route in getting to the Moon. Energy is up, perhaps consumer discretionary falls. Interest rates fall, industrials rise with access to lower-cost capital. The Infrastructure Bill passes, materials up. How do you know if money is flowing into your sector? The daily business shows on FOX and CNBC provide exceptional insight. Another way is by monitoring the ETF that's built from that sector. If the sector ETF is up, that's a good weathervane for your radar stock.

Not only can capital leave sectors, it can also flow out of, and into, countries. Russia's brutal attack on Ukraine led to, among other things, a global worry on commodity shortages. Given Canada's resource-rich economy, the Toronto Stock Exchange (TSX) experienced strong share demand, with its S&P TSX Composite Index rising from 20,744 on February 23, 2022, to 22,086 on April 4, in just six weeks.[80]

NASDAQ provides Sector recommendations for the business cycle in figure 9.40:

---

[80] https://money.tmx.com/en/quote/%5ETSX/price-history.

BUSINESS CYCLE	SECTORS
Peaking	START LOOKING AT: Communication Services, Financials, Materials
Expanding	LOOK AT: Consumer Discretionary, Energy, Industrials, Materials, Real Estate, Technology
Contracting	LOOK AT: Consumer Staples, Health Care, Utilities
Bottoming	START LOOKING AT: Communication Services, Consumer Services, Health Care, Technology

FIGURE 9.40 The Business Cycle and Sector Connection
Source: NASDAQ[81]

Market and sector volatility is a required pulse check for your **EQ** that can be measured by the VIX (Alpha) and the TRIN (a Gamma indicator, like the DJIA, DJTA, NASDAQ, and the NASDAQ 100).

The Chicago Board Options Exchange Volatility Index, known as VIX, is a barometer of near-term investor sentiment built from S&P 500 option price and time-to-expiry swings. The higher the VIX, the more investors might be "climbing the wall of worry." The lower the VIX, the more damn-the-asteroids attitude of investors.

Near-term spikes are often an overreaction to a macro event, and the VIX then retreats. A gradual swelling is more concerning and could signal a market correction. From January 2012 to December 2021, the VIX averaged 17. From January 3, 2022, to June 30, 2022, a period when investors were increasingly concerned about inflation, the VIX averaged 26. The subprime mortgage crisis that started in August 2007 and led to the Lehman Brothers bankruptcy on September 15, 2008, sent the VIX sky-high, with an average of 41 from September 15, 2008, to September 14, 2009, and actually ballooned to 81 on November 20, 2008!

---

[81] https://www.nasdaq.com/articles/your-complete-guide-to-sector-rotation-2021-05-05. Also, RBC has a nice visual on sector rotation. https://www6.royalbank.com/en/di/reference/article/stock market-sectors-and-sector-rotation/ilsa7rci.

At some point, the VIX reaches an apex and that signifies a market bottom is nearing, and it starts poking into that zone at about 35, and often arrives there at 40.

In the late 1960s, Richard Arms created the Arms Index as a measurement of market advances and declines in the context of volume. The ratio, also known as the Short-Term Trading Index (TRIN), is a clever metric:

$$TRIN = \frac{Advancing\ Stocks/Declining\ Stocks}{Advancing\ Volumes/Declining\ Volumes}$$

A TRIN of 1 suggests market equilibrium, below 1 indicates a bullish sentiment, and greater than 1 is bearish. Think about it for a moment: assume more stock prices advanced than declined on the day, that gives you a numerator advance/decline ratio of greater than 1. Now if the denominator volume of the advancing stocks to declining stocks is greater than the numerator, this buy-sell energy presses the TRIN below 1, a bullish view. There are variations of this index that incorporate market capitalizations or other inputs.[82] (Another interesting trend marker, built from multiple moving averages, is the S&P Short-Range Oscillator. When it exceeds 4, the market may be overbought, and less than −4 could mean it's oversold.)

INDICES & SECTOR

The **EQ** seizes four Indices & Sector reference points: the S&P 500 (current, minimum and maximums over the past year), the last two GDP quarter over quarter changes, an ETF weathervane, and the VIX.

Indices and Sector Capsule

- There are 11 sectors and, as a Pro:Active investor, you should readily know your stock's sector placement.

- Sector rotation is a massive cog affecting "to the Moon" success.

■ Valuation

This block is where all the corporate financials collide, and in some ways, it's the most interesting, yet intimidating, module in the Five-Stack. What's the

---

[82] https://www.barrons.com/market-data/stocks/markets-diary for a great daily summary inclusive of advances versus declines.

point of valuation analysis? From as much as the numbers can tell us, do they justify a higher or lower share price (a.k.a. intrinsic value)?

In chapter 6, we revealed the Alpha, Gamma, and Omega Valution indicators; let's hopscotch through them again, with light comment on other metrics. First though, what's the plan here? There are three chunks left in the Five-Stack per figure 9.41, and for valuation, we've assigned our indicators to align with four archetypes: market sentiment, growth, earnings power, and risk.

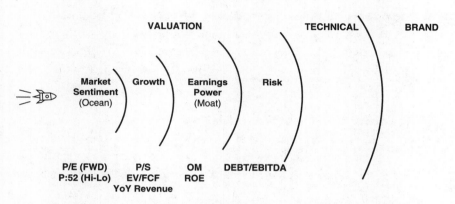

FIGURE 9.41 Valuation and the Five-Stack Discovery

Alpha/Acid Test (5 Metrics)

The five alpha acid-test ratios are **P**rice/**E**arnings (PE FWD), **P**rice/**S**ales (P/S), **E**nterprise **V**alue to **F**ree **C**ash **F**low (EV/FCF), **O**perating **M**argin (OM%), and Debt to EBITDA. All acid-test evaluators have a red flag warning.

PE (FWD) is calculated as the next 12-month Price/Share to Earnings/ Share or as Market Capitalization to aggregate Earnings (a.k.a. Net Income) The PE multiple unmasks the market's sentiment of the company's growth prospects. Too low a PE means light expectations, not necessarily under-valued. Companies with a low PE may be in an overly competitive industry and the ocean is red from their battle wounds. Too high could mean sketchy hope rather than Pro:Active wisdom. Given our futuristic "to the Moon" objective, we use the forward PE, and not the trailing 12 months.

The weak economy in mid-2022 is a gut-punch to market PEs, per the *Wall Street Journal* (a.k.a. WSJ):[83]

- Dow: July 14, 2021 PE @ 26.6, July 2022 @ 17.5, July 2023 (est.) @ 16.6
- S&P 500: July 14, 2021 PE @ 37.7, July 2022 @ 21.1, July 2023 (est.) @ 16.6

The WSJ data confirms how corporate Price Earnings are affected by the broader economy. The **EQ** raises a red flag at 25 or higher.

P/S: Price/Share to Sales/Share (Sales = Revenue)[84] This multiple is especially important to growth stocks, and given that many of them have zero or less earnings (both currently and in the near-term), P/S assumes a role that PE cannot fully provide. The S&P 500 P/S average is around 3, and the **EQ** red flag is 5.

EV/FCF: Enterprise Value to Free Cash Flow Free cash flow generates net income, not the other way around; therefore, it's imperative that in the acid-test group there is one ratio that includes FCF. EV/FCF presents a view of: this is how effective the company is at turning its cash flow into brand value. Recall that:

Enterprise Value = Market Capitalization + Debt − Cash

Free Cash Flow = Operating Cash Flow − (PP&E (n) − PP&E $(n-1)$)[85]

An informative *Forbes* article by David Trainer from June 2021, reveals the range of FCF and EV totals across the 11 company sectors during his Q1, 2021 review period, which I massage into figure 9.42.

The more commonly used EV/EBITDA average across the S&P 500 is about 15 with a generally acknowledged goal seek of under 10. Proportionally, if the EV/FCF average is roughly 60, the **EQ** wants a multiple under 40. The lower the EV/FCF, the better, but like PE and P/S, negative is not good! The **EQ** raises a red flag at 40 or higher.

---

[83] *Wall Street Journal*, July 14, 2022, https://www.wsj.com/market-data/stocks/peyield; Sources: Birinyi Associates; Dow Jones Market Data.

[84] "Sales" and "Revenue" are used interchangeably, although there could be differences if a Company has operating revenue that arises from supplementary sources. The difference between terms is immaterial to the **EQ**. Friendly reminder that some analysts/Fintechs only use LT Debt in EV, and some include Capital Leases.

[85] PP&E is Property, Plant & Equipment and is often called Capital Investment.

SECTOR	FCF ($MM)	EV ($MM)	FCF/EV Yield	EV/FCF Multiple
Energy	$ 19,494	$ 1,584,388	1.2%	81
Materials	$ 67,641	$ 1,331,491	5.1%	20
Industrials	$ 110,325	$ 4,387,403	2.5%	40
Consumer Discretionary	$ 45,029	$ 6,564,458	0.7%	146
Consumer Staples	$ 78,923	$ 3,105,421	2.5%	39
Healthcare	$ 63,431	$ 5,307,618	1.2%	84
Financials	$ 98,025	$ 5,095,816	1.9%	52
Information Technology	$ 312,585	$ 12,076,824	2.6%	39
Communication Services	$ 86,641	$ 1,613,682	–5.4%	–19
Utilities	$ 19,573	$ 1,814,472	–1.1%	–93
Real Estate	$ 32,227	$ 1,119,458	2.9%	35
S&P 500 TOTAL	$ **721,466**	$ **44,001,031**		
Simple Average	$ *65,588*	$ *4,000,094*	*1.6%*	*61*

FIGURE 9.42 Free Cash Flow and Enterprise Value Multiples by Sector[86]
Source: Adapted from [86]

OM: Operating Margin to Sales Operating Margin is a mirror of a company's ability to generate earnings with pricing power. Along with EV/FCF, it's likely the most sector-specific metric in our list. There are many websites that provide the S&P 500 average OM%, and 15% is roughly the norm over the last few years.[87] The **EQ** raises a red flag at 15% or lower.

Debt to EBITDA: Debt (Short Term + Long Term) to Earnings Before Interest, Taxes, Depreciation, and Amortization EBITDA is a "top down" calculation as it descends from revenue, whereas Free Cash Flow is "bottom up" as it starts with net income. Again, both exclude the effects of depreciation and other noncash outlays. The Debt to EBITDA multiple shows the firm's ability to carry its debt obligations. The **EQ** has a red flag of 2.5 or higher.

Alpha/Bold (8)

The Bold **EQ** adds three alpha indicators, the 52 share-price Range, YoY Revenue, and ROE.

---

[86] https://www.forbes.com/sites/greatspeculations/2021/06/07/sp-500--sectors-free-cash-flow-yield-through-1q21/?sh=456209ec3f44.
[87] CSIMarket.com is a good data aggregating site. https://csimarket.com/Industry/industry_Profitability_Ratios.php?sp5

P 52 (Hi–Lo): Highest and Lowest Share Prices over the Last Year   Eyeballing where your potential buy price fits in that 365-day zone is a clean compass visual. You want to be mindful of the share-price midpoint per its last 365 days and your price target.

Q/Q YoY Revenue: Percentage Change in Quarterly Revenue   Q/Q revenue is our proof-point for "did the customer base grow?" Q/Q can be determined by looking at two consecutive quarters, or by comparing the current quarter to the previous year's. The **EQ** adopts the previous year to current year.

ROE: Return on Equity (Net Income to Equity)   This percentage is easy to compute, reasonably insightful, very good for cross-firm analyses, and is consistent in application by fintech and media sites. ROE is also known as the Dupont Formula and it cleverly deconstructs ROE for added intelligence:

$$\text{Dupont ROE} = \frac{\text{Net Income}}{\text{Sales}} \times \frac{\text{Sales}}{\text{Total Assets}} \times \frac{\text{Total Assets}}{\text{Equity}}$$

ROE illustrates the return the company is giving shareholders. The **EQ** views ROE as a growth indicator, not just because of net income, but also because of equity itself. A company record of strong additions to retained earnings from net income growth is a solid progress metric.

Generally, the average company's ROE is in the 15–20% range, but the rate across organizations can be significant if, for example, a firm has a relatively small base of authorized shares (good) or reduced earning contributions to retained earnings (bad).

The following Gamma and Omega metrics are not part of the **EQ**. They are described as they may come up in your CSI pursuits and this brief explanation of some other metrics may be useful.

Gamma (10)

PE (TTM), PEG, P/CF, Div Yield, EV/Sales, EV/EBITDA, Market Cap/EBITDA, Rule of 40, EBITDA Margin, NI/Sales

All these Gamma metrics are well documented on-line (or earlier in this book), but a couple of highlights:

PE TTM: PE Trailing 12 Months, PEG: Price Earnings to Growth, P/CF: Price to Cash Flow   PE TTM and PEG are great multiples, but we chose

PE FWD for our team. Price to cash flow is a tough one. I like this multiple a lot and although it didn't make the cut, I recommend you keep it in the bullpen. As the investing world expands with more shared knowledge, P/CF (and its cohort P/EBITDA) shall take a bigger role in the general discourse.

DY: The Dividend Yield, Annual Dividend to Share Price Dividends are paid quarterly and normalize to an annual 3–5% yield although "the typical S&P 500 stock pays less than 1.4% right now" according to a February 2022 US News & World Report study.[88] Having divvy stocks in your portfolio is a prudent move, and they're not hard to find, as ~75% of the S&P 500 rewards shareholders with dividends. Adding DY to the **EQ** is a good idea if dividend accruals are critical to your portfolio.

Note that if you buy a stock on, or after, the ex-dividend date for that quarter, you are not entitled to the dividend. If you sell before the record date, which is usually within a few days after the ex-dividend date, you will not receive that quarterly dividend.

Some financial platforms report another dividend measure: the dividend payout which is a ratio of dividends to net income.

EV/Sales: Enterprise Value to Sales This is an insightful metric for spotting undervalued stocks. A January 2022 review by NYU's Aswath Damodaran of listed companies yielded an average multiple of about 3.76, so getting underneath that would be your objective.[89]

Enterprise Value to EBITDA and Market Capitalization to EBITDA The widely used EV/EBITDA multiple is a good contrast of a firm's total value to the proceeds from its revenue less direct (COGS) and indirect (SG&A) costs. Market cap to EBITDA is similar but excludes LT Debt and Cash.

Figure 9.43 is a mug shot of four conceptually similar ratios; each has its merits, and EV/FCF is our pick. Note a couple things:

- NFLX is in line with APPL on EV/Sales, but is way different on EV/FCF due to its negative cash flow (at time of information sourcing, April 5, 2022).

---

[88] Jeff Reeves, "9 Highest Dividend-Paying Stocks in the S&P 500," *U.S. News &World Report* (February 9, 2022), https://money.usnews.com/investing/dividends/slideshows/high-paying-dividend-stocks-in-the-s-p-500.
[89] Aswath Damodaran, NYU Stern School of Business, https://pages.stern.nyu.edu/~adamodar/New_Home_Page/datafile/psdata.html.

from figure 6.7	APPLE	TESLA	Freeport-McMoRan	WALMART	KELLOGG	DISNEY	NETFLIX
	AAPL	TSLA	FCX	WMT	K	DIS	NFLX
EV/Sales	8	22	3	1	2	4	6
EV/EBITDA*	23	121	7	13	11	27	29
Market Cap/EBITDA*	23	126	7	11	9	24	27
EV/FCF*	29	324	14	41	26	194	−1,389

FIGURE 9.43   EV and Market Cap Ratios, April 2022

- TSLA, due to its significant market cap, has EV ratios that are in interstellar space.

- If the EV/EBITDA and Market Cap/EBITDA are close (e.g. APPL, FCX), that's because the amount of long-term debt they carry is either very low or it's offset by large cash holdings.

Given figure 9.43, which of the seven companies do you think has the highest trailing PE and which the lowest? Which company would have more cash than debt on its balance sheet? Pencil in your answers and check back to figure 6.7.

156

NAVIGATION

Highest and Lowest PE TTM   Cash Greater Than LT Debt

_____

_____

_____

_____

The Rule of 40 (Revenue Growth + EBITDA Margin > 40%)   The Rule of 40 combines the pace of revenue growth with EBITDA margin. This percentage is a valuable corporate energy indicator, with both inputs coming from the income statement. However, the Alpha indicators already cover growth through Q/Q YoY, and having OM% makes the EBITDA margin superfluous in our **EQ**.

NI/Sales: Net Income to Sales (a.k.a. Profit Margin)   This is a well-used indicator, but we made a choice to use the broadly similar OM in the **EQ**. Per a _FactSet_ review of profit margins:

> The blended (combines actual results for companies that have reported and estimated results for companies that have yet to report) net profit

margin for the S&P 500 for Q3 2021 is 12.3%, which is above the year-ago net profit margin and above the five-year average net profit margin (10.9%).[90]

Omega (8)

The eight Omega metrics are ROA, R/Capital, Price to Book, Current Ratio, Cash/Share, EBIT/Interest, Debt/Equity, and Turnovers.

ROA: Return on Assets   This ratio illustrates how good the Company is at generating a profit given what it has to work with. It's a common metric, and it's very sector-specific given the capital intensity (PP&E) of some companies.

- Numerator: Net Income or Net Income – Dividends

- Denominator: Assets or Net Operating Assets

R/Capital: Return on Capital or Capital Effectiveness   There are countless old-school "Capital" ratios, with variations of:

- Numerator: EBITDA, EBIT, Operating Income, NOPAT, EBIAT, Net Income, Net Income – Dividends

- Denominator: Debt + Equity (sometimes with Cash subtracted out and possibly adjusted for Capital Leases, Retained Earnings, and other classifications)

These many Return methods lead to bewildering ratio death-stars from one financial source to the next as each defines the inputs differently, especially around the word "Capital" (as covered in chapter 5). If you like return ratios, just ensure each sourced metric is using similar inputs.

P/B: Price to Book, Price/Share to Book Value/Share   P/B can also be calculated by Market Capitalization/Equity, just as PE can also be determined by Market Capitalization/Earnings. Book Value is Assets – Liabilities (i.e. Equity), and is sometimes called the "accounting value" of the company or

[90] John Butters, "S&P 500 Is Reporting Third Highest Net Profit Margin Since 2008 For Q3," *FactSet* (October 18, 2021), https://insight.factset.com/sp-500-is-reporting-third-highest-net-profit-margin-since-2008-for-q3.

what remains after all claims are made if a company were to cease operation. The Price to Book evaluation often reduces Assets by any Intangible holdings (i.e. non-physical assets such as Goodwill, Trademarks held, etc.).

Price to Book should be 1.0 or higher as the future expectations for the company should logically exceed its accounting value.

Current Ratio: Current Assets to Current Liabilities and Cash/Share These two are liquidity ratios. The **EQ** addresses liquidity through EV/FCF and Debt/EBITDA. The Current Ratio should be 1.25 or higher, and many analysts prefer 1.75 to 2. Excessive Cash/Share can herald future M&A activity or share buybacks.

Earnings Before Interest and Taxes to Interest Expenses EBIT to Interest Expense gives the firm's ability to pay its debt. The ratio must be 1.0 at a minimum, but 2.5+ (i.e. the reverse of Debt to EBITDA of 2.5 and below) is a good bar to keep in your head.

Debt to Equity or Debt to Debt+Equity Debt to Equity is in reference to a firm's capital structure, and what might be the optimal mix. There are long-debated theories on the right structure, if any. For the **EQ**, our need is to capture the company's capacity to pay its debt, which we include through the Debt/EBITDA ratio.

Turnover Ratios: Assets, Receivables, and Inventory These "how good is the day-to-day management of the firm" ratios are indicative of a firm's efficiency, and they can be very sector-specific.

- **Asset Turnover:** Revenue/Assets reveals how well the company uses its Assets to drive Revenue, and the higher the ratio, the better.

- **Inventory Turnover:** Cost of Goods Sold/Inventory shows how efficient the firm is at getting its inventory out-the-door. The higher the ratio the better, and for added "time" appreciation, divide the Inventory Turnover number into 365 for a view of how many days Inventory is sitting inside the organization. In other words, a high inventory Turnover gives a better "days" calculation when divided into 365:

    365 / (Cost of Goods Sold/Inventory)

- **Receivables Turnover:** Sales/Accounts receivable, tells how quickly the company is getting paid. As with Inventory Turnover, divide the Receivables Turnover figure into 365 to see how many days it's taking for the company to get paid, on average. A more efficient collections group would give a company a higher Receivables Turnover, which yields faster cash turnarounds throughout the year:

365 / (Sales/Accounts Receivable)

The other side of the Receivables Turnover is Accounts Payable Turnover. How a company manages its turnover of Inventory, Receivables, and Payables contributes to its cash conversion cycle and is captured in the OCF part of the Cash Flow Statement. If the Inventory and Receivables "days" calculation adds to considerably more than the Payables "days" for a sustained period, the company will eventually have to reset its internal processes.

VALUATION

The **EQ** pulls five acid-test indicators: PE FWD, PS, EV/FCF, OM%, and Debt/EBITDA. The bold view adds three more: P52, YoY Quarterly Revenue, and ROE.

Valuation Capsule

- Valuation tools are best reviewed against other companies in the same sector.

- Red flags may be slightly recalibrated, better or worse, based on whether the economy is expanding or contracting.

- Alpha indicators are split into acid test and bold; the latter category supplements acid test with more metrics (this is done for the technical discovery chunk as well in the next section).

■ Technical (Momentum)

This piece of the Five-Stack is a rearview-mirror look at volume and price movements to flesh out existing share-price strength and its likely future path. As with valuation, there are hundreds of technical nuggets to pan for in the information river. Figure 9.44 shows our Five-Stack technical trip.

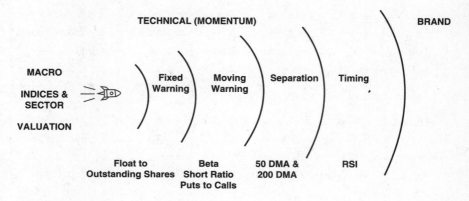

FIGURE 9.44 Technical and the Five-Stack Discovery

We *Occamize* our acid-test and bold technical gauges to a dashboard of fixed warning, moving warning, separation, and timing toward an end-state of marking when it might be time to get in or to get out.

Trading on momentum flow asks you to accept two premises:

- That past share pricing and volumes can foretell the future; and,

- Investor confidence, and therefore momentum flow, can quickly decelerate or accelerate from the "herd leaving instinct" or "fear of missing out" (FOMO).

These are generally accepted positions, and the pictorial support that technical charting can bring to your radar understanding is compelling. Sometimes though, the mathematical depth of these technical gauges could have us getting lost-in-space, so the **EQ** is built on the most elegantly simple and useful measurements.

Alpha/Acid Test (3 Metrics)

The bedrock evaluators for the **EQ** are float to outstanding shares and the 50 and 200 DMAs.

Float to Outstanding Shares This normally static percentage is known before you press the buy button. In 2021, almost 700 SPACs were dangled in front of investors, and many of their share prices sank due to the expiry of lockup shares which gradually diluted the float. In medieval times, rather than producing more gold and silver coins, the Kings and Queens would allow their mints to, literally, shave off some of the existing coins to melt into new coins or secretly use more copper than gold. This practice of "debasing" is akin to what many newly issued stocks levy on their shareholders. Look back to Palantir (PLTR) in February 2021:

> (Markets Insider)—Palantir's stock sank on Thursday after a lockup expiration freed some 80% of the company's shares to trade on the open market. When the Denver-based firm went public via a direct listing back in September, early investors were forced to hold their shares due to a lockup clause. Now that the clause has expired, it means a number of big investors in Palantir could be looking to cash out amid the recent rally in the share price. If they do, it could drive the stock down significantly.[91]

There's always a gap between float and outstanding shares for growth companies as they require shares to reward and attract talent. Amazon has about a 10% difference, not alarming at all, especially given their majestic share-price run-up! But if you see a 20%+ difference on a flat stock, please keep your mind's eye on it.

50-day Moving Average and 200-day Moving Average   As you would expect, the moving average is the share-price average over a particular time-period, usually calculated as a "simple" average by adding the daily closing share prices and dividing by the number of days. The Exponential Moving Average (EMA) fine-tunes the computation by giving more weight to the recent closing days.

The 50 and 200 are helpful scales, both individually and together, for illustrating when the share price is separating from its recent arc to a new up or down trajectory. Nirvana is:

- Current share price is above both the 50 and 200.

- The 50 is above the 200 or crosses it from below (a.k.a. Golden Cross), a bull pattern. If the 50 dives through the 200, that's the Death Cross.

Through the many, easy-to-use financial platforms, you can pair other short and long term day frequencies, such as a 15 DMA with a 30 DMA, etc. The **EQ** uses the 50 and 200.

---

[91] Will Daniel, "Palantir Slumps as a Lockup Expiration Opens 80% of Its Shares for Trading," *Markets Insider* (February 18, 2021), https://markets.businessinsider.com/news/stocks/palantir-stock-price-analysis-lockup-expiration-cathie-wood-soros-fund-2021-2-1030097725.

Alpha/Bold (7)

The **EQ Technical section** adds four metrics to your toolbox: Beta, RSI, Short Ratio, and Puts to Calls

Beta   This is a volatility metric calculated from the historical movement of your radar stock's share price as tethered to the systemic risk of the broader market.

- Beta = 1, your stock moves precisely with the market

- Beta > 1, your stock is more volatile

- Beta < 1, your stock is less volatile

- Beta < 0 (i.e. a negative number), your stock moves inversely to the broader market. In rare circumstances, a stock can have a beta of zero, meaning it has no correlation to the market.

Beta tells you how your share price will move when the market moves. If your radar stock's beta is greater than 1, then when the market sneezes, your stock catches a cold. On the other hand, if the market starts to rally, your higher beta stock could benefit from a slingshot effect. And you would expect a higher return for higher betas as you are carrying more risk.

Kellogg and Walmart are both in the consumer staples section. In the panel, write in your answer to:

- Would both be above 1, equal to 1, or below 1?

- Which one would have the lowest beta?

KELLOGG AND WALMART BETAS

The answer is provided in chapter 11.[92]

---

[92] Betas are from Yahoo! Finance on March 25, 2022.

Relative Strength Indicator (RSI)

RSI is a quick-view numerical scale from zero to 100 that suggests whether a stock is overbought (above 70) or oversold (below 30), calculated by averaging the upward price changes in a stock to the downward price changes over a time period, usually 14 trading days.[93] The RSI line is then plotted underneath the running share price for a possible break-out view. A falling RSI indicates that the current timing is bearish and a rising RSI is bullish, but when the RSI gets to the 70/30 zones, a reversal is likely in order. Just as the 14-day period can be toggled, so can the 70/30 indicators on most financial platforms.

Assume that on three trading days over a couple week period, Walmart's share price fell from Day 1 to Day 2, and then rose on Day 3. How do you think the RSI moved in that time frame? Circle up or down in the "Walmart RSI" box.

WALMART RSI

Change from Day 1 to Day 2: Up or Down
Change From Day 2 to Day 3: Up or Down

Figure 9.45 shows the Walmart and Kellogg RSIs over three days.

	March 15, 2022		March 23, 2022		March 25, 2022	
	Share Price	RSI	Share Price	RSI	Share Price	RSI
Walmart (WMT)	$ 145.78	64	$ 141.95	54	$ 143.45	56
Kellogg (K)	$ 61.32	43	$ 61.58	52	$ 62.82	52

FIGURE 9.45   Walmart and Kellogg RSIs, March 15, 23, 25, 2022

I add Kellogg to help your RSI learnings, but also to mention that comparing RSIs is not a cross-firm evaluation mechanism. Technical is lower in the Five-Stack as its outputs are more specific to the radar stock, and not so much for comparative insight.

Short Ratio: Shorted Shares to Float All fintech platforms ratio the shorted shares to the float or outstanding shares. The **EQ** uses the float as it

---

[93] Developed by J. Welles Wilder Jr. and explained in his book *New Concepts in Technical Trading* (Trend Research, 1978)

represents the shares immediately in-play. The influence of large shorting on a share's price is a real factor, and at times an unwinnable development for the Pro:Active investor.

Shorting is where the stock is borrowed from a financial insititution with the promise to repay at some future date. If the stock falls to where the "shorter" makes the desired profit, the shorter buys the stock and repays the financial institution with the same number of borrowed shares, netting the difference between the share price at time of borrowing and the proceeds from the subsequent purchase.

The **EQ** tracks the short ratio and you should be curious if it's 10%+, and especially so if it's 25%+.

Another short metric is the short interest ratio, which is the number of shorted shares divided by the average trading volume, and is meant to show the number of days it takes for all the short sellers to cover their position; the higher the number, the more shorting of the stock.

Puts to Calls (Buys)   Chapter 14 describes options, so for now, just note that a put option is the right to sell a stock to a put seller, whereas a call is the right to buy a stock from a call seller, with both transactions bolted to a predetermined price and time frame. The more puts, the higher the negative sentiment of the stock's future share price.

- Puts to Calls = 1, risk equilibrium

- Puts to Calls > 1, risk is higher (bear)

- Puts to Calls < 1, risk is lower (bull, especially if .7 or less)

As with the valuation section, the following gamma and omega metrics are not part of the **EQ**. They are described as they may come up in your CSI pursuits and this brief explanation of some other metrics may be useful.

Gamma (3)

The three useful evaluators are MACD, Chart Visuals, and Maximum Pain.

Moving Average Convergence Divergence (MACD)   MACD is a cousin of RSI, and it prompts when to buy or sell via cross-overs of the "MACD" line to a "Signal" line. The former is derived by subtracting and plotting the 26 day EMA from the more focused 12-day EMA. The signal line is a plot of the 9-day EMA. When the MACD 26-12 line moves above the signal 9-day line, that is a bullish (buy) point, and when it submarines to below the 9-day, it's bearish (sell) event.

Note that Walmart's MACD was above the signal line on March 15 and 23, and basically equal to it on March 25.

Chart Visuals   It's enlightening to scope a chart's share price over, say, the last 3 or 4 months (actually, it's kind of fun!). For charting, there are no parameters other than to set your time frame. Although chart visuals are not in our alpha toolbox, they are astronomically useful, and being familiar with some of the charting terms allows you to sort whether the share price is exhibiting bull or bear tendencies:

Bull

- **Higher Highs & Higher Lows:** This pattern exudes confidence as sellers are running out of steam. Charting experts draw support and resistance lines across the share-price pattern to create triangles, wedges, and pennants that could suggest further pricing upside.

- **Reverse Head & Shoulders:** A downward price wave (shoulder) followed by an even lower wave (head) and then to another shoulder with a share price that "breaks the neckline" means the stock might have bottomed.

- **Double or Triple Bottoms:** Similar to the reverse head & shoulders, the share price has tested a bottom two or three times, found its support, and will now travel north.

- **Cup and Handle:** This is an interesting, and surprisingly common, visual of a share price that drifts down and then up in a curvature (the cup), followed by a handle extension.

Bear

- **Lower Highs & Lower Lows:** The reverse of the bull scenario, with sellers overwhelming buyers.

- **Head & Shoulders:** The share price has found resistance and it breaks south below the "neckline."

- **Double or Triple Tops:** The stock can't punch through a ceiling despite two or three tries, and is now positioning for a downward turn.

- **Gap Filling:** Assume ZBF closed at $20 on Friday. Over the weekend, there was positive news that ZBF will be the only grocery tenant in the newest, largest mall in America; hence, the stock opens at $25 on Monday. Some investors believe this close-to-open gap must be filled someday, i.e. no matter what happens to the share price over the near term, at some point, the share price will retreat to fill that gap.

Consolidation

- If a share price is flatlining for an extended period, it's considered to be consolidating into a wider base and readying for an upward breakout upon some positive news.

Figure 9.46 sketches the visual descriptions.

166

NAVIGATION

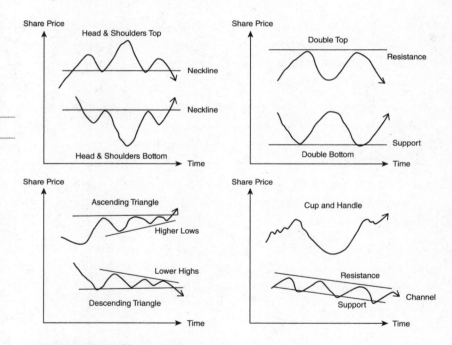

FIGURE 9.46 **Technical Patterns**

Maximum Pain (Max Pain) With options, there are head-on crashes of those who believe a share price will rise (call buyers and put sellers) and those who think it will fall (call sellers and put buyers), all explained in chapter 14. Max pain is the share price at which the greatest number of expired option contracts would lose money. The theory is that there is a gravitational force that drives a share price to its max pain level.

Omega (2)

The two charts are Bollinger Bands® and Fibonacci Ratios. Both tools can be helpful and, thanks to the assistance of financial platforms, the visuals are easily illustrated.

Bollinger Bands The average share price is plotted over a period, usually 20 or 30 days, with an upper band and a lower band profiling variations to the simple moving average. When the share price moves closer to the upper band, the shares are overbought and when the share price moves to the lower band, shares are oversold. The bands widen with increased share pricing volatility and narrow when the share prices are more stable. Specialists of this method believe that the widening or narrowing will often shortly reverse, suggesting a new pricing trend. With our Walmart example, its share price hit the upper band on March 15 and retreated to just above the Bollinger 20-day average on March 23 and 25.

Fibonacci Ratios Conceptually like the Bollinger banding approach, here the share price chart is sliced into horizontal layers between a peak price and a trough price using the Fibonacci sequence percentages of 23.6%, 38.2%, and 61.8%, supplemented with 0, 50%, and 100%, to indicate lines of support or resistance.

The history to this sequence model is from mathematician Leonardo Fibonacci (1175–1250), who noted that beginning with the number 1, each of the following numbers is the sum of the two preceding numbers (1, 1, 2, 3, 5, 8, 13, 21, 34, etc.). This gets esoteric really, really fast; suffice to say that the percentage differences arise from dividing a number by other sequence numbers: if you divide a sequence number by the next number, you get 61.8% (e.g. 5 divided by 8), by two numbers to the right yields 38.2% (5/13), and three numbers is 23.6% (5/21), all along the sequence. As share prices move up or down within the percentage horizontal dividers, Algos often set buy and sell actions.

TECHNICAL (MOMENTUM)

The **EQ** aggregates three acid-test indicators: Float to Outstanding Shares, 50 DMA, and the 200 DMA. The bold view tosses in Beta, RSI, Short Ratio, and Puts to Calls.

Technical (Momentum) Capsule

- The visual guidance of technical indicators adds to your buy and sell confidence level.

- Sizing up a stock's share-price movements by looking at a chart is a beneficial input to your curiosity quest.

▓ Brand

As a Pro:Active investor, your *Sisu* is the courage you possess on your "to the Moon" investment voyage. Can *Sisu* apply to a brand, as well as a person? Very much so, but there is another attribute that is perhaps more specific to a company: the element of "time." Brands, and their competitive advantage, must evolve and adapt as noted by the great Charlie Munger:

> Yet while moats can be powerful, they are not unassailable. The key for investors, according to Munger, is to be able to differentiate companies with ephemeral competitive advantages from those with true structural economic moats.[94]

168

NAVIGATION

If you could describe the essential quality of great companies in one word, i.e. a corporate *Sisu*, what could it be, and please write it in the following box.

THE *SISU* EQUIVALENT FOR A FIRM:

Many brands have a starburst of success, then fade to mediocrity. Others find a way of adapting to changing business environments and produce long-run growth for your portfolio. Their pivots and innovations are a

---

[94]Yahoo! Finance, *Charlie Munger: How to Identify a Resilient Economic Moat,* by John Engle of GuruFocus.com, December 22, 2020, https://finance.yahoo.com/news/charlie-munger-identify-resilient-economic-230238899.html.

Shackleton-type characteristic, and the *Sisu*-like word is rooted in Munger's statements and taken from John Engle's article: *Resilient*. Like Tom Brady evaluating the defensive scheme in mere moments, *Resilient* companies audible when necessary and go forward. Here's part of an incredible example of *Resiliency* and knowing your *Why*, from Lesley Stahl's December 2018 *60 Minutes* interview with Elon Musk:

> **Elon Musk:** It was life or death. We were losing $50, sometimes $100 million a week. Running out of money.
>
> **Lesley Stahl, voice-over:** His two assembly lines weren't churning out cars fast enough. Failure was imminent, until his lightbulb moment, create a third assembly line in a big tent in the Tesla parking lot. Musk was a champion of automation. So his original assembly lines were full of robots. But the robots kept breaking down. Walk along this new line in the tent, and all you see are, well, humans. He tweeted: "Excessive automation at Tesla was a mistake. To be precise, my mistake. Humans are underrated."
>
> **Elon Musk:** People are way better at dealing with unexpected circumstances than robots.
>
> **Lesley Stahl, voice-over:** He pushed his workers hard to meet the 5,000-a-week deadline. But he pushed himself even harder, out on the factory floor day and night troubleshooting and fixing work-line slowdowns.
>
> **Elon Musk:** I think there was like literally one week where I actually worked 120 hours and just didn't leave the factory. I didn't even go outside. I wanted to make it clear to the team. They needed to see that however hard it was for them, I would make it worse for me.
>
> **Elon Musk:** The whole point of Tesla is to accelerate the advent of electric vehicles. And sustainable transport and trying to help the environment. We think it's the most serious problem that humanity faces. I'm not sure if you know it, but we open sourced our patents, so anyone who wants to use our patents can use 'em for free.[95]

Elon certainly had *Sisu* and the brand had *Resiliency*—a double rainbow for investors!

As with the other Five-Stack slabs, the **EQ** allocates brand attributes to alpha, gamma, and omega. An added notation about brand is that it's more of a lead indicator, whereas valuation and technical are lag data that the **EQ** is weaving to a future state.

---

[95] Lesley Stahl, "Tesla CEO Elon Musk: The 60 Minutes Interview," *60 Minutes,* CBS NEWS (December 9, 2018), https://www.cbsnews.com/news/tesla-ceo-elon-musk-the-2018-60-minutes-interview/.

Alpha/Acid Test & Bold (4 Metrics)

The four references for the **EQ** canvas are Moat and Ocean, Black Swans, Executive Guidance, and Upgrades/Downgrades.

Moat and Ocean   The clarity of a firm's *Why*, its commitment to relentless innovation, and the passion of its employees all determine the breadth of a firm's moat. The **EQ** supplements the moat description by noting in figure 9.47 where the firm floats: in an ocean of newfound blue-water opportunity or a sea of cut-throat, price-driven red. Your partially subjective placement of the firm in the desired "A" or "B" quadrant follows your valuation and technical review.

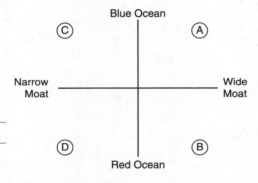

FIGURE 9.47   **Moat & Ocean Location**

170

NAVIGATION

Black Swans   Speculating what could go wrong is part of the Pro:Active makeup. You need to look at your radar stocks through both a rose-colored and a what-the-hell lens.

Executive Guidance   You can get a great read on the company's CEO—and other executives—when they deliver earnings reports (quarterly/annual), usually before or after the bell. Anyone can call the toll-free number, and it's time well spent to catch the figure 9.48 inputs. This is where you will, ideally, hear financial confidence, innovative pursuits, focused direction, and passion for the brand. The CEOs/CFOs will step through a nest of financials, and it's guaranteed they will speak to:

- Topline: Revenue
- Bottomline: Net Income

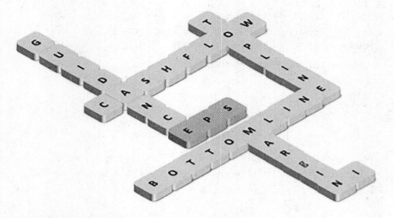

FIGURE 9.48 The ER Puzzle

- Cashflow: OCF and/or FCF

- Margins: EBITDA, Operating, EBIT, and/or Profit

- **g**: past growth across the business

- Earnings per Share

And most importantly: **GUIDANCE!** This is the end-zone play and the analysts are waiting to bellow "Touchdown!" or "Miss!" Most CEOs are conservative in their forecasts and analysts must winch directional words from them. Depending on what they say, the after-hours market can be hallelujah or punishing. Here's an example: on February 24, 2022, Zscaler (ZS) released its Q2 ER. This is part of the Zacks summary:

Zscaler (ZS) Q2 Earnings and Revenues Beat Estimates, Up Y/Y

- Zscaler ZS delivered better-than-anticipated second-quarter fiscal 2022 performance.

- The company reported non-GAAP earnings of 13 cents per share, which beat the Zacks Consensus Estimate of 11 cents per share. The bottom line grew 30% year over year.

- Zscaler's second-quarter fiscal 2022 revenues were $255.6 million, surpassing the Zacks Consensus Estimate of $242 million. The top line improved 63% from the prior-year reported figure.

- During the second quarter of fiscal 2022, Zscaler's calculated billings increased 59% year over year to $367.7 million.

- Zscaler's Zero Trust Exchange platform acted as a key catalyst in the second quarter. The company benefited from sustained demand for its products, given the healthy environment of the global security market. Increased cyber and ransomware risks, coupled with accelerated digital transformation, contributed significantly to growth.

- In the second quarter, Zscaler continued to win multiple customers in each of its three market segments: financial services, enterprise market, and federal. Its net dollar-based retention rate was over 125%.

- Remaining Performance Obligations (RPO) representing Zscaler's committed noncancelable future revenues were $1.95 billion as of January 31, significantly up 90% year over year.

- Cash flow generated through operating activities was $48.3 million, down from the previous quarter's $93.3 million. Consequently, free cash flow stood at $29.4 million, significantly lower than $83.4 million in the first quarter of fiscal 2022.[96]

The ER reads pretty well for ZS, aside from the FCF. So what happened to their share price after the ER release?

> Cybersecurity software maker Zscaler saw its stock fall as much as 18% on Thursday after the company issued quarterly earnings guidance that was slightly less than analysts had predicted.[97]

172

NAVIGATION

Zscaler, Inc. (ZS)
NasdaqGS - NasdaqGS Real Time Price. Currency in USD

☆ Add to watchlist

221.85 –41.53 (–15.77%)   **221.05** –0.80 (–0.36%)
At close: 04:00PM EST   After hours: 04:11PM EST

Light guidance slaughtered what was a pretty good set of numbers!

Analyst Upgrades and Downgrades   The recommended buy/sell action, coupled with price targets, moves share prices. Sourcing just one analyst is a bad move like taking only one Valuation metric. Collectively though, the analyst recommendations are an **EQ** reference-point.

---

[96] Zacks Equity Research, Friday, February 25, 2022, 8:50 a.m., https://ca.finance.yahoo.com/news/zscaler-zs-q2-earnings-revenues-155003393.html.

[97] Jordan Novet, "Zscaler Tumbles After Issuing Light Earnings Forecast," CNBC (February 24, 2022), https://www.cnbc.com/2022/02/24/zscaler-tumbles-after-issuing-light-earnings-forecast.html and the price drop picture is from https://ca.finance.yahoo.com/quote/ZS?p=ZS&.tsrc=fin-srch.

As with the valuation and technical sections, the following gamma and omega metrics are not in the **EQ**.

Gamma (3)

The three gamma indicators are share buybacks/splits, Accounting Integrity, and ESG.

Share Buybacks/Splits   Reducing the float can be a good move. And the reverse action of stock splits is not bad either. Both actions reveal an executive team that wants to improve shareholder returns, they're just taking different shuttles. These executive/board decisions are not made lightly, and a lot of intra-corporate discussion is held on their merits.

Accounting Integrity   This is a binary: companies and their auditors act according to generally accepted accounting principles or they don't. Accounting irregularities are rare, but they do happen and are a reason to bail. More common is a less serious restating of past reporting due to some newfound information. Financial firms that specialize in shorting stocks are often the first to spot the accounting issue.

Environmental, Social, and Governance   The influence of ESG on a company's makeup, ethics, and operative practices is a snowball that's starting to roll. Companies are increasingly codifying their sustainability and ESG commitments, and in some cases, linking executive compensation to the results. Here's the front page on the Siemens website:

> Our Sustainability report: strong results, continued acceleration.
>
> We have achieved further progress towards meeting our sustainability ambitions. At our Capital Market Day in June 2021, we set ourselves ambitious environmental, social and governance (ESG) targets with our new strategic framework DEGREE. In our Sustainability Report for fiscal 2021, we have published information today on our progress toward achieving these targets.[98]

Google Finance provides a Company's CDP Climate Change Score: "A score provided by CDP (formerly the Carbon Disclosure Project) that rates a company on its climate transparency and performance." Figure 9.49 shows the scores of Apple and Walmart with A– and Kellogg was a step behind at B:

---

[98] https://new.siemens.com/global/en/company/sustainability.html (March 28, 2022).

CDP CLIMATE CHANGE SCORE
A−

CDP CLIMATE CHANGE SCORE
B

FIGURE 9.49 CDP Scores[99]

ESG scores are elbowing into the mainstream of collective valuation metrics, and we will see more of them going forward.

Omega (2)

The two omega indicators are Activists and Meme Stocks.

Activists Activists are dissatisfied shareholders with a variety of grievances, such as that the share price is lagging its peers due to ineffective leadership, or that parts of the business should be spun off, or the ESG commitment is ineffectual. In the short term, activism is not helpful, but over the longer term, these efforts may be just what the retail investor ordered.

Meme Stocks In Q1–Q2, 2021, Reddit-driven traders punched above their weight, and to the surprise of many stock watchers, they catapulted several "meme" stocks to outer space. On March 1, 2022, the *Wall Street Journal* provided an interesting look back with graphs that correlate GameStop's share price increases with its number of mentions on Reddit, and illustrated in figure 9.50.

(WSJ)—In 2021, amateur traders baffled professional asset managers by coordinating in forums such as Reddit's WallStreetBets to propel unloved companies such as videogame retailer GameStop to absurd highs. Data by fund tracker VandaTrack confirms that space companies rode the same "meme stock" wave—particularly Virgin Galactic. Its highs in February of 2020 and summer of 2021 were linked to strong retail inflows and highly correlated with mentions on the irreverent forum. At its 2020 peak, Virgin

[99] https://www.google.com/finance/quote on April 14, 2022 for each of WMT, K, and AAPL.

Daily share price

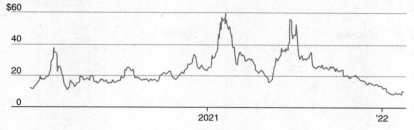

Daily mentions on Reddit

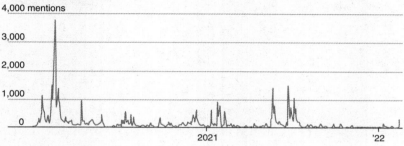

FIGURE 9.50 **GME Share Price and Reddit Mentions**

Galactic was the fourth favorite stock among users, receiving 31% of all mentions.[100]

There's a snooty tendency to dampen the market participation of the meme players given that the rapid price increases of many of their stocks vaporized. Sure, but what's not talked about enough is the colossal addition of liquidity and stock players that Reddit brought to the benefit of overall market froth. Reddit added fun and color to the moonscape, and I hope these newfound players continue to fire up their rockets.

BRAND

The **EQ** spans four Alpha indicators: Moat and Ocean, Black Swans, Guidance, and Analyst Views.

[100] Jon Sindreu, "Reddit Traders Took Space Stocks to the Moon—Re-entry Could Be Ugly," *Wall Street Journal* (March 1, 2022), https://www.wsj.com/articles/reddit-traders-took-space-stocks-to the Moon-re-entry-could-be-ugly-11645785002.

■ Brand Capsule

■ Evaluating brand heft, although subjective, is just as important to the **EQ** as the more common valuation and technical analyses.

PART IV

THE EQUALIZER

CHAPTER 10

The Double Eye

Imagination and Ideating

I don't want it to be a Song, I want it to be an Anthem.[1]

Dolly Parton

From your CSI, you imagine investment possibilities for your radar. Once stocks (or ETFs) make the sensor grade as possible investment choices, you ideate what to buy and what not to buy through the **EQ** that guides your courageous flight to the Moon! The entire **EQ** comprises the following:

- Three "to the Moon" maps (a.k.a. canvases), and

- Five investment doodling worksheets.

This is your Anthem and completing them is as easy as getting into your spacesuit.

As noted in the Introduction, I'm fortunate that I came across some game-changing books over my business career, beginning with the power of visual thinking from Dan Roam's bestselling 2008 book *The Back of the Napkin*:

> Visual thinking means taking advantage of our innate ability to see—both with our eyes and our mind's eye—in order to discover ideas that are oth-

---

[1] Dolly Parton describing her song "9 to 5" from *Dolly Parton: Here I Am* on Netflix (2020).

erwise invisible, develop those ideas quickly and intuitively, and then share those ideas with other people in a way that they simply "get."[2]

Dan brilliantly discusses how we can solve problems and build solutions by slathering ideas with hand-drawn sketches to create profound insight. The beauty of Dan's approach is that you don't need to be a da Vinci to sketch, as it's really a fun collision of deduction and simple visuals. Sure, but is there a way to *creatively* think? Yes, and Michael Michalko shows the way with *Thinkertoys* (as presented in chapter 7):

> Creators are joyful and positive. Creators look at "what is" and "what can be" instead of "what is not." Instead of excluding possibilities, creators include all possibilities, both real and imagined. . . and more importantly, creators are creative because they believe they are creative. . . . By changing your perspective, you expand your possibilities until you see something that you were unable to see before.[3]

Michael extends his model to cool techniques for "mind pumping" and, in short, creating creativity from fractionation of challenges to combining attributes towards new perspectives. Now that I had Dan's and Michael's superior thinking and creativity guidance, how do I get the investment *Why*, CSI efforts, and Pro:Active mindset on paper? Thankfully, I found the *Strategyzer* series, and their canvas tools are dazzling:

> A strategic management tool to simultaneously visualize, analyze and manage the *business models* you are improving and growing and the future *business models* you are searching for and testing.[4]

I highlighted "business models" in italics. If you replace those words with "investment portfolio," then you are contributing to the *Why* on the to the Moon path.

The **EQ** canvases and worksheets are inspired and named after the courageous NASA space programs: Mercury, Gemini, Apollo, and Skylab. I'm

---

[2] Dan Roam, *The Back of the Napkin* (Penguin Group, 2008): 4

[3] Michael Michalko, *Thinkertoys*, 2nd edition (Ten Speed Press 2006): xiv and xvii. I combined a couple of his great insights to the above panel.

[4] Alex Osterwalder, Yves Pigneur, Fred Etiemble, Alan Smith, *The Invincible Company* (Wiley, 2020): 4. Emphasis added.

pleased to share from NASA's website the wondrous efforts and sacrifices made by the organization and its people:

> For six decades, NASA has led the peaceful exploration of space, making discoveries about our planet, our solar system, and our universe. At home, NASA research has made great advances in aviation, helped to develop a commercial space industry, enrich our economy, create jobs, and strengthen national security. Outside the United States, our international partnerships shine as examples of diplomacy. Space exploration has brought together people of diverse backgrounds working for the good of all humankind.
>
> As we celebrate NASA's first 60 years of achievement, we honor the sacrifice that came with it: the tragic loss of lives including aviation pilots and the crewmembers of Apollo 1, Challenger, and Columbia. Sacrifice has also come in the countless hours dedicated NASA personnel—on the ground and in space—have spent away from families to plan and execute missions. The next decade promises to be full of adventures that only science fiction writers dreamed of and only NASA and its partners will accomplish.[5]

EQ Canvases

Through the integrated canvases, you are creating your personal value proposition, a plan on achieving your *Why* through wealth creation. It's exactly what businesses do for their customers: create solutions that enable their clients to achieve their *Why* and generate returns for shareholders. The only difference to the **EQ** is that you're creating a portfolio for just one shareholder, yourself.

Our **EQ** canvas creations are visual and in a rich linear sequence that enables you to imagine, clarify, and evaluate stock purchase opportunities. This optical approach leading to discovery is the **EQ** juice: it begins to flow as you see the big-picture and your CSI gears whirl.

Here's an overview of the canvases, with more elaboration provided in chapter 11:

- **Mercury:** this canvas is your point-in-time financial profile. It combines your *Why* with a Pro:Active dashboard of specific information on your current stock holdings, your portfolio value, and the capital available to invest.

---

[5] https://www.nasa.gov/specials/60counting/overview.html.

- **Gemini:** this is the "ideate" canvas where you list the stocks (or ETFs, options) that are on your CSI radar, both those that are existing in your portfolio (and may be contemplating selling) and those that you are exploring and considering buying. There is both a short-form "acid-test" canvas and the longer-form "bold" canvas; you use the one that meets your needs and time-availability:

  - **Gemini Acid Test:** Here you allocate your radar stocks (existing and exploring) per our four stock groupings: growth commercial, growth start-up, value secular, and value cyclical.

  - **Gemini Bold:** this canvas provides a more informative layout by slotting your radar stocks into one of the eleven sectors, with a further cut into the four stock groupings.

- **Apollo:** here you capture the output of your Five-Stack Discovery and create one Apollo for each stock in your exploration quest. There are two Apollo canvases to choose from:

  - **Apollo Acid Test:** Includes the macro register, the indices & sector business cycle data, valuation & technical metrics, plus brand considerations.

  - **Apollo Bold:** This canvas includes all inputs from Apollo acid test, but with added macro register, valuation, and technical detail.

EQ Worksheets

There are five worksheets to assist your Mercury, Gemini, and Apollo completions, grouped into a set called Skylab.

- What-if: for doodling investment ideas gushing from one possibility

- Personal Development: this is where you document your learnings and measure your commitment

- Investment Tracking: an easy-to-fill spreadsheet to record the macro register, sector, valuation, and technical indicators

- Gauge Warnings: a dashboard of warning signs and conditions from chapter 12

- Gauge Checks: a rundown of helpful touchpoints from chapter 15

How to Get Started

Depending on your available time and proficiency, you'll likely swap between acid test and bold to reach your highest confidence level. In fact, on all canvases, feel free to adjust the inputs and build a more awesome canvas as you creatively see fit!

Of course, it takes time to complete these canvases, but not as much as you might think. The biggest challenge with Mercury is determining your *Why*. You should update Mercury once per month, and that won't amount to more than 30 minutes. Perhaps you'll capture your *Why* with a cool Roam-type drawing!

Gemini is more of a weekly commitment of about 20 minutes. Your first Apollo will take about 30 minutes, and with repetition, you should be cracking them off at 20 minutes or less per stock—especially if you're familiar with a good stock screener program.

The canvases likely appear a little cluttered when viewed on a book page, but once you print the blank sheets from www.wiley.com\go\frank\tothemooninvesting, I'm sure you'll get it and have them sitting on your lap for notes as you listen to podcasts or watch business shows.

You might be wondering "Why can't this be a software program where I just enter minimal data and the canvases spit out the grand design?" Honestly, I think that could be a future hybrid path between the pencil and the digital, and I might end up there some day. But for now, I want to ensure we secure the power of "ideate mapping" rather than just "digital entering."

One question you may have: what is the minimum number of canvases I need to complete to be considered Pro:Active? That's a tough question. But there is a Mendoza line.[6] If you really don't have the time or mental effort to fully use these tools, or maybe you want to ease in for now, then the minimum is Gemini bold. At the very least, you must ensure a sector awareness and robust diversification of your portfolio.

---

[6]"The Mendoza Line is baseball jargon for a sub-.200 batting average, the absolute minimum threshold for competence at the Major League level. It derives from light-hitting shortstop Mario Mendoza, who failed to reach .200 five times in his nine big league seasons. When a position player's batting average falls below .200, the player is said to be 'below the Mendoza Line.'" https://en.wikipedia.org/wiki/Mendoza_Line.

■ Capsule

- ■ The "to the Moon" arc is guided by the **EQ**.

- ■ The **EQ** comprises visual canvases: Mercury, Gemini, and Apollo, enhanced by the Skylab worksheets, that powerfully map your flight.

- ■ Each of Gemini and Apollo present a choice between a simpler acid test and a more thorough bold view.

- ■ Although the **EQ** has a set of recommended alpha indicators, the gamma and omega metrics in the evaluation matrix are there for you to source and replace an alpha indicator if you have a better idea.

CHAPTER 11

Visual Investment Maps to Guide You!

*When LeBron passes you the ball, you don't just hold it
and yell, "Oh my God oh my God, LeBron James just passed
me the ball!" No. You crossover the sucker who's trying to
guard you, and you drive the lane furiously.*[1]

Beastie Boys

■ Mercury

It's time to make some noise and get "investment furious" as we begin with
our first canvas, Mercury, in figure 11.1. The inputs required to complete
Mercury are straightforward, with the first step writing in your *Why* on the
upper left and your dashboard of financials on the right, inclusive of "h
Crypto" where you record any Crypto (Bitcoin, etc.) investments. Note that
your total of dividend paying stocks is captured, even though DY is not an
Alpha metric. Mercury's lower part is where you jot any radar stock prospects triggered by your trendspotting & correlation analyses.

---

[1] Michael Diamond and Adam Horovitz, *Beastie Boys Book* (Spiegel & Grau, 2018): 217.

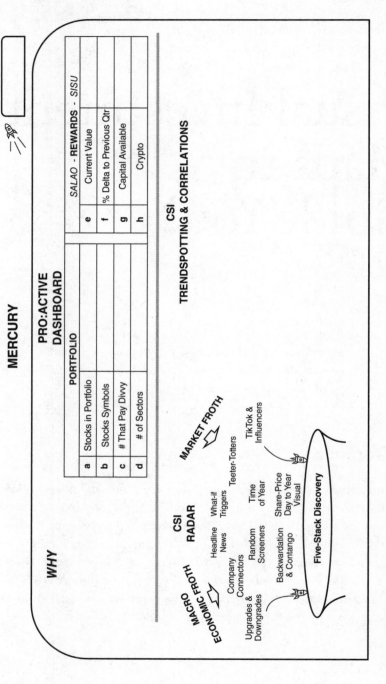

FIGURE 11.1 Mercury Canvas

■ Gemini

Gemini is where "thinking" really erupts. For the acid-test canvas in figure 11.2, you map your existing and exploring stocks with the four stock groupings to ensure a visual recognition and acceptance of having diversity in your portfolio. There are three ETF weathervanes on the left side. If you're looking at ExxonMobil, then, say, check out XLE. If it's moving north, place an *x* above the separation line (and pencil XLE on the separation line). The weathervanes are useful if you're exploring more than one stock (or you could use more than one ETF per stock). List your stock symbols on the right side of Gemini according to the eight categories from chapter 6:

■ 1 a) Growth Commercial: *Existing* and *Exploring*

■ 1 b) Growth Start-Up: *Existing* and *Exploring*

■ 2 a) Value Cyclical: *Existing* and *Exploring*

■ 2 b) Value Secular: *Existing* and *Exploring*

I recommend you use stock symbols, e.g. CSCO rather than the name Cisco, as it's good to have these abbreviations second nature in your head.

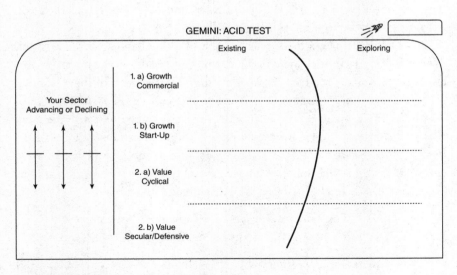

FIGURE 11.2 Gemini Acid Test Canvas

Growth Commercial	Growth Start-up	Value Cyclical	Value Secular
• industry disruptor	• newer listing	• mature listing	• mature listing
• positive EBITDA	• negative EBITDA	• positive EBITDA, Net Income may miss on some Quarters	• positive Net Income
• Net Income might be positive	• unproven biz model		• proven biz model
• proven biz model	• operational execution unknown	• proven biz model	• consistent Dividend
• scale & scope opportunities in-play	• might be awaiting patent or pharma certification	• growth is largely Organic	• growth is largely Organic
• CEO "In-front"		• revenues move with Business Cycle expansion or contraction	• a safe-haven equity investment
• high Dynamic growth	• scale & scope opportunities being developed		• favored by Buy n' Hold investors

FIGURE 11.3 Growth and Value Traits

Here's a reminder thumbnail on the four stock groupings in figure 11.3:

Gemini bold in figure 11.4 takes the diversity factor to a thorough level by illustrating all 11 sectors, with quadrants for each of our four stock groupings. You enter the stock symbols of your current portfolio (a.k.a. existing), and similarly with the ones you are thinking of buying (a.k.a. exploring, and these should be circled). Gemini bold is definitely more detailed than Gemini acid test: 44 quadrants for bold and only 8 for acid test. But don't let that deter you; your brain's muscle memory will have you mastering this fuel input in no time.

The 11 sectors are in three rows: top 3, middle 4, and 4 on the bottom. Each row has an intuitive grouping: energy, industrials, and materials have a common "we make the base ingredients" bond with much of their revenue accrued from other businesses. Consumer discretionary, consumer staples, healthcare, and financials are, in practice, directly linked to consumer purchasing behaviors. Information technology, communications services, utilities, and real estate are not as symmetrical of a group, but they do have a common thread in that much of their revenue is derived from government. You can envision a parallel to the GDP formula:

$$GDP = \textbf{G}overnment\ Purchases + \textbf{C}onsumer\ Spending$$
$$+ \textbf{B}usiness\ \textbf{I}nvestments + \textbf{N}et\ Trade\ (\textbf{Ex}ports - \textbf{Im}ports)$$

Let's do an example. Assume you own Walmart (WMT) and Kellogg (K) in your portfolio of five stocks. Both are in the consumer staples sector. Further assume you are exploring our grocery start-up, ZettaByte Foods (ZBF).

GEMINI: BOLD

Radar

Existing

• Pencil-in the Stock Symbol to the applicable Quadrant

Exploring

• Pencil-in and Circle the Stock Symbol to the applicable Quadrant

🐂 Sector does well in a Bear market

🐗 Sector does well in a Bull market

Your Sector
Advancing or Declining

Energy 🐂	
1a: Growth Comm	1b: Growth Start-Up
2a: Value Cyclical	2b: Value Secular

Materials 🐗	
1a: Growth Comm	1b: Growth Start-Up
2a: Value Cyclical	2b: Value Secular

Industrials 🐗	
1a: Growth Comm	1b: Growth Start-Up
2a: Value Cyclical	2b: Value Secular

Consumer Discretionary 🐗	
1a: Growth Comm	1b: Growth Start-Up
2a: Value Cyclical	2b: Value Secular

Consumer Staples 🐂	
1a: Growth Comm	1b: Growth Start-Up
2a: Value Cyclical	2b: Value Secular

Health Care 🐂	
1a: Growth Comm	1b: Growth Start-Up
2a: Value Cyclical	2b: Value Secular

Financials 🐗	
1a: Growth Comm	1b: Growth Start-Up
2a: Value Cyclical	2b: Value Secular

Information Technology 🐗	
1a: Growth Comm	1b: Growth Start-Up
2a: Value Cyclical	2b: Value Secular

Communication Services 🐗	
1a: Growth Comm	1b: Growth Start-Up
2a: Value Cyclical	2b: Value Secular

Utilities 🐂	
1a: Growth Comm	1b: Growth Start-Up
2a: Value Cyclical	2b: Value Secular

Real Estate 🐂	
1a: Growth Comm	1b: Growth Start-Up
2a: Value Cyclical	2b: Value Secular

FIGURE 11.4 Gemini Bold Canvas

Here's a March 8, 2022, Zacks piece on WMT:

> **Walmart Inc.** WMT is on track to enrich its customers' experience by enhancing its supply-chain network. The retail behemoth unveiled plans of opening a 1.8M plus square-foot fulfillment center in southern Pennsylvania. The facility, which is expected to begin operations in Spring 2022, will contribute to Walmart's growing supply-chain network and e-commerce capabilities.[2]

And on March 10, 2022, Zacks provided on K:

> Iconic food maker **Kellogg** (NYSE: K) has been working to shift its business toward growth-oriented niches, notably in the snack space. It completed a major business overhaul right as the coronavirus pandemic hit, obscuring the progress it has made. That, however, isn't the only issue the company is facing today, as it also has to get its legacy cereal business back on track. And that's going to take some time.[3]

Per Yahoo! Finance on March 10, 2022, 15 of 21 analysts have a strong buy or buy on WMT (beta = .53) and only 3 of 21 have that on K (beta = .57). It's self-evident that these two stocks are not on the same planet. Through the process of elimination, the Gemini bold cyclical versus secular assignment proceeds like this:

- Both companies belong to consumer staples.
- Neither would be considered by the market to be growth; both would be Value.
- Walmart is viewed by analysts as a stronger buy.
- Walmart has more capability to withstand weaker business cycles than Kellogg.
- A secular company often has a lower beta than a cyclical.

For the **EQ**, Kellogg (K) is value cyclical and Walmart (WMT) is value secular, figure 11.5.

---

[2] Zacks Equity Research, *Walmart's (WMT) New Fulfillment Center to Boost E-commerce*, Zacks Equity Research (March 9, 2022), https://ca.finance.yahoo.com/news/walmarts-wmt-fulfillment-center-boost-141102267.html.

[3] Reuben Gregg Brewer, *This High-Yield Food Stock Won't Be Back to Full Speed for Another 6 Months, Motley Fool* (March 10, 2022), https://www.fool.com/investing/2022/03/10/high-yield-food-stock-not-back-full-speed-kellogg.

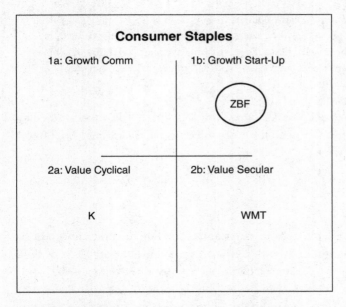

FIGURE 11.5 Cyclical Versus Secular Assignments

Now that you have the visual clarity, the questions in your head blossom:

- Why overweight the portfolio with another consumer staples stock (when your portfolio is only five stocks to begin with)?

- Does ZBF present that much of an upside to WMT? If so, perhaps you should jettison K and load up on ZBF?

- If you really want a growth start-up, and insist on keeping K and WMT, why not eject ZBF and move to another sector?

Apparently, the Kellogg executive received a sneak peak of this manuscript and completed a What-if (chapter 7) given the lagging share price: on June 21, 2022, Kellogg announced a breakup into three companies and, per its chairman and CEO Steve Cahillane, "This will unlock and create opportunity for all three businesses."[4]

Finally, don't assume that stocks have the same share-price trajectory just because they are in the same sector! Jason Zweig hammers home a similar point in his really good commentary within *The Intelligent Investor*:

---

[4] https://news.yahoo.com/kellogg-pops-plans-spin-off.

If you look at a large quantity of data long enough, a huge number of patterns will emerge—if only by chance. By random luck alone, the companies that produce above-average stock returns will have plenty of things in common. But unless those factors *cause* the stocks to outperform, they can't be used to predict future returns.[5]

Gemini is deep-space pondering by you as a Pro:Active investor. Seeing the choices likely sparks a need for more information. Incoming! Apollo just landed for you.

■ Apollo

Apollo is where we "epic up" our maps and reach the go versus no-go decision on a particular stock. As with Gemini, you can use the acid-test or bold view. At the sheet's top, write the company name and the date you are completing the canvas. Then the fun begins, but where do you get all the data inputs from? The beauty of Apollo lies in its crisp layout, which you plaster with easily sourced information from the many financial platforms—from Yahoo! Finance to Google Finance—or gleaned from podcasts, TV shows, and your personal network.

The acid-test canvas in figure 11.7 is separated into the Five-Stack Discovery: macro (1 section), indices & sector (1), valuation (1), technical (1), brand (4 subsections), and one area for the big question: list three reasons why you want to buy this stock.

- **Macro:** incorporates the simpler register.

- **Indices & Sector:** has a sketch of the business cycle (figure 11.6). You enter the most recent GDP (Q/Q), n, and for the prior quarter, $n - 1$.

  - If n and $n - 1$ are positive, you place them on the expanding side of the business cycle.

[5] Benjamin Graham, *The Intelligent Investor, A Book of Practical Counsel*, revised edition—updated with new commentary by Jason Zweig (Harper, 2006): 45.

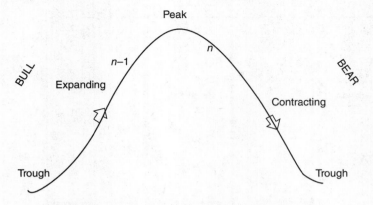

FIGURE 11.6 GDP Assignments to the Business Cycle

- If n and $n-1$ are negative, you place them on the contracting side of the business cycle.

- For example, in May 2022, the most recent GDP quarters would be Q1, 2022 (n) and Q4, 2021 ($n-1$). Q4, 2021 was a positive 6.9%YoY (annualized) and Q1, 2022 is a 1.6% decline.

- You also enter the current S&P 500 total, as well as its minimum and maximum over the last 52 weeks, plus the VIX to this section. Remember, VIX is a confident versus nervous marker of investor sentiment and not an empirical "go to." For that reason, we just record VIX as-is, and don't get trapped in our thinking by its precise pace.

- **Valuation:** Metrics for price/earnings (FWD), price/sales, enterprise value/free cash flow, operating margin, and debt/EBITDA. Red flags are shown for help.

- **Technical:** Just three values, float/outstanding shares, 50 DMA and 200 DMA.

- **Brand (4 subsections):** (a) moat & ocean quadrant where you place the stock symbol; (b) What could go wrong? Fill the black swan section

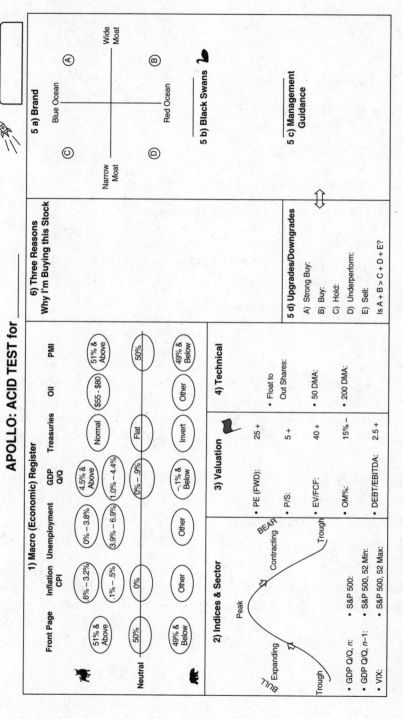

FIGURE 11.7 Apollo Acid Test Canvas

with your existing concerns or future what-ifs; (c) Add recent management guidance; and (d) analyst recommendation totals from strong buy down to sell.

- **Why Do You Want to Buy This Stock?** Given your Gemini allocations and the Five-Stack data, can you answer this question with three responses? When you're buying shares, view it as: should I lend this company my capital? Sure, your secondary market purchase does not flow into their cash register, but that company's executive and often the employees receive bonuses that are tied to an increasing share price. Your purchase adds to that upward froth; do they merit your contribution?

Apollo bold in figure 11.8 is cleaved into the same Apollo acid-test groups: macro (1 section), indices & sector (1), valuation (1), technical (1), brand (4 subsections), and the big question. Let's look at the similar and accretive information required for bold:

- **Macro:** incorporates the more detailed register.
- **Indices & Sector:** exactly the same as acid test.
- **Valuation:** adds three metrics: 52-week hi-lo range (just write the lowest and highest share prices over the last year), YoY revenue growth (i.e. from last year's quarter to current quarter), and ROE.
- **Technical:** adds four indicators: beta, RSI, short ratio, and puts/calls.
- **Brand (4 subsections):** mimics acid test.
- **Why Do You Want to Buy This Stock?** Again, like the acid test.

The Apollo canvases do not kick out a prescriptive response, i.e. by filling in all the data points, the alchemy reveals a score of 90 out of a possible 100 signaling a buy, etc. Instead, it's a descriptive connection of qualitative and quantitative reasoning leading to a go or no-go decision.

Scribing Mercury, Gemini, and Apollo into one flight map provides visual focus and affirmation to your efforts; furthermore, these maps are yours and you can upcycle them if you have better category and metric ideas. Next, to assist your moon shot, Skylab brings transformative idea pads.

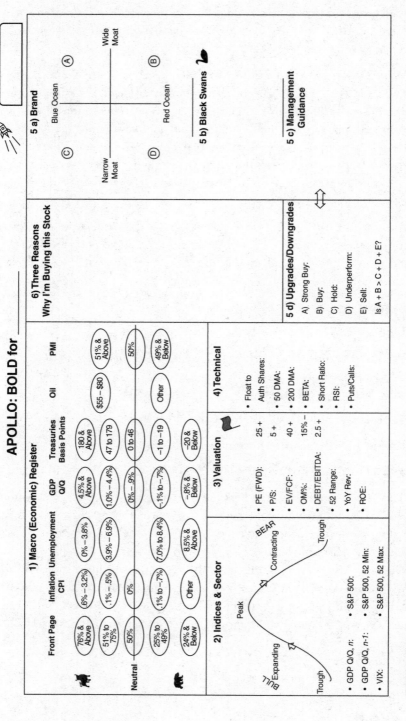

APOLLO: BOLD for _____

1) Macro (Economic) Register

Front Page	Inflation CPI	Unemployment	GDP Q/Q	Treasuries Basis Points	Oil	PMI
76% & Above	6% – 3.2%	0% – 3.8%	4.5% & Above	180 & Above	$55 – $80	51% & Above
51% to 75%	1% – 5%	3.9% – 6.9%	1.0% – 4.4%	47 to 179		
Neutral 50%	0%	0%	0% – 9%	0 to 46		50%
25% to 49%	.1% to –.7%	7.0% to 8.4%	–.1% to –.7%	–1 to –19	Other	49% & Below
24% & Below	Other	8.5% & Above	–8% & Below	–20 & Below		

2) Indices & Sector

Peak

BEAR
Contracting

BULL
Expanding

Trough   Trough

- GDP Q/Q, n: • S&P 500:
- GDP Q/Q, n-1:   • S&P 500, 52 Min:
- VIX: • S&P 500, 52 Max:

3) Valuation

- PE (FWD):   25 +
- P/S: 5 +
- EV/FCF: 40 +
- OM%:   15% –
- DEBT/EBITDA: 2.5 +
- 52 Range:
- YoY Rev:
- ROE:

4) Technical

- Float to
- Auth Shares:
- 50 DMA:
- 200 DMA:
- BETA:
- Short Ratio:
- RSI:
- Puts/Calls:

6) Three Reasons Why I'm Buying this Stock

5 a) Brand

Blue Ocean

Ⓐ   Wide Moat

Ⓒ   Ⓑ

Narrow Moat   Ⓓ   Red Ocean

5 b) Black Swans

5 c) Management Guidance

5 d) Upgrades/Downgrades

A) Strong Buy:
B) Buy:
C) Hold:
D) Underperform:
E) Sell:

Is A + B > C + D + E?

FIGURE 11.8   Apollo Bold Canvas

■ Skylab

There are five Skylab worksheets for reminding, logging, and brainstorming to assist your canvas populating.

A: What-if Worksheet

Enter an event into the center circle and pencil three possible outcomes from the event (branch 1), with offshoots to levels 2, 3, and 4. Cut or add branches as you see fit, as illustrated in figure 11.9.

B: Personal Development

Being a Pro:Active Investor takes effort. This worksheet in figure 11.10 is for you to record *and prove* that you are serious. I always chuckled when the 7x Grand Slam (Singles) tennis superstar John McEnroe would yell at judges, "You can't be serious!" Exactly. If you want to be a professional umpire or a Pro:Active investor, you have to be serious!

C: Investment Tracking

This Excel table in figure 11.11 is for you to record Apollo data across your broader portfolio. It's not necessary that you complete this worksheet; just view it as a total portfolio comparison tool if you need it. The inputs run

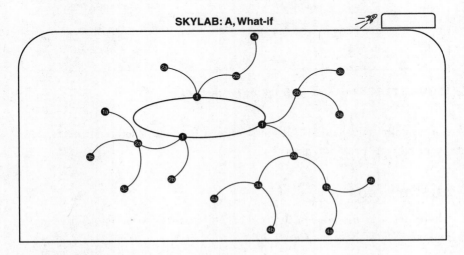

FIGURE 11.9   **What-if Worksheet**

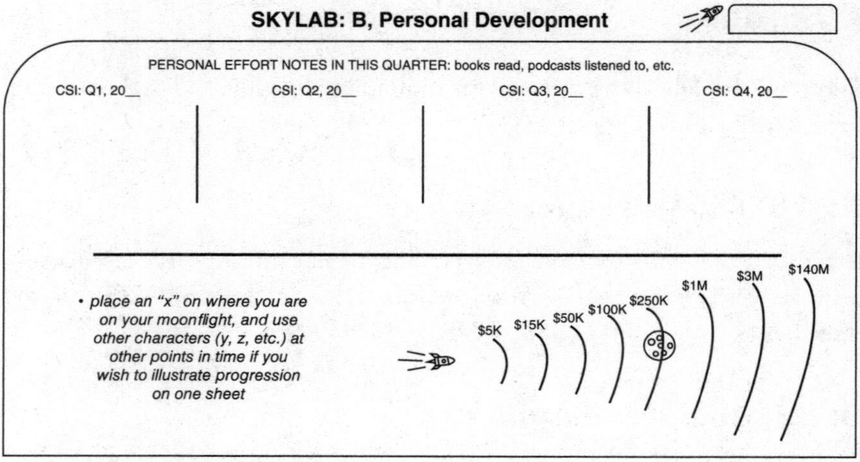

FIGURE 11.10 Personal Development Worksheet

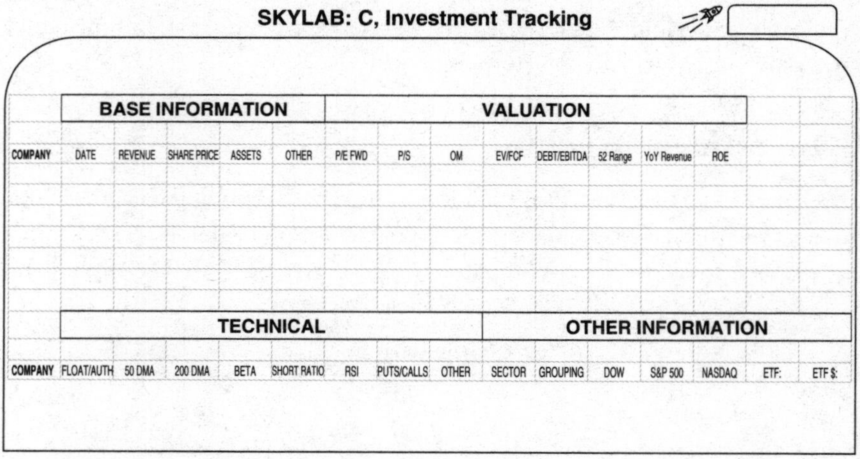

FIGURE 11.11 Investment Tracking Worksheet

horizontally, with added "Other" columns for your preferred metrics (or overwrite any provided ones).

D: Warnings

These perilous meteors in figure 11.12 are part of your Pro:Active radar and we review them in chapter 12.

E: Checks

These helpful principles and suggestions in figure 11.13 are explained in chapter 15.

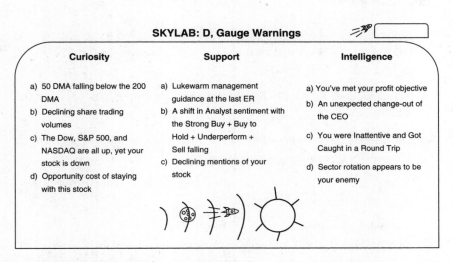

SKYLAB: D, Gauge Warnings

Curiosity	Support	Intelligence
a) 50 DMA falling below the 200 DMA	a) Lukewarm management guidance at the last ER	a) You've met your profit objective
b) Declining share trading volumes	b) A shift in Analyst sentiment with the Strong Buy + Buy to Hold + Underperform + Sell falling	b) An unexpected change-out of the CEO
c) The Dow, S&P 500, and NASDAQ are all up, yet your stock is down	c) Declining mentions of your stock	c) You were Inattentive and Got Caught in a Round Trip
d) Opportunity cost of staying with this stock		d) Sector rotation appears to be your enemy

FIGURE 11.12   Worksheet, 11 Warnings

SKYLAB: E, Gauge Checks

Curiosity	Support	Intelligence
a) When You Buy a Stock, You Buy a Sector	a) Buy in Chunks	a) Corporate Profits Matter
b) Selling Too Soon Hurts	b) Stay Close to Your Canvases	b) Don't Buy IPOs Right Out of the Gate
c) FOMO & Gambling	c) Ignore Penny Stocks and Their Promoters	c) Remember the Importance of Volume
d) Don't Panic	d) Get Familiar With a Stock Screener	d) CEOs Can be Rock-Stars or Rock-Heads
e) It's a Journey to-the-Moon, Not a Sprint	e) If a Website says "Click-Here" for More Information, Run	e) Don't Over-Fuel
	f) Set Your Antennas to Information Satellites	f) Markets fall Faster than they Rise

FIGURE 11.13   Worksheet, 17 Reminders

■ Capsule

- Skylab worksheets are your MacGyver tools to boost your radar and **EQ**.[7]

- You should see symmetry among your visuals. Assume your radar identifies a start-up called Interstellar Jets (ISJ). Let's assume that:

  - The presidential approval is 48%, CPI is 6%, unemployment is 5%, GDP growth −2%, the Treasury 2T − 10T differential is flat, oil is $90, and the China PMI is 50%.

  - Annualized GDP is −2% for the last quarter (n), and is −3% for the previous quarter ($n − 1$).

  - The Industrial Select Sector SPDR XLI (a.k.a. Standard and Poor's Depository Receipt) closed red yesterday.

  - ISJ appears to be in a blue ocean, but they have no competitive advantage, other than being a first mover.

  ISJ's visuals are shown in figure 11.14.

  The other Five-Stack Discovery components may add upside support, but the visuals suggest a lot of incoming flak to your rocket flight. If you remain convinced on ISJ, remember to buy in tranches.

---

[7] MacGyver is the problem-solving hero in the TV series of the same name—he could engineer solutions to any crisis!

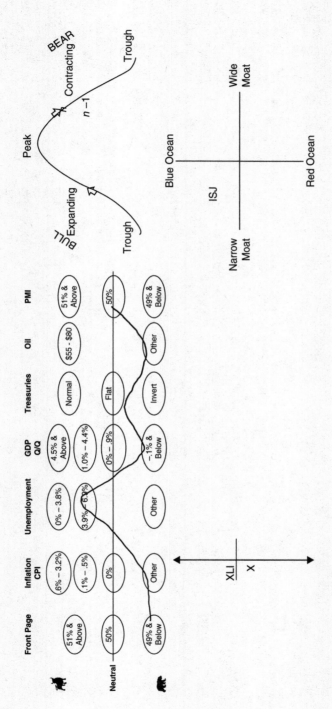

FIGURE 11.14 ISJ Visuals

PART V

To the Moon!

CHAPTER 12

Execution of Your Stock Trade

Stops and Limits

Everyone has a plan till they get punched in the mouth.[1]

Mike Tyson

The **EQ** supports when to buy, but how do you know when to sell? Stocks have this peculiar trait of taking the stairs up, but the elevator down. Are there indicators that suggest you've overshot the moon and you're now rocketing too close to the sun, Icarus-like? Yes, there are a few CSI pivot-points to sort through before we hit execution considerations:

■ Curiosity

These observations should generate a stress test of your stock and portfolio:

- **50 DMA falling below the 200 DMA:** This technical indicator is kryptonite when it happens. Your conviction will be tested, and it might be right to visit why you hounded this stock in the first place and perhaps recalibrate.

---

[1]https://www.sun-sentinel.com/sports/fl-xpm-2012-11-09-sfl-mike-tyson-explains-one-of-his-most-famous-quotes-20121109-story.html.

- **Declining share trading volumes:** Falling volumes, especially with sagging share prices, means the buy side is likely running away. Hopefully you protected your portfolio with stops! Not all trades work out: view them as "badges of courage" and don't beat yourself up. Complete a back-test to your Apollo canvas to where/why you went wrong, and learn from the misstep.

- **The Dow, S&P 500, and NASDAQ are all up, yet your stock is down:** Being cross-threaded to the market can be an omen. But don't panic, this can happen. The real question is, is it a one- or two-day occurrence or are you seeing a potential dumpster fire? Has something changed fundamentally from your **EQ**? Are you sufficiently diversified to ride out the situation? Generally, if you did a thorough **EQ**, a dip is just part of the trip.

- **Opportunity cost from holding on:** Most of us have only so much investment capital. While you're waiting for ZBF to catch fire, you may be missing other opportunities. Also, not having all your capital invested and having some sideline cash ready to go is a smart move.

■ Support

Are you watching for flares popping from your stocks? Here are a few to be aware of:

- **Lukewarm management guidance at the last ER:** This is probably the most aggravating prophecy of them all. The days immediately before and after ER are highly frothy, and the analysts are looking for any scrap of info to justify a move in or out. A blasé CEO performance can bring short-term turbulence. Having said that, the CEO's guidance is just one piece of the brand, and it's best to let the story unfold a bit after ER.

- **A shift in analyst sentiment with the Strong Buy + Buy to Hold + Underperform + Sell ratio falling:** Institutional money is critical to accelerated share gains. Try and find the reasoning for the downgrades before you sell.

- **Declining mentions of the company on social media (e.g. Reddit, etc.):** Sometimes the money starts to move to another sector or stock, and you company becomes Pluto: way, way out there.

■ Intelligence

Your ability to make sense of the facts can mach-up your flight to the Moon. Let's look at a few situations:

■ **You've met your profit objective:** The beauty here is that you control the outcome. You're up 33% in a few months, now what? There's no right answer. Let's look at when to sell from this angle:

> (SOFI)——As an investor, it's important to understand the average return on stocks and what it can mean for portfolio growth over the long term. Overall, the **average stock market return is 10%** annually in the U.S.——but realistically, that figure is more like 6% to 7% when accounting for inflation.
>
> It's rare that the stock market average return is actually 10% in a given year. When looking at nearly 100 years of data—from 1926 to 2020—the yearly average stock market return was between 8% and 12% only eight times. In reality, stock market returns are typically much higher or much lower.[2]

If the average return is 10%, and you've rocketed much further, then it seems prudent to take some money off the table. Just as you should buy in chunks, you should do the same on the sell side.

■ **An unexpected change in the CEO:** Unless it's a planned retirement, announcing a CEO change is usually a board corrective decision. I wouldn't parachute all your shares the next day, but unloading a piece of your stock for reinvesting elsewhere till matters sort themselves out is not a bad idea.

■ **You lapsed into a Buy 'n Hold and got caught in a round trip:** You bought at $9, it went to $18, and you thought you'd let it ride. But, to use the apt phrase of William McChesney Martin, the Fed chairman from 1951 to 1970, "the chaperone (i.e. the Fed) ordered the punch bowl removed just when the party was really warming up" and you ended up doing a 360 to $9.[3] All stocks wobble up and down

---

[2] Rebecca Lake, "What Is the Average Stock Market Return," sofi.com (October 11, 2021), https://www.sofi.com/learn/content/average-stock-market-return/

[3] https://en.wikipedia.org/wiki/William_McChesney_Martin: "William McChesney Martin Jr. (December 17, 1906–July 27, 1998) was an American business executive and federal government official. He served as the ninth chairman of the Federal Reserve from 1951 to 1970." There are variations of William's clever phrase, also see https://idioms.thefreedictionary.com/take+away+the+punch+bowl.

on the road north, but in this situation, is that 100% run-up going to strike twice?

- **Sector rotation appears to be your enemy:** A major macroeconomic event can lead to rebalancing of portfolios by the institutions, and your stock can drown in their wake. If interest rates quickly rise, money may move from consumer discretionary to consumer staples overnight. You can't fight the tape.

As a Pro:Active investor, these "sell" pivot-points are part of your radar recognition, no different than being on guard for when to "buy." The **EQ** strategy is more growth-oriented than the often-used 60/40 approach (and that means more attention is required to your leader-board):

> For decades, investors have relied on 60/40 portfolios—a mix of 60% stocks and 40% bonds—and since the financial crisis, such a passive mix of stocks and bonds provided steady and attractive returns. But rising stagflation risks and growing geopolitical and policy uncertainties are unlikely to favor passive investing going forward. In the latest episode of *Exchanges at Goldman Sachs*, **Christian Mueller-Glissmann**, head of asset allocation research in GS Research, and **Maria Vassalou**, co-CIO of multi-asset solutions in the firm's Asset Management Division, discuss the changing investment landscape.
>
> **Expect lower real returns**. Real returns for 60/40 portfolios, which have averaged about 5% annually for the last 100 years, are likely to be lower going forward, Mueller-Glissmann tells *Exchanges* host **Allison Nathan**. "I think it'll be much more difficult to achieve that 5% real return which we had over the long run, especially through passive investing, and certainly, quite difficult to get anywhere close to where we were in the last cycle." [4]

There is a heavy topic that's not included in our canvases, and that's the US debt of over $30 trillion. [5] Someday, this bad boy should be taken to the *Yellowstone* train station. What does a debt correction look like? Increased taxes, currency devaluations, reduced services, off-loaded government functions, much higher user pay, massive immigration to lower it per capita, etc., etc. Elon Musk points out the debt danger:

---

[4] From Goldman Sachs, "How Rising Stagflation Risks Are Changing the Investment Playbook" (April 14, 2022), briefings@gs.com. Emphasis not added.
[5] https://www.usdebtclock.org/ and https://www.usdebtclock.org/world-debt-clock .html (Canada).

"True national debt, including unfunded entitlements, is at least $60 trillion—roughly three times the size of the entire US economy. Something has got to give," Musk tweeted Thursday . . . The US national debt currently sits at just over $30 trillion but, as Musk points out, that does not factor in unfunded entitlements and future obligations.[6]

This book and its canvases are not about government policy or political views; the subject is only raised for your trendspotting and correlations as a potential black swan that could override your best stock market plays, that's all.

■ Launching Your Rocket

For the Pro:Active investor, 5% returns (14 years for your money to 2X) is not representative of the "to the Moon" direction. There'll be investment scars along your flight, but most importantly, you'll learn. It's absolutely true: no risk, no reward.

In the following box, write in your worst investment and what you learned from it. If you've not made a bad investment or not invested at all, write in the rate of return that you want before you sell a stock. Then check back after a few months and see if it still holds true.

MY LEARNING INVESTMENT

Alright, you've completed your **EQ** and now you're ready to punch-in the code from figure 12.1 and launch your rocket.

All buy and sell stock orders can be time-stamped, such as good for today only, or good till canceled, or just for the next 30 days (most platforms have different rules on durations). You can also add "trailing" conditions, usually expressed as a percentage, to each of stop market and stop limit orders so that your order pricing moves with the current share price and protect your profits.

---

[6]https://www.foxbusiness.com/politics/elon-musk-warns-skyrocketing-national-debt-something-has-got-to-give.

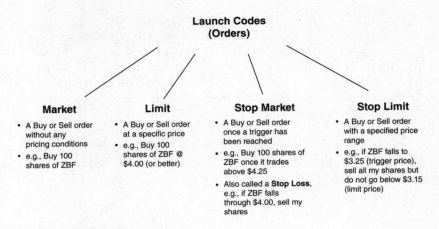

FIGURE 12.1 Launch Codes

Assume ZBF is trading at $4.50, and you have a stop loss at $4.00. Due to a good ER, ZBF quickly rises to $6.00. Your circuit breaker is too far away from the current $6.00 share price to be of protective use to you. By trailing, you set an active stop loss that moves with the share price and protects your downside risk. The skill is in setting a trailing price that does not get activated by the regular gyrations of the stock. Note that your trailing stop can rise, but does not ever decrease. If your trail stop was 10% on ZBF, then when it went to $6.00, your stop would be reset at $5.40, and not static like the $4.00 stop loss. If ZBF moved to $10, your trailing stop would be reset to $9.00.

You can also use trailing stops when shorting stocks. Assume you believe ZBF will go down in price, you could do a *trailing buy* order. If ZBF starts to move up, your trailing stop will trigger and buy you out of the short trade.

■ Capsule

- ■ Protecting your downside through stops is part of being a Pro:Active investor.

- ■ Frequently tailor your warning list and add to the Skylab worksheet as you create your **EQ** strategy.

CHAPTER 13

Information Satellites

> *... and no one—not rock stars, not professional athletes, not software billionaires, and not even geniuses—ever makes it alone.*[1]
>
> Malcom Gladwell

There are many, many information sources to add throttle power. Like the stars in the sky, some shine brighter than others. I enjoy reading or hearing their quotes, news bites, and thoughts; you can forge your support (CSI) from them. They're like satellites ready to transmit information if you're open to their signals. And it's not just about business or economics, the incisive columns and books by nonfiction (or fiction!) writers can assist you on the ideate front. I allocate my satellites to three groups in figure 13.1.

Other information streams are the discussion forums: Reddit (r/wallstreetbets, etc.), Yahoo! Finance, and a flock of others. These message boards are a bubbling cauldron of interesting insight, political diatribes, biased comments, entertainment, know-nothing, know-it-alls, history helpers, and projections on when ER is going to be. On the upside, you can bag some intelligent data geeks on the board, e.g. "BABA ER is Friday and the stock has fallen more than 1.5% after ER on 7 of the last 8 Quarters." Stuff like

---

[1] Malcom Gladwell, *Outliers: The Story of Success*, (Little, Brown, 2008): 115.

BUSINESS & ECONOMIC LEADERS

Jerome Powell, Jamie Dimon, Bill Ackman, Warren Buffet, Charlie Munger, Michael Jordan, Carl Icahn, Ray Dalio, Tim Cook, Jeff Bezos, Mary Barra, Elon Musk, James Farley, Marc Benioff, Whitney Herd, Robert F. Smith, Robert Reich, Peter Thiel, Steven Levitt, Larry Kudlow, Cathie Wood

SHOWS & PODCASTS

CNBC Fast Money/Options Action: Melissa with Guy, Dan, Tim, Steve, Karen, Bonawyn, Nadine, Brian, Jeff, Pete, Mike, Tony, & Carter, plus insightful guests like Tom Lee, Gene Munster—all are amazing ... Fast Money with the energizing Jim Cramer ... fun, self-help gurus Jeffrey & Jennifer Gitomer podcast ... Investopedia website ... Skyview Trading and their simplified You Tubes ... Fox Business & CNBC websites are a great way to start the day ... Morgan Stanley Five Ideas ... Briefings From Goldman Sachs ... Robinhood Snacks ... The Barron's Daily

JUST REALLY SMART PEOPLE

Malcom Gladwell, Michael Lewis, Sebastian Junger, Simon Sinek, Nassim Nicholas Taleb, Neil Degrasse Tyson, Jared Diamond, Jon Krakauer, Van Jones, Rex Murphy

FIGURE 13.1   Some Great Information Satellites

that. Reddit has some really special writers that are intelligent AND funny. Overall, though, just enter these forums carefully.

As you accelerate from your radar stocks and ollie through the **EQ**, you will see symmetry among the inputs in figure 13.2 toward your stock selection choice, and satellite beacons can reinforce your confidence.

■ Capsule

■ Information and media sources surround your flight; select some to assist your trek.

■ Message forums are interesting, helpful, *and* biased. Be careful!

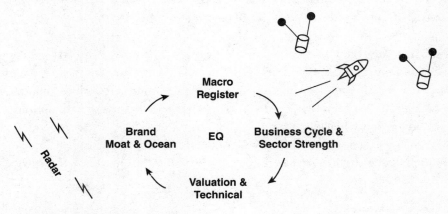

FIGURE 13.2   Your Journey

CHAPTER 14

Other Plays

Options, Shorting, and Crypto

There are strange things done in the midnight sun
By the men who moil for gold;
The Arctic trails have their secret tales
That would make your blood run cold;[1]

Robert W. Service

There are other asset-related tools to mine and condensing them to one chapter means we shall focus on their *Why* and not so much on trading tactics.

■ Options

Let's begin by noting the massive rise in option trading from 4.2 billion contracts in 2017 to more than doubling to 9.9 billion in 2021.[2] Do options

---

[1] Robert W. Service (1874–1958), "The Cremation of Sam McGee," https://www.poetry-foundation.org/poems/45081/the-cremation-of-sam-mcgee.
[2] Per The Options Clearing Corporation and Business Wire, https://www.businesswire.com/news/home/20220104005239/en/OCC-Clears-Record-Setting-9.93-Billion-Total-Contracts-in-2021.

have a *Why?* They surely do, and that's to allow an investor to expand one's financial might through leverage.

Options are a derivative in that its value is derived from another asset—a publicly traded stock. Rather than buying or selling a stock, an option contract allows you to allocate your capital per your view of the stock's directional movement. For example, instead of buying 100 shares of ZBF @ $5 per share, you instead buy an option (always in groups of 100) for a small premium that gives you the *right* to buy the 100 shares at a "strike price" within a certain time frame.

Like any trade, there is (1) a buyer and (2) a seller (a.k.a. option writer), plus a stock is either (3) going up or (4) heading down. That means there are four overarching option positions according to the investor's share-price forecast:

Believe the Share Price will Rise (Bullish)

- **Call Buyer (i.e. goes long):** pays a premium for the *right* to buy the stock at the strike price

- **Put Seller:** keeps the premium, receives any dividends, and has the *obligation* to buy the stock at the strike price

Believe the Share Price will Fall (Neutral to Bearish)

- **Call Seller:** keeps the premium, receives any dividends, and has the *obligation* to sell the stock at the strike price

- **Put Buyer (i.e. goes long):** pays a premium for the *right* to sell the stock at the strike price

Emphasis is required on "right" and "obligation." The buyer, given the relationship between the share price and the strike price, has the right to exercise the contract or let it expire worthless. The seller is obligated to complete the contract if the buyer enacts the right. Here is the *buyer's* POV for a bought call or a bought put:

- **Call:** if the share price does *not* go above the strike price, the option expires worthless.

- **Put:** if the share price does *not* go below the strike price, the option expires worthless.

- The buyer's profit is the net between the share price and strike price, less the premium.

Some extreme examples will bring it home:

Dylan believes ZBF's current share price of $4.50 will rise in the next 60 days. Instead of paying $450 for 100 shares on the market today, he buys a call at a premium of $.20 ($20 in total, 100 × $.20) for the right to buy the shares at a $5 strike price. Dylan is controlling $500 of potential shares for a price of $20, and his break-even price is $5.20 per share. Joss is on the other side of the trade and believes ZBF will fall. She receives a $20 premium for making shares available through selling a $5 Call.

- **Scenario 1:** On or before the contract expiry, ZBF goes to $6. Dylan exercises his *right* to "call in" the contract as he's now "in the money," sells the shares in the market at $6, and his long position nets $100 less $20 for the premium. Joss is *obligated* to provide the shares at $5. She may or may not be out: if she sold a covered call, meaning she had the shares and, say, had bought them a year ago at $3, she is still up and has the premium. If Joss sold a naked call, she must go to market and cover her position.

- **Scenario 2:** On or before the expiry, ZBF goes to $3. Dylan would not exercise his *right* (why would he call in at $5 when he can buy at market for $3?). From Dylan's viewpoint, the option expires worthless, and his loss is the premium he paid. For Joss, "nothing to see here, folks," and she gained the premium.

Dylan's opportunity is sketched in figure 14.1.

And now the flip side:

Danielle thinks ZBF's current share price of $4.50 is overvalued. She buys a put at a premium of $.20 ($20) for the *right* to push the shares to a put seller at a $4 strike price. Joaquin takes the reverse position, he sells a put thinking there is no way ZBF will fall. He receives a $20 premium for agreeing to buy the shares at $4 if they are "put" to him.

- Scenario 1: On or before the expiry, ZBF goes to $3. Danielle exercises her *right* and nets $100 ($4 strike price − $3 share price × 100) less $20 for the premium. Joaquin is *obligated* to buy the shares at $4.

- Scenario 2: On or before the expiry, ZBF goes to $5. Danielle would not exercise her option (why would she source shares at $5 and put them at $4?). From Danielle's viewpoint, her loss is the premium, and the option contract expires unsuccessfully. For Joaquin, it's a happy event and he has the premium.

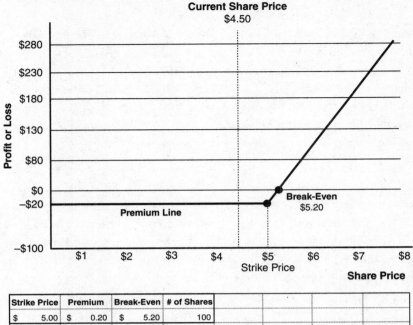

Current Share Price
$4.50

Strike Price	Premium	Break-Even	# of Shares				
$ 5.00	$ 0.20	$ 5.20	100				

Strike Price	$ 3.00	$ 4.00	$ 5.00	$ 5.20	$ 6.00	$ 7.00	$ 8.00
Net	–$ 20.00	–$ 20.00	–$ 20.00	$ –	$ 80.00	$ 180.00	$ 280.00

TO THE MOON!

FIGURE 14.1 A Call Purchase

Danielle's opportunity can be roughed out per figure 14.2.

You likely noticed that the basic constructs of Dylan's and Danielle's options are the same, they just have parallax views: one believes the share price shall rise, the other it will fall. For example, when the share price is $2 from the strike price, they each gain $180.

RISK EXPOSURE OF A CALL SELLER TO A PUT SELLER

_____

_____

_____

Record in the panel who assumes more risk, a naked call seller or a put seller?

Note that during the options contract, when they are ahead, Dylan and Danielle could resell their contract to the market or exercise their rights. Let's collect our learnings into figure 14.3:

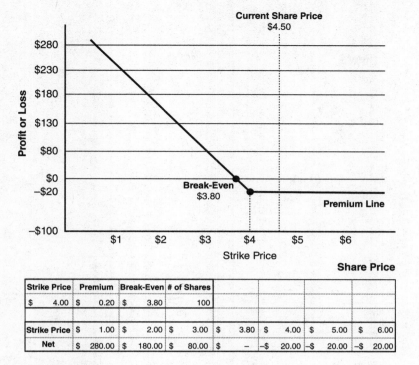

Strike Price	Premium	Break-Even	# of Shares
$ 4.00	$ 0.20	$ 3.80	100

Strike Price	$ 1.00	$ 2.00	$ 3.00	$ 3.80	$ 4.00	$ 5.00	$ 6.00
Net	$ 280.00	$ 180.00	$ 80.00	$ –	–$ 20.00	–$ 20.00	–$ 20.00

FIGURE 14.2   A Put Purchase

The four option positions are complete, and we can now scout the strike price to share-price relationship for an options Buyer through three "moneyness" terms:

In The Money (ITM)

- **Calls:** the share price when you purchased the contract or during the contract is higher than the strike price

- **Puts:** the share price when you purchased the contract or during the contract is lower than the strike price

Out of The Money (OTM)

- **Calls:** the share price when you purchased the contract or during the contract is lower than the strike price

- **Puts:** the share price when you purchased the contract or during the contract is higher than the strike price

- Note that Dylan and Danielle bought OTM options

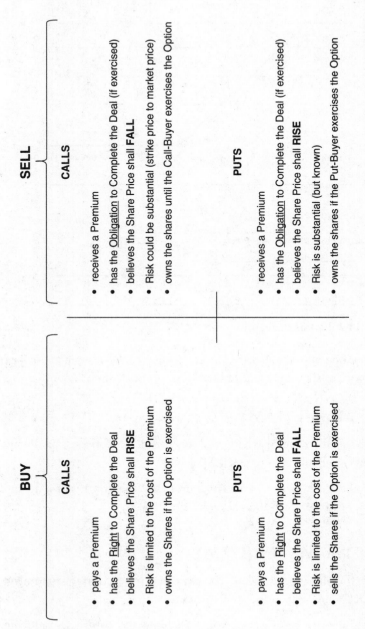

BUY

CALLS

- pays a Premium
- has the <u>Right</u> to Complete the Deal
- believes the Share Price shall **RISE**
- Risk is limited to the cost of the Premium
- owns the Shares if the Option is exercised

PUTS

- pays a Premium
- has the <u>Right</u> to Complete the Deal
- believes the Share Price shall **FALL**
- Risk is limited to the cost of the Premium
- sells the Shares if the Option is exercised

SELL

CALLS

- receives a Premium
- has the <u>Obligation</u> to Complete the Deal (if exercised)
- believes the Share Price shall **FALL**
- Risk could be substantial (strike price to market price)
- owns the shares until the Call-Buyer exercises the Option

PUTS

- receives a Premium
- has the <u>Obligation</u> to Complete the Deal (if exercised)
- believes the Share Price shall **RISE**
- Risk is substantial (but known)
- owns the shares if the Put-Buyer exercises the Option

FIGURE 14.3 Call and Put Summary

At The Money (ATM)

The strike price and share price are equal.

For an option newbie, this might seem like a bizarro world. But if you sequence your thinking, it will become clear:

Where do you think the share price is going: rising or falling?

- Rising: buy calls or sell puts

- Falling: sell calls or buy puts

How much risk do you want to carry?

- Minimal: then take the buy side (risk is limited to the loss of the premium)

- Maximum: take the sell side

How do I know if I'm making money?

- By comparing the share price to the strike price (with recognition of the premium)

- The strike price is fixed during the contract; the share price revolves around it

The thinking sequence for the ITM and OTM fields is shown in figure 14.4.

When you purchase your option, you could be ITM, OTM, or ATM on Day 1, and the premium will regulate accordingly per its components of intrinsic and extrinsic value. The difference between the share price and the strike price is the intrinsic value of the option premium, which brings us to the inherent wizardry of options, the extrinsic factors of time (to contract

		In the Money	Out of the Money
⇧ Share Price	Buy a Call	Share Price > Strike Price	Share Price < Strike Price
	Sell a Put	Share Price > Strike Price	Share Price < Strike Price
You Believe	Sell a Call	Share Price < Strike Price	Share Price > Strike Price
Share Price ⇩	Buy a Put	Share Price < Strike Price	Share Price > Strike Price

FIGURE 14.4 ITM and OTM Moneyness Summary

expiry) and volatility. The premium is also affected by dividends (which are retained by the options seller) and interest rates, but it's time and volatility that we shall briefly examine.

Intrinsic Value = Share Price − Strike Price (reversed for Puts)
Extrinsic Value = Time Value + Volatility
Premium = Intrinsic + Extrinsic Value

When you buy a stock, there is no "sell" clock ticking—assuming you did not purchase on margin. You sell when you believe the time is right and you control the end state insofar as when to walk away. Options are different. If you bought an OTM Call and the share price is flatlining, the end of the runway quickly approaches.

Assume that ZBF's share price is $5 and there is a call at $4.50 with a $.75 premium. The intrinsic value is $5 − $4.50 = $.50. If the premium is $.75, then there is $.25 of extrinsic value:

- The longer the time to contract expiration, the higher the premium, as you're being granted more time to surpass your strike price.

- Each stock has a Historical Volatility (HV) of its price movements and an Implied Volatility (IV) per market maker and analyst views of how the stock will move in the future. Both HV and IV are buried in the premium. The higher the volatility, the higher the option premium.

Let's visualize the rhythm of time, share prices, and volatility on your options trade. You can enter the trade at an ATM, OTM, or ITM position. The chance of hitting your strike price is narrower on an OTM trade—but you pay a lower Premium for being OTM. As you move from the time "*n*" when you purchased the option to time "0" at contract expiry, the probability of achieving your strike price (or better) declines due to time decay. But success is also affected by the push and pull of share price and volatility direction, portrayed in figure 14.5.

Volatility is a measurable risk element that is provided in all option chains, in what are called the "Greeks," overviewed as follows (without the heavy math on how they are derived):

- Delta: a guide metric of the option premium change with a $1.00 move in the share price.

  - Ranges from 0 to 1 for calls and 0 to −1 for puts.

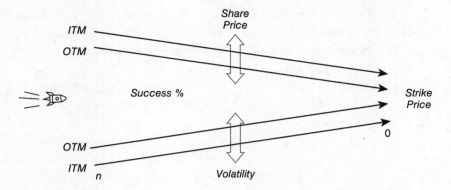

FIGURE 14.5 Factors Affecting Success

- A zero Delta means the option value does not change with movements in the share price and a 1 Delta is full correlation. Sometimes Deltas are referred to in non-decimal format, i.e. instead of .75, the chain shows 75.

- Delta also mimics a position of owning the shares. If the ZBF call has a .70 Delta, and the share price increased $1, then your long position value should rise by $.70, or $70 in total (of course, if you owned 100 shares, you would be sitting on a $100 gain). Delta also serves as a probability guess that the option will expire "In The Money"; in other words, the ZBF call has a 70% chance of reaching ITM.

- Gamma: the pace of Delta change given the share-price change.

- Assume a Gamma of .10.

- When the ZBF share price moved up $1, the Delta becomes .80. On the next share-price increase of $1, the call value increases by $.80.

- Theta: the theoretical daily decay of the option premium (holding other factors constant).

- If Theta was −$.02, then the call value would decline by 2 cents per day (remember, your full total decay is multiplied by 100).

- Vega: measures the effect on an option price given a 1% change in the asset's implied volatility.

- Rho: gauges the option's pricing sensitivity to changes in the risk-free rate.

There are tons of ways to buy and sell options in combination on the same stock and at different expiry dates, and you'll hear strategies like credit spreads, collars, strangles, and others. All are a means of better managing risk toward the desired return.

The Apollo bold **EQ** includes the Put to Call ratio: knowing this number is a helpful motion detector on your radar stock, and a ratio greater than one points to bearish sentiment.

Perhaps someday there can be an **EQ** specific to options, but that'll require a lot more insight than was provided here. Metaphorically, we covered options up to the Kármán line, the boundary 62 miles (100 kilometers) above Earth that defines where Earth's atmosphere ends and outer space begins; in other words, there's a lot more to know about options. But we made headway and for option gains, the star points in figure 14.6 of your starting ITM versus OTM position, whether you are buying or selling, Delta and Gamma warnings, time to contract expiry, and how you leg in and out of risk management through spreads and other strategies, will determine your success.

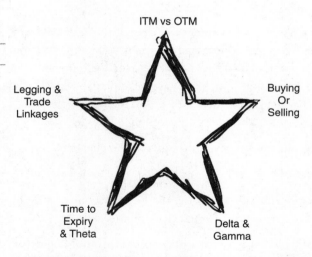

FIGURE 14.6 Interconnected Factors Affecting Options Success

■ Shorting Stocks

You can bet that stocks are going up by buying shares, buying calls, or selling puts. And you can take the other side if you think the share price is going to decline: selling calls, buying puts, or shorting the stock.

Shorting stocks is uncomplicated from a *transactional* view: you establish a margin account with your financial platform, agree to pay interest and assign some financial collateral to support your activity, borrow the shares, wait for the share price to fall, then close out at your target low, replace your borrowings with the bought shares, and net the borrowed versus replaced share proceeds.

But shorting stocks is complicated from a *risk* view: what if you're wrong? The stock starts to rise, do you wait it out? If the gap between the share price at borrowing and the market price begins to really stretch, you'll likely have to "cover" per your collateral obligation. Remember, during this shorting period, you are paying margin-account interest (and the lender keeps the dividend, if any). How long can you sweat the share-price movement? Your risk exposure is undefined.

Is shorting, in terms of risk, more like a call seller or a put seller?

RISK EXPOSURE OF SHORTING

_____

_____

_____

The Apollo bold **EQ** includes a short ratio of the number of shorted shares divided by the float. A curious thing about the short ratio is that when it gets very high, say 25% and above, it's setting up for either a stock face-plant or blastoff due to covering.

For example, GameStop (GME) rose from $19.95 on January 12, 2021, to $347.51 in 10 trading days to January 27. During the rapid share price rise, a pile-on occurred with investors buying huge volumes of near-term call options, adding accelerant to the short squeeze fire as the market makers acted to balance their underlying position through buying shares. This rare event was colloquially called a "gamma squeeze" and it arises from the market maker's objective to be both Delta neutral and provide liquidity (i.e. make money on the way up or on the way down as their gain is in the bid/ask).

■ Crypto

Economics 101 tells us that money has three properties: a medium of exchange, a unit of account, and a store of value. Crypto adds two more inherent qualities: it's decentralized versus the government's fiat currency and its underlying mathematical algorithms and blockchain protocols have value that can be levered into other fields. Having some proportion of your capital in Crypto may be warranted given current government noninterference and Crypto's expanding acceptability. Yet, there are likely a few chapters to be written in the "Where Is This Crypto Thing Heading" book, and not all Crypto coins will endure. Furthermore, many national governments are reviewing the merits of digitizing their currency—China has already started. One component of a "Central Bank Digital Currency" (CBDC) is that it enables person-to-person digital transactions without going through a third party, which is a Crypto attribute. The practical relationship between Crypto and CBDC is yet to be characterized, so be aware. Non-Fungible Tokens are noted only in that the monetizing of digital assets through blockchain technology is an exciting asset-growth realm that may become part of your capital allocation.

■ Capsule

- Selling calls (naked) carries more risk than selling puts as the share price in selling calls can leap many orders higher than the strike price, whereas with selling puts, your downside maximum is boxed by the share price not being able to descend below $0.

- Lower Delta means lower odds of finishing ITM.

- Short squeezes and Gamma squeezes are two different events. When combined, it can be hyper-parabolic to the share price!

- Options, shorting, and Crypto may be part of your asset growth plan; like stock selections, they too possess risk.

CHAPTER 15

Helpful Principles and Touchpoints

Houston, Tranquility Base here. The Eagle has landed.[1]

Neil A. Armstrong

Sports has loads of similarities to investing. Both require brain memory to become proficient, both need some type of game plan, both require agility toward changing circumstances, both have rules, and both teeter on a risk–reward relationship.

Tennis and baseball have two unique characteristics: neither are anchored to a clock and they track errors. In baseball, a batter drives a hard ground ball between the second baseman and the shortstop. The second baseman makes a tough, diving play. He just barely brushes the ball with his outstretched glove and the ball gets by him. It's recorded as an error, perhaps unfairly. In tennis, your opponent rips a topspin forehand to the corner, you sprint and blast it back with such ferocity that your foe can only stroke a weak lob to the baseline. You get there in plenty of time and, unlike Serena, you return the ball into the net. Yikes, an "unforced" error.

I like the way tennis does it. "Unforced" makes you feel a bit guilty. Like there is no way you should have made that mistake, c'mon! It's highly probable that the majority of sports errors are more mental than physical, more cognitive than equipment related, more thinking about the next play than being in the moment. Having a flight list of principles and touchpoints can

---

[1] Neil Armstrong, July 20, 1969.

reduce your investing unforced errors. Following is some summary guidance from the previous chapters, as aligned to the CSI.

■ Curiosity

There is a cosmos of opportunity **and** risk! Here are reminder guides for your curiosity quotient:

- **When you buy a stock, you buy a sector:** If the sector is speeding north, that's a huge magnetic pull to your stock choice. Just remember the reverse setup: if a sector is slowing or going south, that can be a headwind for your stock.

- **Selling your entire position too soon can be painful:** You don't have to close out entirely; just protect your house.

- **Manage your FOMO:** Chasing fireballs because of your "fear of missing out" is a prompting voice in your head that you have to squelch. Buying dips, quiet brands, and those that are sweetly dislocated from the current share price per your Apollo is a better strategy. Beyoncé was in your city last night and you missed the concert. Well, Megan Thee Stallion is coming next week, so get ready. There's also the often referred to "3 Day Rule": when a stock has a significant drop, even though you may think it's bottomed, wait 3 days before you dive in. Let the stock find itself before you buy.

- **Don't panic:** There is a reaction spectrum that spreads from Hyper-Selling (HS) to Holding on for Dear Life (HODL). As a Pro:Active investor, you have to find a HS <> HODL balance, and that comes from your clinical canvas views. Down markets eventually wash out, and your **EQ** may prove correct!

- **It's a journey to the Moon, not a sprint:** Getting there takes a lot of effort; in fact, the Saturn V rocket that launched Apollo 11 had an incredible 32 million horsepower![2]

---

[2] Elizabeth Landau, "Amazon CEO Says Discovery Is Apollo 11 Rocket Engines," CNN (July 19, 2013), https://www.cnn.com/2013/07/19/tech/innovation/amazon-apollo-engines/index.html.

By recognizing high-growth opportunities, you add thrust to your rocket. Still though, don't set your expectations at three-baggers for every stock in your portfolio. Recall your *Why* and be realistic about returns.

■ Support

There are several habits that you can log to reinforce your "to the Moon" expedition. Following are some that should help:

- **Buy in chunks:** Build a core position, and then add capital given the investment risk.

  - Higher Risk Selection: 1/3, 1/3, 1/3 (a.k.a. 33%, 33%, 33%, rounded)

  - Lower Risk Selection: 1/2, 1/4, 1/4 (a.k.a. 50%, 25%, 25%)

- **Stay close to your canvases:** Jump back into the gimbal rig if you have to by rereading chapters in this book for reinforcement of Pro:Active steps, understanding market dynamics, and serious trendspotting. Contrasting one company's **EQ** to another's can reaffirm your initial conviction and decrease the chance of getting toasted.

- **Ignore penny stocks and their promoters:** Many hedge funds and ETFs won't touch a share price below $5. For a "name brand" that's fallen, you can go lower, but a good stop is $3.

- **Get familiar with a stock screener:** You should be as adept as if you're learning a second language, and it doesn't take a lightyear either. The ability to buzz combinations of companies and financials is a truly amazing tool, whereupon feeding the screened data into Gemini and Apollo becomes effortless.

- **If a website says "Click Here" for more information, run away:** I pass on these divining rod teasers. Often you have to listen through a table-pounding 45-minute screed for a 5-minute offer. To switch-up the psychic words of killingly funny Chris Rock: there's no champagne in the champagne room!

- **Set your antennas to information satellites:** Find your go-to sources. There are so many that it's truly overwhelming. Look for succinct and bite-sized facts, with some directional opinion. I've become a big fan of Robinhood Snacks, the Barron's Daily, and Jim Cramer's Investing Club for just those reasons; I can read any one of them in less than five minutes, and there's no "click here for this super-duper offer."

Also, having a helpful network of friends—actually collaborators—is like igniting afterburners on your rocket.

■ Intelligence

We can expedite our flight path by reasoning through events that surround us. Here are some reminders:

- **Corporate profits matter:** The **EQ** leans to growth, but at some point, companies have to make money. If it's always a "next quarter" story, it might be time to fade your trade.

- **Don't buy IPOs right out of the gate:** This ties in with FOMO. Wait a bit before you pounce. Look for a share-price pattern, what are volumes like, see if the big money is rushing in, and how the lockup is proceeding. This all nurtures your Gemini and Apollo canvases. My rule of thumb is a minimum of 90 days for a good luminol read.

- **Remember the importance of volume:** You want to be in a trend of higher highs and higher lows. When volume chokes, share prices can plummet. Volume is a force multiplier on price, not the other way around.

- **CEOs can be rock stars or rock heads:** The best ones have many common traits, and one they share: a respect and commitment to shareholders that goes well beyond their comp envelope. Watch for insider buying; it's generally a positive move, but if it doesn't match guidance, then it might be a trapdoor.

    I read where Jack Welch, the legendary GE CEO, said you could rank your people as A's, B's, and C's. Similarly, one of the premises of Jim Collins in *Good to Great* was getting the right people on the bus. The same applies to CEOs, some are rock star A's, some are middling B's, and some are rock head C's that will torch your stock.

- **Don't over-fuel:** Your flight can only pack so many stocks. Too many, and gravity slows you down. You just don't have enough time to properly care 'n feed 20 stocks, no matter how smart you are.

- **Markets fall faster than they rise:** Your portfolio can quicky overcook, and that's why stop losses and trailing stops have to be in your jetpack.

You probably have a few thoughts or principles that you really like too. I kindly ask you to write them in the following box.

OTHER GUIDING THOUGHTS

_____

_____

_____

_____

■ Capsule

- Please add to the CSI guide list with your better ideas!
- Developing your CSI consistency will add the power of good habits to your investment practices.

CHAPTER 16

Arrival

Two roads diverged in a wood, and I—
I took the one less traveled by,
And that has made all the difference.[1]

Robert Frost

On our flight to the Moon, we looped around a constellation of raw information in figure 16.1 that culminated in the **EQ**.[2]

■ Getting to the Moon

Some of you wish to monetize your *Why* achievement. I get that. But it's really about what you started with, not your total. If your flight began with $2,000 and you achieved a 25-bagger, your $50,000 is a lot more impressive than someone who had $250,000 given to them and they doubled it to $500,000.

---

[1] From "The Road Not Taken" by Robert Frost, the great American poet (1874–1963), https://www.poetryfoundation.org/poems/44272/the-road-not-taken.
[2] Planet and ring images are from https://www.bing.com/images/search.

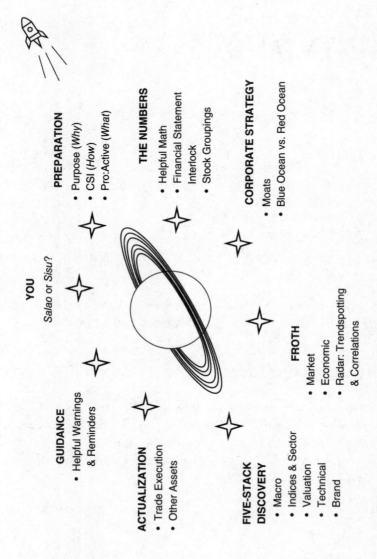

PREPARATION
- Purpose (*Why*)
- CSI (*How*)
- Pro:Active (*What*)

THE NUMBERS
- Helpful Math
- Financial Statement Interlock
- Stock Groupings

CORPORATE STRATEGY
- Moats
- Blue Ocean vs. Red Ocean

YOU

Salao or Sisu?

FROTH
- Market
- Economic
- Radar: Trendspotting & Correlations

GUIDANCE
- Helpful Warnings & Reminders

ACTUALIZATION
- Trade Execution
- Other Assets

FIVE-STACK DISCOVERY
- Macro
- Indices & Sector
- Valuation
- Technical
- Brand

FIGURE 16.1 All the Information That Was Reviewed!

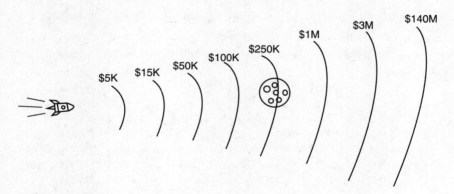

FIGURE 16.2 Financial Flight

Is that answer still not good enough for you? OK, then, if you insist. Given the Moon is about 250,000 miles from Earth, once your portfolio gets to $250,000, you've landed on the Moon—your rocket made it as per figure 16.2![3] Note that to the Moon 4x is pretty much a portfolio of a million bucks!

For the Aussies, Brits, Canadians, and others, you toggle the $250,000 to your currency exchange, as done in figure 16.3.[4] And if you demand the currency per kilometer rather than miles per your rocket's odometer, that's provided as well. All fun!

		per mile	per km
miles to the Moon	250,000		
km to the Moon	400,000		
USD/AUD	$ 1.40		
USD/GBP	$ 0.74		
USD/CAD	$ 1.27		
		per mile	per km
AUD $ required	$ 350,000	$ 1.40	$ 0.88
GBP £ required	£ 185,000	£ 0.74	£ 0.46
CAD $ required	$ 317,500	$ 1.27	$ 0.79

FIGURE 16.3 Getting to the Moon!

---

[3] https://www.nasa.gov/sites/default/files/files/Distance_to_the_Moon.pdf.
[4] Per FX rates on June 4, 2022, https://www.xe.com/currencyconverter.

If you're fortunate to have already landed on the Moon, heads-up that Mars is 140 million miles from Earth. For most of us, some Moon back 'n forth might be a more achievable flight path than Mars in our economic goal setting!

> The next phase of NASA exploration, Artemis, shall make two fascinating leaps forward: (1) the first woman on the moon and (2) exploring, for the first time, the Moon's South Pole. Much like Shackleton's goal to be the first human to traverse the southernmost territory on Earth, Artemis will launch toward exciting discoveries of the Moon's South Pole.

I hope this book met your learning and entertainment needs, and that you ended your read by seeing what I see: that we retail investors can make money in the market through the **EQ** by articulating a purpose (*Why*), having a continually engaged CSI approach (*How*), and a Pro:Active mindset (*What*).

It's now your time, Moonwalker.

■ Capsule

- ■ The Rocket is launched by your *Why*, and not by an end-state dollar figure.
- ■ Your **EQ** shall navigate you to the Moon!

This is Major Tom to Ground Control
I'm stepping through the door[1]

David Bowie

You need your support network—your Ground Control—to test your decisions. These moments of review need not happen daily on every trade, but certainly a periodic check-in with some outside thinking will positively contribute to your Pro:Active direction.

The markets have their own language. You'll come across words, terms, and phrases that you just won't hear anywhere else. It would have been easier to provide a Glossary, but you need shape and context; hence this chapter is written in a special way. I've incorporated market jargon in a screenplay dialogue between two people, Keisha and D'Wayne, and I **highlight** key words for you to retain. I hope you like it.

FADE IN:

INT. DENVER COCKTAIL LOUNGE – LATE AFTERNOON

MAIN TITLES OVER

D'WAYNE is sitting at a small table by himself. He is dressed for his work's casual Friday. As he sips his beer, "Space Oddity" plays in the background. The Lounge is busy with people piling in for their end-of-week reward.

---

[1] Lyrics from "Space Oddity," David Bowie, 1969. https://www.azlyrics.com/lyrics/davidbowie/spaceoddity.

D'WAYNE

(Rising from his seat to hug an approaching Keisha)

Goddess, thanks for meeting me!

KEISHA

Ha, all good! Besides, I couldn't resist the whistle of your buy train.

D'WAYNE

That one there's for you.

KEISHA

(Sips her beer, looking at the beer's label)

Hmmm . . . nice. Just you here in Orbit City? Where are your **apes**?

D'WAYNE

Just me, no investing friends today. Orbit what?

KEISHA

Jetsons, the cartoon from the '60s.

D'WAYNE

Geez Girl, is there isn't anything you don't know. That's like 30 years before you were born!

KEISHA

(laughing)

Well, Howard U has given me rewards. Anyway, your message sounded thirsty. I only have 30 minutes, honey, as I'm going to the Nuggets–Lakers game.

D'WAYNE

Got it. Anyway, you really steered me into a **3 bagger** with Palantir. Got in, got out! Again, thank you, and that's why I ordered these **tendies**! And now I want your magical *Sisu* to override my awful *Salao*. Feel me?

KEISHA

(laughing)

Can't get enough chicken tenders to reward my wins! Not every trade 3 bags to 200%. I'm glad it worked out. What are you adding to your sweet **diamond-hand**?

D'WAYNE

(eager)

I'm going **long** on a **SPAC** between Top Notch Capital and a private uranium producer called Wapiti Minerals, to be traded under Wapiti.

KEISHA

You're going for **growth** versus **value**, ok. You know I don't like **Special Purpose Acquisition Companies**. They mostly bypass the deep rinse you get with an **IPO**. I heard of Top Notch, they became a **unicorn** fairly quickly. Just the new Wapiti or doing a **pair-trade** with another **asset**?

D'WAYNE

Agreed, the **Initial Public Offering** process would be better. Just going with Wapiti, full **conviction**. But I've done my homework. Yeah, Top Notch became a unicorn with a valuation of over 1 billion in less than a year. It's trading at $9.25 on the **NYSE** with a reasonable **beta** of 1.6. The quick-view financials show well: **Debt to EBITDA** is less than 2. But the **PS multiple** is kinda up there at 4. Of course, there is no **PE** for a couple of years.

KEISHA

Slow down bloodhound, no freestyle! You're biting into the middle of the pizza. Let's start at the **EQ** edge. **Macro-wise**, tell me those factors first, and how they correlate to Wapiti.

D'WAYNE

Right, right! **GDP** quarter to quarter was up, and is projected high again next **Q**, so some good tailwind there.

KEISHA

The **pace and value of all American goods and services** is a key economic driver, about $24 trillion a year. But you should also look at **year over year** as Q4 might be bigger than Q3 anyway due to the rise in retail and travel from Thanksgiving and Christmas. I believe **y-o-y** is only 2.9%.

D'WAYNE

Good point! The Bureau of Labor Stats gave the **jobless numbers** last week and unemployment is a low 2.8%.

KEISHA

That's healthy. I imagine this company is **capital-intensive**. Recent **Fed minutes** give me a sense they're going to raise the **FFR**.

D'WAYNE

Yeah, they are spending a lot on new Property, Plant, & Equipment to get the mine rolling. Sure, the **Federal Open Market Committee monetary policy** is sounding **hawkish** like they want the economy to slow and slay inflation. But the Federal Funds Rate is a low 1.25% and Prime is 4.25%, so even a quarter point increase doesn't set off Defcon 1, I think.

KEISHA

I don't disagree with you. You know, in 2021, there were over 1050 IPOs/SPACS and not even 500 in 2020.[2] Is this SPAC thing getting to be a **crowded trade**?

---

[2] https://stockanalysis.com/ipos/2021/.

D'WAYNE

Maybe, but more reason to go with a **blue-ocean** Company. My only macro concern is the rising price of oil, it broke 90 bucks **boe** last week.

KEISHA

You're right, oil prices are two-faced. Are **barrels of equivalent** prices going up because of **demand** and the economy is doing well? Or is it more a case of **supply** restrictions caused by **OPEC**?

D'WAYNE

I believe it's more demand given the good employment numbers and the rising **China PMI**. It's not about the **Organization of Petroleum Exporting Companies**. The **Dow's been** up 8 out of the last 10 trading sessions too, so that's good.

KEISHA

Yeah, in this interconnected world of almost 8 billion people, the butterfly in the China forest means we even make the **Purchasing Managers Index** a part of our macro **dashboard**. I like the **S&P** as a better gauge than the Dow though, the movements of 500 stocks instead of 30 are more meaningful. Anyway, the **Macro** dashboard is fine—let's move into the sector analysis. Of the **11 sectors**, they're obviously in **materials**. Is there any acknowledged **sector-rotation** into materials?

D'WAYNE

Great question. This stock is definitely a **cyclical** and not a defensive **secular**.

KEISHA

Yup. And if **inflation** rears its ugly head, then your cyclical growth stocks might get punished. I always like to have some cash parked in the **less volatile seculars**; they are boring, but you can sleep at night.

D'WAYNE

So you're concerned?

KEISHA

Not just yet. Jumping back to macro, the **2 and 10-year Treasury spreads** are at the front of the inflation bus. Their **yield difference** is tightening. Just keep your eye on it. First though, what's your **PT** and **Mendoza Line**?

D'WAYNE

My **price target** is $14 and anything below $12 in the next six months would be an unforced error. I need all your time, should we blast to valuation? Like I said earlier, **PS** is 4, **EV to EBITDA** is a low 15, and **EV to FCF** is 30.

KEISHA

That's barely OK on the **Price to Sales**. **EBITDA** is high-school and **FCF** is college level for valuations, Stormtrooper. Is the **Enterprise Value** inflated due to a lot of debt on the balance sheet? You gotta be careful with **EV**.

D'WAYNE

Wapiti is not **over-leveraged** at all. And **EBIT** is **5 times** their interest payments. And like I said, **Debt to EBITDA** is under 2.

KEISHA

FCF is likely down if they're investing in a new mine?

D'WAYNE

Yes, **Free Cash Flow** is taking a bit of a hit, **H1 to H2** is about a 15% decline, not material in my view.

KEISHA

I'm ok with the first half of the year drop to the second half. **Operating Margin**, any degradation there?

D'WAYNE

OM is holding steady at 35%.

KEISHA

Good stuff. Describe some of the **share price movements** over the past couple of months.

D'WAYNE

Sure. On **Momentum**, indicators are strong. The **50-day** has never been below the **200 DMA**.

KEISHA

Good to know the **Daily Moving Average** info is solid. What about the **visuals**? And have **trading volumes** been increasing?

D'WAYNE

There was a **double-bottom** at $8.50, so that's the **support level**, and I feel good about that. **RSI** has tracked in the middle between 50 and 60. It's been a great case of **higher highs** and **higher lows**.

KEISHA

That's a good **floor** given its now at $9.25. What about the difference between the **Float** and **Outstanding shares**? Is there the possibility of a **lockup expiry** or significant **dilution**?

D'WAYNE

I knew you'd ask that! The difference is less than 10%. No flooding of the market with added shares to bring down the share price.

KEISHA

All right, what's the street saying, what was **guidance** at the last **ER**?

D'WAYNE

Analysts are 5 Buys, 2 Hold, and 1 Sell. Average **PT** is about $11.50. Management guidance was strong on **top line**. Nothing on **Net Income** of course as they are not there yet.

KEISHA

Generally, those Analyst Price Targets are for 2 to 3 quarters out, a year max. My last Valuation question is the **13-F** from last quarter. Any big hedge or capital funds moving in?

D'WAYNE

Yes, a few actually. Lightpoint Moneta, Saturn Fixed Capital, and the crazy wealthy McDeer Family Foundation.

KEISHA

Good stuff, eases into our last review piece on the Brand. **CEO**, rock head or rock star?

D'WAYNE

Definitely a star. He took Red Sparrow resources from **OTC** at under a $1 to the **NYSE** at $22 in less than two years. They even pay a 4% **dividend** now!

KEISHA

Impressive! What's this firm's **Buffett moat**? Is it as wide as a football field or are we talking a narrow bowling lane?

D'WAYNE

It's their guaranteed production. They are one of the few mining companies in North America that, as a matter of their **value proposition**, ensures that area Native tribes have an **equity stake** in the mine. This eliminates **business interruptions** around regional water usage and contributes to their *Why* of being the first green mining company.

KEISHA

So you're saying they are in the **Blue Ocean** with a wide **moat**?

D'WAYNE

I am.

KEISHA

And their competition in this **B2B** sell-cycle?

D'WAYNE

That would be **business-to-business** offshore companies like Taiga Uranium and Ulan Mining & Minerals.

KEISHA

(air quotes on "nuclear")

No, their competition is the public's fear of the word "nuclear." Think broader. All these new discount airlines are not challenging other airlines—they are competing against buses and cars. Nuclear "fear" is your **black swan**.

D'WAYNE

Hmmm, you have a good point there. But only 20% of US electricity is powered by nuclear.[3] I'm an **early adopter** of uranium and nuclear opportunity.

KEISHA

That's always the fundamental question on stock selections: **timing**. Sounds like you did your **EQ** homework. Anyway, I recommend a **core position** of around 33% of your projected investment, and then **scale up** in two separate **tranches** over the next few weeks.

D'WAYNE

(worried)

So it's a strong buy, right?

KEISHA

Yup, print it. I'm going to set a **buy stop** at $10.00 and join you. You know my buy high and sell higher strat. Might pick up some $11.00 **OTMs** too. I think this could go **parabolic.** Anything else?

D'WAYNE

Great, we achieved the mind-meld! One more thing, any of your Spock logic on ZBF?

KEISHA

What are you doing with that stonk?

D'WAYNE

I'm still in that trade. Sold some **LEAP covered calls.** Exec gave good guidance last **ER**, and the **RSI** seems to have bottomed around 35 or so. It's getting close to **ATM** now.

KEISHA

Those multiyear **Long-term Equity Anticipation Securities calls** will give you **premium candy**. But I read ZBF is charging into the Midwest and Canada in a year. They are **growth,** soon to be **commercial.** You might need to clock your points now. Maybe close out or **spread** and buy some calls. You could sell **puts** too for air-cover.

D'WAYNE

---

[3] https://www.eia.gov/energyexplained/electricity/electricity-in-the-us.php.

Vetting with you always helps. I'm going to exit. Awesome as usual; thanks, She-Dog.

KEISHA

(smiling)

Gotta jet, Astro. **To the Moon** on this one. And, of course, Go Bisons!

This appendix provides the monthly Consumer Price Index (All Items) for the United States from 2012 to 2021 (percent, growth rate same period previous year, not seasonally adjusted).

- CPI 2012–2021 data is provided in figure B.1.

- The 2012–2021 year over year Data *count* (n) is 120.

- The *mean* ($\bar{x}$) is 1.9% and one *Standard Deviation* (s) is 1.3%. *Range* ($\bar{r}$) at one s is .6% to 3.2%.

- Removing the COVID extreme 2020 months of April, May, June, and July generates much the same output (to one decimal place).

- CPI in H1 2022: January 7.5%, February 7.9%, March 8.5%, April 8.3%, May 8.6%, and June 9.1%.

Monthly CPI, Y/Y							
2012-01-01	2.9	2015-01-01	-0.1	2018-01-01	2.1	2020-01-01	2.5
2012-02-01	2.9	2015-02-01	0.0	2018-02-01	2.2	2020-02-01	2.3
2012-03-01	2.7	2015-03-01	-0.1	2018-03-01	2.4	2020-03-01	1.5
2012-04-01	2.3	2015-04-01	-0.2	2018-04-01	2.5	2020-04-01	0.3
2012-05-01	1.7	2015-05-01	0.0	2018-05-01	2.8	2020-05-01	0.1
2012-06-01	1.7	2015-06-01	0.1	2018-06-01	2.9	2020-06-01	0.6
2012-07-01	1.4	2015-07-01	0.2	2018-07-01	2.9	2020-07-01	1.0
2012-08-01	1.7	2015-08-01	0.2	2018-08-01	2.7	2020-08-01	1.3
2012-09-01	2.0	2015-09-01	0.0	2018-09-01	2.3	2020-09-01	1.4
2012-10-01	2.2	2015-10-01	0.2	2018-10-01	2.5	2020-10-01	1.2
2012-11-01	1.8	2015-11-01	0.5	2018-11-01	2.2	2020-11-01	1.2
2012-12-01	1.7	2015-12-01	0.7	2018-12-01	1.9	2020-12-01	1.4
2013-01-01	1.6	2016-01-01	1.4	2019-01-01	1.6	2021-01-01	1.4
2013-02-01	2.0	2016-02-01	1.0	2019-02-01	1.5	2021-02-01	1.7
2013-03-01	1.5	2016-03-01	0.9	2019-03-01	1.9	2021-03-01	2.6
2013-04-01	1.1	2016-04-01	1.1	2019-04-01	2.0	2021-04-01	4.2
2013-05-01	1.4	2016-05-01	1.0	2019-05-01	1.8	2021-05-01	5.0
2013-06-01	1.8	2016-06-01	1.0	2019-06-01	1.6	2021-06-01	5.4
2013-07-01	2.0	2016-07-01	0.8	2019-07-01	1.8	2021-07-01	5.4
2013-08-01	1.5	2016-08-01	1.1	2019-08-01	1.7	2021-08-01	5.3
2013-09-01	1.2	2016-09-01	1.5	2019-09-01	1.7	2021-09-01	5.4
2013-10-01	1.0	2016-10-01	1.6	2019-10-01	1.8	2021-10-01	6.2
2013-11-01	1.2	2016-11-01	1.7	2019-11-01	2.1	2021-11-01	6.8
2014-12-01	1.5	2016-12-01	2.1	2019-12-01	2.3	2021-12-01	7.0
2014-01-01	1.6	2017-01-01	2.5			Mean, all months	1.9
2014-02-01	1.1	2017-02-01	2.7			Standard Deviation	1.3
2014-03-01	1.5	2017-03-01	2.4			Mean + 1 s	3.2
2014-04-01	2.0	2017-04-01	2.2			Mean - 1 s	0.6
2014-05-01	2.1	2017-05-01	1.9			Mean + 2 s	4.5
2014-06-01	2.1	2017-06-01	1.6			Mean - 2 s	-0.7
2014-07-01	2.0	2017-07-01	1.7	Mean, w/o 2020 April, May, June, July			1.9
2014-08-01	1.7	2017-08-01	1.9			Standard Deviation	1.3
2013-09-01	1.7	2017-09-01	2.2			Mean + 1 s	3.2
2014-10-01	1.7	2017-10-01	2.0			Mean - 1 s	0.6
2014-11-01	1.3	2017-11-01	2.2			Mean + 2 s	4.5
2014-12-01	0.8	2017-12-01	2.1			Mean - 2 s	-0.7

FIGURE B.1   CPI %, 2012–2021[1]

---

[1] "Board of Governors of the Federal Reserve System (US), Consumer Price Index: Total All Items for the United States, retrieved from FRED, Federal Reserve Bank of St. Louis; https://fred.stlouisfed.org/series/CPALTT01USM659N, May 19, 2022. CPI weightings are rounded. The $\bar{x}$ to two decimal places for 2012-2021 is 1.89%, and without the COVID extreme months, it is 1.94%. Minor summary differences may appear due to rounding.

This appendix provides the monthly Unemployment Rate for the United States from 2012 to 2021 (percent, seasonally adjusted).

- Unemployment 2012–2021 data is provided in figure C.1.

- The 2012–2021 10-year Unemployment Data *count* (n) is 120, the *mean* ($\bar{x}$) is 5.7% and one *Standard Deviation* (s) is 1.9%. Range ($\bar{r}$) at one s is 3.8% to 7.6%.

- Removing the COVID extreme 2020 months of April–December (i.e. three quarters) is material: $n = 111$, $\bar{x}$ is 5.4%, s is 1.5%, and $\bar{r}$ at one s is 3.9% to 6.9%.

- Unemployment in H1 2022: January: 4.0%, February 3.8%, and March through June is 3.6%.

Monthly Unemployment							
2012-01-01	8.3	2015-01-01	5.7	2018-01-01	4.0	2020-01-01	3.5
2012-02-01	8.3	2015-02-01	5.5	2018-02-01	4.1	2020-02-01	3.5
2012-03-01	8.2	2015-03-01	5.4	2018-03-01	4.0	2020-03-01	4.4
2012-04-01	8.2	2015-04-01	5.4	2018-04-01	4.0	2020-04-01	14.7
2012-05-01	8.2	2015-05-01	5.6	2018-05-01	3.8	2020-05-01	13.2
2012-06-01	8.2	2015-06-01	5.3	2018-06-01	4.0	2020-06-01	11.0
2012-07-01	8.2	2015-07-01	5.2	2018-07-01	3.8	2020-07-01	10.2
2012-08-01	8.1	2015-08-01	5.1	2018-08-01	3.8	2020-08-01	8.4
2012-09-01	7.8	2015-09-01	5.0	2018-09-01	3.7	2020-09-01	7.9
2012-10-01	7.8	2015-10-01	5.0	2018-10-01	3.8	2020-10-01	6.9
2012-11-01	7.7	2015-11-01	5.1	2018-11-01	3.8	2020-11-01	6.7
2012-12-01	7.9	2015-12-01	5.0	2018-12-01	3.9	2020-12-01	6.7
2013-01-01	8.0	2016-01-01	4.8	2019-01-01	4.0	2021-01-01	6.4
2013-02-01	7.7	2016-02-01	4.9	2019-02-01	3.8	2021-02-01	6.2
2013-03-01	7.5	2016-03-01	5.0	2019-03-01	3.8	2021-03-01	6.0
2013-04-01	7.6	2016-04-01	5.1	2019-04-01	3.6	2021-04-01	6.0
2013-05-01	7.5	2016-05-01	4.8	2019-05-01	3.6	2021-05-01	5.8
2013-06-01	7.5	2016-06-01	4.9	2019-06-01	3.6	2021-06-01	5.9
2013-07-01	7.3	2016-07-01	4.8	2019-07-01	3.7	2021-07-01	5.4
2013-08-01	7.2	2016-08-01	4.9	2019-08-01	3.7	2021-08-01	5.2
2013-09-01	7.2	2016-09-01	5.0	2019-09-01	3.5	2021-09-01	4.7
2013-10-01	7.2	2016-10-01	4.9	2019-10-01	3.6	2021-10-01	4.6
2013-11-01	6.9	2016-11-01	4.7	2019-11-01	3.6	2021-11-01	4.2
2014-12-01	6.7	2016-12-01	4.7	2019-12-01	3.6	2021-12-01	3.9
2014-01-01	6.6	2017-01-01	4.7			Mean, all months	5.7
2014-02-01	6.7	2017-02-01	4.6			Standard Deviation	1.9
2014-03-01	6.7	2017-03-01	4.4			Mean + 1 s	7.6
2014-04-01	6.2	2017-04-01	4.4			Mean - 1 s	3.8
2014-05-01	6.3	2017-05-01	4.4			Mean + 2 s	9.5
2014-06-01	6.1	2017-06-01	4.3			Mean - 2 s	1.9
2014-07-01	6.2	2017-07-01	4.3		Mean, without 2020 April - Dec		5.4
2014-08-01	6.1	2017-08-01	4.4			Standard Deviation	1.5
2013-09-01	5.9	2017-09-01	4.3			Mean + 1 s	6.9
2014-10-01	5.7	2017-10-01	4.2			Mean - 1 s	3.9
2014-11-01	5.8	2017-11-01	4.2			Mean + 2 s	8.4
2014-12-01	5.6	2017-12-01	4.1			Mean - 2 s	2.4

FIGURE C.1   Unemployment %, 2012–2021[1]

---

[1] Board of Governors of the Federal Reserve System (US), Unemployment Rate, retrieved from FRED, Federal Reserve Bank of St. Louis; https://fred.stlouisfed.org/series/UNRATE#0, May 19, 2022. Minor summary differences may appear due to rounding.

This appendix provides the quarterly Real Gross Domestic Product for the United States from 2012 to 2021 (percent change from preceding period, seasonally adjusted annual rate).

- GDP 2012–2021 data is provided in figure D.1.

- The 2012–2021 10-year GDP annualized quarter over quarter *count* (n) is 40, the *mean* ($\bar{x}$) is 2.4%, one Standard deviation (s) is 7.6%, and Range ($\bar{r}$) at one s is −5.2% to 10.0%.

- Removing the 2020 COVID counts of Q1 (−5.1%), Q2 (−31.2%), and Q3 (+33.8%) is material as shown in the second number column of figure D.1 where $n = 37$, $\bar{x} = 2.7\%$, $s = 1.7\%$, with $\bar{r}$ at one s being 1.0% to 4.4%.

- Figure D.2 illustrates the *counts* by GDP Q/Q % group, excluding the extreme COVID quarters. The 37 Q/Q *counts* are assigned to 19 bands of .5% ranging from −2.00% to 7.49%. The highest cluster is from 2.00% to 2.49% at 7 data points.

- The GDP for Q1, 2022 decreased at an annual rate of 1.6% (Third Estimate) and a decline of .6% (Second Estimate) for Q2, 2022.

Quarter	Q/Q	Q/Q
2012-01-01	3.3	3.3
2012-04-01	1.8	1.8
2012-07-01	0.7	0.7
2012-10-01	0.4	0.4
2013-01-01	3.5	3.5
2013-04-01	0.6	0.6
2013-07-01	3.2	3.2
2013-10-01	2.9	2.9
2014-01-01	−1.4	−1.4
2014-04-01	5.2	5.2
2014-07-01	4.7	4.7
2014-10-01	1.8	1.8
2015-01-01	3.3	3.3
2015-04-01	2.3	2.3
2015-07-01	1.3	1.3
2015-10-01	0.6	0.6
2016-01-01	2.4	2.4
2016-04-01	1.2	1.2
2016-07-01	2.4	2.4
2016-10-01	2.0	2.0
2017-01-01	1.9	1.9
2017-04-01	2.3	2.3
2017-07-01	2.9	2.9
2017-10-01	3.8	3.8
2018-01-01	3.1	3.1
2018-04-01	3.4	3.4
2018-07-01	1.9	1.9
2018-10-01	0.9	0.9
2019-01-01	2.4	2.4
2019-04-01	3.2	3.2
2019-07-01	2.8	2.8
2019-10-01	1.9	1.9
2020-01-01	−5.1	
2020-04-01	−31.2	
2020-07-01	33.8	
2020-10-01	4.5	4.5
2021-01-01	6.3	6.3
2021-04-01	6.7	6.7
2021-07-01	2.3	2.3
2021-10-01	6.9	6.9
Mean	2.4	2.7
Standard Deviation	7.6	1.7
Mean + 1 s	10.0	4.4
Mean - 1 s	−5.2	1.0
Mean + 2 s	17.6	6.1
Mean - 2 s	−12.8	−0.7

FIGURE D.1   GDP %, 2012–2021[2]

---

[2] Board of Governors of the Federal Reserve System (US), Release Tables: Real GDP and Its Components, Quarterly, Seasonally Adjusted, retrieved from FRED, Federal Reserve Bank of St. Louis; https://fred.stlouisfed.org/release/tables?eid=155790&rid=269, May 19, 2022. Minor summary differences may appear due to rounding.

Data Group	MIN	MAX	Data-Points per Group
	Min	Max	
1	−2.00	−1.51	
2	−1.50	−1.01	1
3	−1.00	−0.51	
4	−0.50	−0.01	
5	0.00	0.49	1
6	0.50	0.99	4
7	1.00	1.49	2
8	1.50	1.99	5
9	2.00	2.49	7
10	2.50	2.99	3
11	3.00	3.49	6
12	3.50	3.99	2
13	4.00	4.49	
14	4.50	4.99	2
15	5.00	5.49	1
16	5.50	5.99	
17	6.00	6.49	1
18	6.50	6.99	2
19	7.00	7.49	
		TOTAL	37

FIGURE D.2 GDP % by Band, 2012–2021

This appendix provides the daily Federal Reserve of the United States 10-Year Treasury Constant Maturity Minus 2-Year Treasury Constant Maturity spreads from 2012 to 2021 (percent, not seasonally adjusted), and then summarized in basis point format.

- The 2- and 10-Year T-Note spread over 2012–2021 yields a *count* (n) of 2502, *mean* ($\bar{x}$) of 113 basis points (1.13%), and one Standard Deviation (s) is 66 basis points (.66%), Range ($\bar{r}$) at one s is 47 (.47%) to 179 (1.79%) basis points. The size of the data set precludes it from being listed.[1]

- There is a stark difference between the 2012–2021 data and January 3, 2022–June 30, 2022 data (figure E.1). This recent and smaller data set gives a n of 124, $\bar{x}$ of 35 basis points, one s is 24 basis points, and $\bar{r}$ at one s is 11 to 59 basis points.

---

[1] Board of Governors of the Federal Reserve System (US), 10-Year Constant Maturity Minus 2-Year Constant Maturity, retrieved from FRED, Federal Reserve Bank of St. Louis; https://fred.stlouisfed.org/series/T10Y2Y, July 14, 2022. Minor summary differences may appear due to rounding.

2-Year & 10-Year Basis Spread					
2022-01-03	0.85	2022-03-01	0.41	2022-05-02	0.26
2022-01-04	0.89	2022-03-02	0.36	2022-05-03	0.19
2022-01-05	0.88	2022-03-03	0.33	2022-05-04	0.27
2022-01-06	0.85	2022-03-04	0.24	2022-05-05	0.34
2022-01-07	0.89	2022-03-07	0.23	2022-05-06	0.40
2022-01-10	0.86	2022-03-08	0.23	2022-05-09	0.44
2022-01-11	0.85	2022-03-09	0.26	2022-05-10	0.37
2022-01-12	0.82	2022-03-10	0.26	2022-05-11	0.25
2022-01-13	0.79	2022-03-11	0.25	2022-05-12	0.28
2022-01-14	0.79	2022-03-14	0.27	2022-05-13	0.32
2022-01-17		2022-03-15	0.30	2022-05-16	0.30
2022-01-18	0.81	2022-03-16	0.24	2022-05-17	0.27
2022-01-19	0.79	2022-03-17	0.26	2022-05-18	0.21
2022-01-20	0.75	2022-03-18	0.17	2022-05-19	0.21
2022-01-21	0.74	2022-03-21	0.18	2022-05-20	0.18
2022-01-24	0.76	2022-03-22	0.20	2022-05-23	0.21
2022-01-25	0.76	2022-03-23	0.19	2022-05-24	0.26
2022-01-26	0.72	2022-03-24	0.21	2022-05-25	0.27
2022-01-27	0.63	2022-03-25	0.18	2022-05-26	0.29
2022-01-28	0.63	2022-03-28	0.11	2022-05-27	0.27
2022-01-31	0.61	2022-03-29	0.06	2022-05-30	
2022-02-01	0.63	2022-03-30	0.04	2022-05-31	0.32
2022-02-02	0.62	2022-03-31	0.04	2022-06-01	0.28
2022-02-03	0.63	2022-04-01	-0.05	2022-06-02	0.27
2022-02-04	0.62	2022-04-04	-0.01	2022-06-03	0.30
2022-02-07	0.62	2022-04-05	0.03	2022-06-06	0.31
2022-02-08	0.61	2022-04-06	0.11	2022-06-07	0.23
2022-02-09	0.58	2022-04-07	0.19	2022-06-08	0.25
2022-02-10	0.42	2022-04-08	0.19	2022-06-09	0.21
2022-02-11	0.42	2022-04-11	0.29	2022-06-10	0.09
2022-02-14	0.40	2022-04-12	0.33	2022-06-13	0.03
2022-02-15	0.47	2022-04-13	0.33	2022-06-14	0.04
2022-02-16	0.51	2022-04-14	0.36	2022-06-15	0.13
2022-02-17	0.48	2022-04-15		2022-06-16	0.14
2022-02-18	0.45	2022-04-18	0.39	2022-06-17	0.08
2022-02-21		2022-04-19	0.32	2022-06-20	
2022-02-22	0.38	2022-04-20	0.25	2022-06-21	0.10
2022-02-23	0.41	2022-04-21	0.22	2022-06-22	0.10
2022-02-24	0.42	2022-04-22	0.18	2022-06-23	0.08
2022-02-25	0.42	2022-04-25	0.18	2022-06-24	0.09
2022-02-28	0.39	2022-04-26	0.23	2022-06-27	0.12
		2022-04-27	0.24	2022-06-28	0.10
		2022-04-28	0.22	2022-06-29	0.04
		2022-04-29	0.19	2022-06-30	0.06
				Mean	35
				Standard Deviation	24
				Mean + 1 s	59
				Mean - 1 s	11
				Mean + 2 s	83
				Mean - 2 s	-13

FIGURE E.1   2- and 10-Year Spread, January 3, 2022 to June 30, 2022

This appendix provides the monthly Spot Crude Oil Price for West Texas Intermediate (WTI) from 2012 to 2021 (dollars per barrel, not seasonally adjusted).

- Per figure F.1, the 2012–2021 Oil monthly spot price yields a *count* (n) of 120, *mean* ($\bar{x}$) of \$65.72, one Standard Deviation (s) is \$22.31 giving a Range ($\bar{r}$) at one s of \$43.41 to \$88.03. Half of one s is \$11.16 and covers almost 40% of n giving a $\bar{r}$ of \$54.56 to \$76.88.[1]

- The macro register target for oil, given its broad dispersion and our knowledge of cost inputs, will be set to less than one Standard Deviation, giving a Range of \$55 - \$80 for the **EQ**.

- WTI in H1 2022: January \$83.22, February \$91.64, March \$108.50, April \$101.78, May \$109.55, and June \$114.84.

---

[1] Board of Governors of the Federal Reserve System (US), Spot Crude Oil Price: West Texas Intermediate (WTI), retrieved from FRED, Federal Reserve Bank of St. Louis; https://fred.stlouisfed.org/series/WTISPLC, July 14, 2022. Minor summary differences may appear due to rounding.

WTI Monthly Spot Price							
2012-01-01	100.24	2015-01-01	47.22	2018-01-01	63.70	2020-01-01	57.52
2012-02-01	102.25	2015-02-01	50.58	2018-02-01	62.23	2020-02-01	50.54
2012-03-01	106.19	2015-03-01	47.82	2018-03-01	62.73	2020-03-01	29.21
2012-04-01	103.33	2015-04-01	54.45	2018-04-01	66.25	2020-04-01	16.55
2012-05-01	94.70	2015-05-01	59.27	2018-05-01	69.98	2020-05-01	28.56
2012-06-01	82.41	2015-06-01	59.82	2018-06-01	67.87	2020-06-01	38.31
2012-07-01	87.93	2015-07-01	50.90	2018-07-01	70.98	2020-07-01	40.71
2012-08-01	94.16	2015-08-01	42.87	2018-08-01	68.06	2020-08-01	42.34
2012-09-01	94.72	2015-09-01	45.48	2018-09-01	70.23	2020-09-01	39.63
2012-10-01	89.57	2015-10-01	46.22	2018-10-01	70.75	2020-10-01	39.40
2012-11-01	86.66	2015-11-01	42.44	2018-11-01	56.96	2020-11-01	40.94
2012-12-01	88.25	2015-12-01	37.19	2018-12-01	49.52	2020-12-01	47.02
2013-01-01	94.69	2016-01-01	31.68	2019-01-01	51.35	2021-01-01	52.00
2013-02-01	95.32	2016-02-01	30.32	2019-02-01	54.95	2021-02-01	59.04
2013-03-01	93.05	2016-03-01	37.55	2019-03-01	58.15	2021-03-01	62.33
2013-04-01	92.07	2016-04-01	40.75	2019-04-01	63.86	2021-04-01	61.72
2013-05-01	94.80	2016-05-01	46.71	2019-05-01	60.83	2021-05-01	65.17
2013-06-01	95.80	2016-06-01	48.76	2019-06-01	54.66	2021-06-01	71.38
2013-07-01	104.61	2016-07-01	44.65	2019-07-01	57.35	2021-07-01	72.49
2013-08-01	106.57	2016-08-01	44.72	2019-08-01	54.81	2021-08-01	67.73
2013-09-01	106.29	2016-09-01	45.18	2019-09-01	56.95	2021-09-01	71.65
2013-10-01	100.54	2016-10-01	49.78	2019-10-01	53.96	2021-10-01	81.48
2013-11-01	93.86	2016-11-01	45.66	2019-11-01	57.03	2021-11-01	79.15
2013-12-01	97.63	2016-12-01	51.97	2019-12-01	59.88	2021-12-01	71.71
2014-01-01	94.62	2017-01-01	52.50			Mean	65.72
2014-02-01	100.82	2017-02-01	53.47			Standard Deviation	22.31
2014-03-01	100.80	2017-03-01	49.33			Mean + 1 s	88.03
2014-04-01	102.07	2017-04-01	51.06			Mean - 1 s	43.41
2014-05-01	102.18	2017-05-01	48.48			Mean + 2 s	110.34
2014-06-01	105.79	2017-06-01	45.18			Mean - 2 s	21.10
2014-07-01	103.59	2017-07-01	46.63			.5 s	11.16
2014-08-01	96.54	2017-08-01	48.04			Mean + .5 s	76.88
2014-09-01	93.21	2017-09-01	49.82			Mean - .5 s	54.56
2014-10-01	84.40	2017-10-01	51.58				
2014-11-01	75.79	2017-11-01	56.64				
2014-12-01	59.29	2017-12-01	57.88				

FIGURE F.1 West Texas Intermediate, Spot Crude Oil, $/barrel, 2012–2021

This appendix provides the daily Chicago Board Options Exchange Volatility Index (VIX) from 2012 to 2021 (percent, adjusted close).

- The VIX for 2012–2021 yields a *count* (n) of 2516, *mean* ($\bar{x}$) of 17, and one Standard Deviation (s) is 7, Range ($\bar{r}$) at one s is 10 to 24. The size of the data set precludes it from being listed.[1]

- Per figure G.1, the 2022 VIX from January 3 to June 30 yields n of 124, $\bar{x}$ of 26, one s is 5, and $\bar{r}$ at one s is 21 to 31.

- It was interesting to run the data from September 15, 2008, the day of the Lehman Brothers declared bankruptcy, for one year to September 14, 2009. The VIX had a n of 252 and $\bar{x}$ of 41 (data set not illustrated).

---

[1] https://finance.yahoo.com/quote/%5EVIX/history?p=%5EVIX, sourced May 16, 2022. Minor summary differences may appear due to rounding.

from Yahoo Finance, Jan 3, 2022 to June 30, 2022					
Date	Adj Close		Adj Close		Adj Close
2022-01-03	17	2022-03-03	30	2022-05-02	32
2022-01-04	17	2022-03-04	32	2022-05-03	29
2022-01-05	20	2022-03-07	36	2022-05-04	25
2022-01-06	20	2022-03-08	35	2022-05-05	31
2022-01-07	19	2022-03-09	32	2022-05-06	30
2022-01-10	19	2022-03-10	30	2022-05-09	35
2022-01-11	18	2022-03-11	31	2022-05-10	33
2022-01-12	18	2022-03-14	32	2022-05-11	33
2022-01-13	20	2022-03-15	30	2022-05-12	32
2022-01-14	19	2022-03-16	27	2022-05-13	29
2022-01-18	23	2022-03-17	26	2022-05-16	27
2022-01-19	24	2022-03-18	24	2022-05-17	26
2022-01-20	26	2022-03-21	24	2022-05-18	31
2022-01-21	29	2022-03-22	23	2022-05-19	29
2022-01-24	30	2022-03-23	24	2022-05-20	29
2022-01-25	31	2022-03-24	22	2022-05-23	28
2022-01-26	32	2022-03-25	21	2022-05-24	29
2022-01-27	30	2022-03-28	20	2022-05-25	28
2022-01-28	28	2022-03-29	19	2022-05-26	28
2022-01-31	25	2022-03-30	19	2022-05-27	26
2022-02-01	22	2022-03-31	21	2022-05-31	26
2022-02-02	22	2022-04-01	20	2022-06-01	26
2022-02-03	24	2022-04-04	19	2022-06-02	25
2022-02-04	23	2022-04-05	21	2022-06-03	25
2022-02-07	23	2022-04-06	22	2022-06-06	25
2022-02-08	21	2022-04-07	22	2022-06-07	24
2022-02-09	20	2022-04-08	21	2022-06-08	24
2022-02-10	24	2022-04-11	24	2022-06-09	26
2022-02-11	27	2022-04-12	24	2022-06-10	28
2022-02-14	28	2022-04-13	22	2022-06-13	34
2022-02-15	26	2022-04-14	23	2022-06-14	33
2022-02-16	24	2022-04-18	22	2022-06-15	30
2022-02-17	28	2022-04-19	21	2022-06-16	33
2022-02-18	28	2022-04-20	20	2022-06-17	31
2022-02-22	29	2022-04-21	23	2022-06-21	30
2022-02-23	31	2022-04-22	28	2022-06-22	29
2022-02-24	30	2022-04-25	27	2022-06-23	29
2022-02-25	28	2022-04-26	34	2022-06-24	27
2022-02-28	30	2022-04-27	32	2022-06-27	27
2022-03-01	33	2022-04-28	30	2022-06-28	28
2022-03-02	31	2022-04-29	33	2022-06-29	28
				2022-06-30	29
			Mean, 2022		26
			Standard Deviation		5
			Mean + 1 s		31
			Mean - 1 s		21
			Mean + 2 s		36
			Mean - 2 s		16

FIGURE G.1 VIX, January 3, 2022 to June 30, 2022

■ Sector Components, Row 1

Energy, Materials, Industrials

SECTOR	INDUSTRY GROUP	INDUSTRY	SUB-INDUSTRY
Energy	Energy	Energy Equipment & Services	Oil & Gas Drilling
			Oil & Gas Equipment & Services
		Oil, Gas & Consumable Fuels	Intergrated Oil & Gas
			Oil & Gas Exploration & Production
			Oil & Gas Refining & Marketing
			Oil & Gas Storage & Transportation
			Coal & Consumable Fuels
Materials	Materials	Chemicals	Commodity Chemicals
			Diversified Chemicals
			Fertilizers & Agricultural Chemicals
			Industrial Gases
			Specialty Chemicals
		Construction Materials	Construction Materials
		Containers & Packaging	Metal & Glass Containers
			Paper Packaging
		Metals & Mining	Aluminum
			Diversified Metals & Mining
			Copper
			Gold
			Precious Metal & Minerals
			Silver
			Steel
		Paper & Forest Products	Forest Products
			Paper Products

Industrials	**Capital Goods**	Aerospace & Defense	Aerospace & Defense
		Building Products	Building Products
		Construction & Engineering	Construction & Engineering
		Electrical Equipment	Electrical Components & Equipment
			Heavy Electrical Equipment
		Industrial Conglomerates	Industrial Conglomerates
		Machinery	Construction Machinery & Heavy Trucks
			Agricultural & Farm Machinery
			Industrial Machinery
		Trading Companies & Distributors	Trading Companies & Distributors
	Commercial & Professional Services	Commercial Services & Supplies	Commercial Printing
			Environmental & Facilities Services
			Office Services & Supplies
			Diversified Support Services
			Security & Alarm Services
		Professional Services	Human Resource & Employment Services
			Research & Consulting Services
	Transportation	Air Freight & Logistics	Air Freight & Logistics
		Airlines	Airlines
		Marine	Marine
		Road & Rail	Railroads
			Trucking
		Transportation Infrastructure	Airport Services
			Highways & Railtracks
			Marine Ports & Services

Source: Adapted from S&P Global; Nasdaq; MSCI and Wikipedia

Consumer Discretionary, Consumer Staples, Health Care, Financials

SECTOR	INDUSTRY GROUP	INDUSTRY	SUB-INDUSTRY
Consumer Discretionary	Automobiles & Components	Auto Components	Auto Parts & Equipment
			Tires & Rubber
		Automobiles	Automobile Manufacturers
			Motorcycle Manufacturers
	Consumer Durables & Apparel	Household Durables	Consumer Electronics
			Home Furnishings
			Homebuilding
			Household Appliances
			Housewares & Specialties
		Leisure Products	Leisure Products
		Textiles, Apparel & Luxury Goods	Apparel, Accessories & Luxury Goods
			Footwear
			Textiles
	Consumer Services	Hotels, Restaurants & Leisure	Casinos & Gaming
			Hotels, Resorts & Cruise Lines
			Leisure Facilities
			Restaurants
		Diversified Consumer Services	Education Services
			Specialized Consumer Services
	Retailing	Distributors	Distributors
		Internet & Direct Marketing Retail	Internet & Direct Marketing Retail
		Multiline Retail	Department Stores
			General Merchandise Stores
		Specialty Retail	Apparel Retail
			Computer & Electronics Retail
			Home Improvement Retail
			Specialty Stores
			Automotive Retail
			Homefurnishing Retail
Consumer Staples	Food & Staples Retailing	Food & Staples Retailing	Drug Retail
			Food Distributors
			Food Retail
			Hypermarkets & Super Centers
	Food, Beverage & Tobacco	Beverages	Brewers
			Distillers & Vintners
			Soft Drinks
		Food Products	Agricultural Products
			Packaged Foods & Meats
		Tobacco	Tobacco
	Household & Personal Products	Household Products	Household Products
		Personal Products	Personal Products

Health Care	**Health Care Equipment & Services**	Health Care Equipment & Supplies	Health Care Equipment
			Health Care Supplies
		Health Care Providers & Services	Health Care Distributors
			Health Care Services
			Health Care Facilities
			Managed Health Care
		Health Care Technology	Health Care Technology
	Pharmaceuticals, Biotechnology & Life Sciences	Biotechnology	Biotechnology
		Pharmaceuticals	Pharmaceuticals
		Life Sciences Tools & Services	Life Sciences Tools & Services
Financials	**Banks**	Banks	Diversified Banks
			Regional Banks
		Thrifts & Mortgage Finance	Thrifts & Mortgage Finance
	Diversified Financials	Diversified Financial Services	Other Diversified Financial Services
			Multi-Sector Holdings
			Specialized Finance
		Consumer Finance	Consumer Finance
		Capital Markets	Asset Management & Custody Banks
			Investment Banking & Brokerage
			Diversified Capital Markets
			Financial Exchanges & Data
		Mortgage Real Estate Investment Trusts (REITs)	Mortgage REITs
	Insurance	Insurance	Insurance Brokers
			Life & Health Insurance
			Multi-line Insurance
			Property & Casualty Insurance
			Reinsurance

Source: Adapted from S&P Global; Nasdaq; MSCI and Wikipedia

■ Sector Components, Row 3

Information Technology, Communication Services, Utilities, Real Estate

SECTOR	INDUSTRY GROUP	INDUSTRY	SUB-INDUSTRY
Utilities	Utilities	Electric Utilities	Electric Utilities
		Gas Utilities	Gas Utilities
		Multi-Utilities	Multi-Utilities
		Water Utilities	Water Utilities
		Independent Power & Renewable Electricity Producers	Independent Power Producers & Energy Traders
			Renewable Electricity
Real Estate	Real Estate	Equity Real Estate Investment Trusts (REITs)	Diversified REITs
			Industrial REITs
			Hotel & Resort REITs
			Office REITs
			Health Care REITs
			Residential REITs
			Retail REITs
			Specialized REITs
		Real Estate Management & Development	Diversified Real Estate Activities
			Real Estate Operating Companies
			Real Estate Development
			Real Estate Services

SECTOR	INDUSTRY GROUP	INDUSTRY	SUB-INDUSTRY
Information Technology	Software & Services	IT Services	IT Consulting & Other Services
			Data Processing & Outsourced Services
			Internet Services & Infrastructure
		Software	Application Software
			Systems Software
	Technology Hardware & Equipment	Communications Equipment	Communications Equipment
		Technology Hardware, Storage & Peripherals	Technology Hardware, Storage & Peripherals
		Electronic Equipment, Instruments & Components	Electronic Equipment & Instruments
			Electronic Components
			Electronic Manufacturing Services
			Technology Distributors
	Semiconductors & Semiconductor Equipment	Semiconductors & Semiconductor Equipment	Semiconductor Equipment
			Semiconductors
Communication Services	Telecommunication Services	Diversified Telecommunication Services	Alternative Carriers
			Integrated Telecommunication Services
		Wireless Telecommunication Services	Wireless Telecommunication Services
	Media & Entertainment	Media	Advertising
			Broadcasting
			Cable & Satellite
			Publishing
		Entertainment	Movies & Entertainment
			Interactive Home Entertainment
		Interactive Media & Services	Interactive Media & Services

Source: Adapted from S&P Global; Nasdaq; MSCI and Wikipedia

Note: *Italic* page references indicate figures.

W

Y